…as the rivers flow…

Daphie Pooyak is Nakota-Cree from Sweetgrass First Nation, Treaty 6 territory. A social media influencer, storyteller, and a traditional knowledge keeper, traditional dancer, and foremost; a mother and grandmother. Daphie travels extensively throughout Indian Country on Turtle Island, she is well respected and known for her teachings, which she generously shares. She is a medicine knowledge keeper, a ceremony woman who devotes her time to those in need of healing and spiritual guidance. Her late grandparents recognized her inherent spiritual gifts when she was only a child and during their time on earth, they brought her to ceremonies to listen to elderly knowledge keepers and oral historians, these keepers of traditional/historical knowledge were keen to pass onto Daphie their teachings.

It was during Daphie's childhood that her grandparents brought her to a Treaty 6 gathering of elders and knowledge keepers, where she was introduced to an elder who spoke of the true meaning of "…for as long the sun shines, the grass grows and the rivers flow…".

Sacred Bundles Unborn

MORNINGSTAR MERCREDI
& FIRE KEEPERS

 FriesenPress

One Printers Way
Altona, MB R0G 0B0
Canada

www.friesenpress.com

Copyright © 2024 by Morningstar Mercredi
www.morningstarmercredi.com
Second Edition — 2024

Cover Artist: Emma Voyageur

ISBN
978-1-03-831776-6 (Hardcover)
978-1-03-831775-9 (Paperback)
978-1-03-831777-3 (eBook)

1. SOCIAL SCIENCE, INDIGENOUS STUDIES

Distributed to the trade by The Ingram Book Company

At the gathering the elder clarified the true meaning of "…the rivers flows…" which is misinterpreted in the English language. The Cree meaning was lost in translation, and in English paraphrased to literally mean 'a river,' which is not the case.

The elder went on to say "…the rivers flow…" is a reference to a woman's water breaking prior to birthing life. When a woman gives birth, her water breaks before her labor intensifies, until she gives birth to her newborn, her sacred bundle, and/or plural should there be more than one newborn.

Therefore, to date, the Crown and Canada have broken the Treaty through the sterilizations of First Nations (Métis and Inuit) in Canada and indeed, throughout Turtle Island.

First Nations, Métis and Inuit women who were sterilized are unable to give life, their water no longer breaks, '…their rivers no longer flow,' decreasing our populations for generations, thus eradicating distinct linguistic groups, catastrophically diminishing our DNA lineages on Turtle Island since time immemorial…

Joseph Naytowhow
"Kamiyo kisikan kisikaw pimohtew"
(Spirit of the Day Guided Being)

"Sterilization according to "nehiyawiwin" (Cree) worldview is "pastahowin," meaning "the breaking of natural law by causing tremendous harm toward a human being.""

Contents

ACKNOWLEDGEMENTS

Thank you, Chief Allan Adam, for listening to me and believing in me when I reached out to you. You took a stand on behalf of all survivors of sterilizations and spoke up in my defense, and for all survivors; despite Indian Act policies protecting the perpetrators and the Canadian government protecting practitioners of sterilizations. ACFN Councilor's, Flossie Cyprean, Mike Mercredi, Teri Villebrun, Hazel Mercredi, your support and advocacy on our behalf as Athabasca Chipewyan First Nation members is valued and appreciated.

I am proud to be part of the Wolf Clan of the K'ai Tailé Dené.

Margo Auger, Chief Administrative Officer at Treaty 8 First Nations of Alberta, matriarch of Treaty 8 office administration, as well as advisor and matriarch for Treaty 8 First Nations. Your advocacy on behalf of all survivors of sterilizations is valued, thank you for your ongoing support on so many fronts. I am proud to walk with you.

Dedicated to my grandchildren, Walker and Nahanni, granny loves you with all my heart. To my only 'miracle' child, my son, Matthew. Life began for me when you were born and you were why I chose to live. This is not for you to carry, it is me letting you know, I was blessed and grounded in love the day you were born. I love you more than words can say. To my beautiful daughter in law, Adrianne, you gifted me with two of the purest, sweetest, strong ancestral souls and I am a better human because of them. Marsi Choo.

No one walks alone and I choose wisely who walks with me as life has taught me, not everyone has my best interest at heart, so why worry about those who don't genuinely care, rather, celebrate those who do. I don't love-bomb. I speak from my heart, sometimes to a fault.

My late grandpa Emile Mercredi told my dad when he was a young man, "If you can count on one hand your friends, consider yourself lucky." I thought my dad was being cynical when he told me this but I was too young and naïve to know the difference.

I am a lucky woman to count on one hand the 'friends' I have known. And the friends I have.

I love you Murray Townsend, you are the epitome of a solid 'brother from another mother.' I am honored you chose to be my 'bro' many moons ago. If not for you this book would not have come to fruition, thank you.

Rita Makkannaw, you are 'my person,' you've known me through many lives. I love you.

Randy and Mousie (Roseanna) LETS RIDE SOON! Knowing both of you are there is all I need to know.

Karen Stote, whatever I did to earn your friendship is beyond me as I hold you in the highest regard, respectfully. I am filled with giggles, laughter and lotsa love for you. You ground me when I'm intensely being me.

Terri Bailey, were it not for you I literally would not be here. You and I know this to be true. In a word. Alive. I am alive, and now living my best life. Love you with all of me.

Sometimes the most loving thing a person can do for themselves is let go, and I have loved myself back to the land of the living, by letting go.

And then there are life's teachers; Yvonne Boyer, Alisa Lombard.

Yvonne, you raised the bar by emulating what being a 'warrior' means, I am humbled and honored to be in your sphere, if even remotely as a shadow. I adore you and my respect for you is boundless.

Alisa Lombard, warrior woman, you are a force of nature and I am grateful for you.

My Cuz, Bunny, keep me laughing at myself, please. XO

Mom and Dad, miss you every day, see you on the other side one day, until then, keep watching over. Love you forever.

Life's lesson. If I stare too long into the void, I will be consumed by it. The void is empty of all that nurtures and sustains life; love, hope, compassion, kindness, caring, laughter, and gratitude.

There is balance in being a warrior and walking in kindness.

Allies & Firekeepers: The synergy of carrying loss of life is formidable, the weight on the heart is indescribably heavy.

One blade of sweetgrass will wilt alone. A field of sweetgrass uplifts each blade and when harvested, a braid of sweetgrass is unbreakable. 'Allies and Firekeepers' stand unified to ensure sterilizations are not only prevented, but stopped completely. It will take a collective to make this happen, a field of sweetgrass rising to heal deeply embedded wounds which are now wide open.

It took generations of First Nations, Métis and Inuit people, as well as allies, to ensure the doors of residentials schools were finally closed. And in 1996 the Gordon Reserve Indian Residential School in Saskatchewan was closed permanently. Although the last Indian hospital's doors were closed in 1981, the legacy of racism remains in many hospitals to date with the ongoing second-class treatment of Indigenous peoples, which has led to death of Indigenous people and certainly, ongoing sterilizations through various methods; Tubal ligation, IUDs and hysterectomies, which are known to be coerced or forced, and without consent.

Collective voices of activists, allies and survivors of sterilization continue to advocate for criminalizing forced or coerced sterilizations in Canada.

Several of the 'Firekeepers' from the first edition remain in the second edition of Sacred Bundles Unborn, in honor of their voices as allies, MARSI CHOO!

The origin of my activism comes from a sacred space within myself. I am empowered because I spoke up and strive to uplift others, that's where this book comes from.

In spirit and with universal love I extend my condolences to ALL 'First peoples' (Indigenous) in countries beyond the shores of Turtle Island who have also been subjected to forced or coerced sterilizations.

All my relations.

FOREWORD BY
UNJALI MALHOTRA

Sacred Bundles Unborn is a sacred work centered around the brave voices of some of the many First Nations, Métis, and Inuit women who were, due to racism in the health care system, sterilized without their permission. These are profoundly painful truths that have long been held in Indigenous communities.

The book's intent is to document some of these injustices in order to ignite people's desire to challenge them and to demand change. This has been led by author Morningstar Mercredi's brave mission for decades; it is a mission borne of her own pain as a result of being involuntarily sterilized. *Sacred Bundles Unborn* also seeks to educate people about how and why forced or coerced sterilization is still happening, especially to Indigenous women and women of colour.

As a woman of colour, who is also a women's health physician and long-time advocate for the reproductive rights of First Nations women, I am honoured to be part of this work and to be asked to write this foreword. I have a lifelong connection to the First Nations and Métis communities, as I grew up on Treaty Six territory, with both of my parents serving these communities as physicians.

My mother was an obstetrician, gifted the name "Angel of the North" by a former Muskoday First Nation Chief. She was a birth worker and remains a protector, warrior, and believer. Because of her, I was always surrounded by First Nations and Métis women, with their warm smiles and laughter, and was able to hear first-hand about their concerns and issues. We were accepted as part of the community, which taught me to stand up and shout for change when needed, to be unaccepting of the ever-present racism and abuses that many want to inflict, and to use my voice and any resources I have to make a difference.

I also have some understanding of the impacts of colonization, inequality, and dispossession since my ancestors were displaced by the Partition of India in the aftermath of colonial rule. I have dedicated my life to reproductive justice, and have held many positions and titles in this area. I have been the medical director of "Options for Sexual Health," overseeing 60 clinics in British Columbia offering sexual and reproductive health care. I have been co-founder and program director at the University of British Columbia Women's Health Residency Program; the chair of Canadian Foundation for Women's Health (the Society of Obstetricians and Gynecologists, Canada Foundation); and board member of the Federation of Medical Women, Canada.

I am also an auntie, a wife, and a mama – Mama being the most important one of all. I love my child more than words can express. I live for her. Having children is more than reproducing. It is a ceremony. It is the passing of love, tradition, culture, and a sacred bond. It is the passing of cells, tissue, blood, and dreams. Any person who wants to experience the heart-wrenching, painful, and joyous feeling of motherhood should never have that right taken from them.

However, under colonialism, First Nations people have endured – and continue to endure – traumatic violations of their parental rights via genocidal policies and systems such as the residential school system, the Sixties' Scoop, the foster care system, and forced, non-consensual, or coerced sterilization in a racist, unsafe health care system.

In 2017, Senator Yvonne Boyer and Dr. Judith Bartlett conducted a review of health policies and practices regarding the coercion of Indigenous women in Saskatchewan. The review confirmed and exposed the racism in health care, obstetrical violence, and reproductive coercion.

In this book, Senator Boyer discusses the long-term and far-reaching impacts of racism, genocide, and colonialism including the loss of culture, tradition, language, with the loss of the ability to reproduce. She speaks about the strength and beauty found in First Nations teachings, personal stories and insights regarding togetherness and community, and the spiritual balance found with birthing. She shares about the relational laws, roles, responsibilities, and loss of valuable and necessary contributions due to eugenics. She shares the eugenics history in Canada and laws that enabled the coerced sterilization of Indigenous women. Anyone interested in this important issue will want to read and follow Senator Boyer's work. She is not only working to change the criminal code to protect Indigenous women and girls, but also to create supports for those who have been victimized by the egregious act of coerced/forced sterilization. She also supported the FNHA's development of a provider consent guide for health care professionals to help them ensure they are obtaining consent properly and with cultural safety.

Another truth of colonization is shared in this book by Indigenous midwives Nathalie Pambrun and Cheryllee Bourgeois. They tell how Indigenous midwives were pushed aside, causing immeasurable harm to communities as they were the protectors and providers of intimate care. The art was nearly lost, but is being revitalized. Today, Indigenous midwives' work weaves together ancestral Indigenous knowledge systems and practices with modern-day medical advances. Indigenous midwives are partners in a reproductive journey, carrying expertise regarding choice and continuity of care in urban communities as well as rural and remote communities.

In 2021, the FNHA's report on the health of women and girls in British Columbia, *Sacred and Strong*, reiterated that racism in health care has led and continues to lead to Indigenous women not accessing routine care today.

It is important to know that coerced sterilization is a widespread and ongoing global issue that is systemic in nature. Dr. Ewan Affleck shares about the sterilization of Inuit women in Canada as a result of racism. Dr. Karen Stote shares about eugenics in Canada and the role of government in systemic reproductive violence and racism. Dr. Stote speaks to the need for systemic change that includes recognition of the humanity of Indigenous people and support for their traditional ways.

Journalist Ann-Sophie Greve Moller shares about Greenland's IUD Campaign, which was designed to curb population growth. This IUD insertion was often done against people's wishes, at ages 13 and younger, as part of an assimilation attempt of Greenlandians into Danish culture. Stories, investigations, the ongoing trauma, and education on the colonization of Greenland by Denmark are all detailed. Doctoral student Patricia Bouchard enlightens readers on the use of sterilization by IUD during this campaign; she explains how large IUDs were used on girls to ensure not only that they couldn't get pregnant but that they could not bear children in the future. This violation broke any trust between people and the health care system.

Dr. Ewan Affleck also speaks about segregated care in Canada (Indian hospitals), the Indigenous community he has settled within, its fertility journey, his journey in learning of coerced sterilization in northern Canada, the impacts of evacuation for birth, and the risks including coerced sterilization that women face when leaving their community.

Keri Cheechoo, PhD, shares haunting poetry describing the painful experiences.

Gary Geddes, PhD, provides insights into racism in the health care system impacting Indigenous women that is ongoing and the root of sterilization.

Genevieve Johnson-Smith, PhD researcher, tells of her lifelong journey of learning about Indigenous history and the atrocities of colonization. As a historian, she notes that she takes seriously her responsibility to speak up and against coerced sterilization.

Dr. Alika Lafontaine provides the perspective of an Indigenous father and physician. He expresses his support for calls for much-needed change to the health care system in view of the tragic stories shared.

Some key things I have learned from experience, and from victims bravely coming forward, is that there are certain times and circumstances where coercion is more likely to occur than others. Coercion more commonly occurs when the patient is away from their community, enduring isolation, and lacking community support and advocacy.

Further, as Mi'kmaq lawyer Alisa Lombard notes in this book, "Free, prior, and informed consent must be properly obtained and given by all parties, and bodily autonomy should be non-negotiable." And, "Correct, complete, and honest information must be provided." Ms. Lombard notes that tubal ligations are never an emergency and offers details of case law. She shares her personal experience and her expertise regarding the legal rights of Indigenous women. She discusses the feelings women have postpartum, which are very much concentrated on the wellbeing of their newborn. This state of mind is absolutely not conducive to conversations about contraception or sterilization. Ms. Lombard also offers education on "implicit bias" and the impacts this has had on Indigenous people in health care.

In addition to postpartum being an inappropriate time to ask for or talk about consent, there are other times or circumstances where doing so would carry the risk of coercion. For example, consent is not valid if it involves threats (perhaps of child apprehension if not cooperative) and fear. When decisions of a non-emergency nature are pressured by time, there can be a great risk to the patient's rights. Any time the voice of women is not leading the care, as it should, there is a risk of coercion.

I know from personal and professional experience that there can be a beautiful connection between provider and patient where experiences are shared and discussed. This should be the goal. However, if this connection is not made, and consent not properly obtained and given, immeasurable harm can be caused to patients and communities. Suzie Basile, PhD, details legal actions taken in Quebec by forced-sterilization survivors. She emphasizes the commonality of coerced sterilization survivors' experiences, including having consent breeched, sharing a mistrust and avoidance of the health care system, being of a young age, and experiencing Indigenous-specific racism in hospitals (such as that experienced by the late Joyce Echaquon). She also details the landscape in Quebec aimed at ending coerced sterilization.

Health care systems rely heavily on processes and forms. These forms guide practice and offer protections. However, often the forms were created to protect the system, not necessarily the patient, and were written in complex medical terms that are hard to understand. They do not take into account patient literacy, let alone medical knowledge. I liken the healthcare system visit to entering a foreign country without a map, translator, or guide. The roads and signs are in another language. The talk is indiscernible and happens around you, not with you. Somebody asks you a question and you agree without understanding what was asked, not wanting to be rude. It is at times when patients are vulnerable.

Consent requires that forms be understandable. Consent should be a conversation. The conversation should be for the person receiving care, not the preferences of those providing care.

Improvements and clarity on consent related to sterilization have been called upon by the United Nations, the Missing and Murdered Indigenous Women and Girls Commission in its final report, and the Canadian Senate.

In my capacity as Women's Health Director in the Office of the Chief Medical Officer at the First Nations Health Authority, I worked with Senator Yvonne Boyer, lawyer Alisa Lombard, and Perinatal Services British Columbia to help women understand their rights when it comes to medical consent. This work included formalizing the questions and processes people have asked to be changed in the contraception counseling process.

To give consent, one must ask many questions: Is the consenting patient in the right frame of mind to have this conversation? Is she focused on another matter at this time (such as her labour, delivery or newborn)? Does the patient feel comfortable in the conversation and understand it is not an emergency? Could this conversation on consent occur at a more appropriate time when the patient is not potentially focused on other, possibly more acute matters?

A good example is having contraception conversations at routine care visits or early in pregnancy versus post-partum. Are supports in place for this person if they need or want them? As Alisa Lombard notes in this book, the postpartum period is one that is focused on the event of pregnancy, and for many women, not on future contraception.

Further within the conversation the future outcome, utility, and needs of any method should be known to the client. Whatever method is recommended, does the person know what the outcome will truly be? If sterilization is recommended, does this person know when they leave care that they cannot have more children? And if using a long-action method of contraception, do they know how it can be removed?

Has the consent been given based on a truthful, open, and honest conversation about what the person's reproductive future holds? Do they know how to access care if needed? Do they feel this is their choice to make freely? These questions are all vital to consent.

Anishinabe midwife and scholar Karen Lawford speaks about the preciousness of children and the impacts colonization has had on the ability of Indigenous people to have children, raise their children, and care for their children. She discusses surgical and chemical sterilizations, the abusive use of pharmaceuticals, and the current and ongoing sterilization of Indigenous women in Canada. She emphasizes that Indigenous people deserve health care that is compassionate, attentive, and responsive to Indigenous relational ethics.

There are many other contributors to this book; I have only mentioned some in this foreword. All of them are known as "Fire Keepers." I have a personal connection with many of them. My work and the other Fire Keepers' work is a collective. We are all working towards a common goal – ensuring the reproductive rights of Indigenous women and eliminating the misogyny and racism that violates these rights.

They are warriors, and I am so proud to work alongside them. I love, respect, admire, and cherish them. They speak in a way that you can feel in your heart and soul, because they hold you and your story with incomparable respect, dignity, and care. Their desire to make change and ensure all women feel safe is in every breath they take.

Many of the Fire Keepers share in this book their own fertility and pregnancy journeys – stories of courage, advocacy, and expertise. They include poets, researchers and artists. I am forever grateful to all of them.

And to Morningstar, one of the most courageous people I have ever met. She has shared her heart-wrenching story, which is a precious gift for us to learn from. Her story is one that she continues to try to heal from, the trauma that lingers and the triggers are visceral. She lives every day with the impacts of genocide, and she has truly risen above the ashes, like a phoenix — strong and bold. She is passionately taking a stand to ensure that other women will not go through what she and so many others have endured, and I am proud to join her in this important fight for justice.

To Be Seen

How loud must I scream for you to hear me.

So used to my silence you seem stunned by the sound of my voice.

Truth, an unfamiliar frequency to your ears.

So accustomed to the echo chamber of yeses that perpetuate
your power.

Yet something feels different, is your reign reaching its final hour?

You may turn away so your eyes won't see, but looking away won't
stop your inner ear from receiving the sound of me.

The sounds of screaming now penetrate your thin skin.

  The sound of wombs crying for those unborn, born, and their
  future kin.

    The sound of women and those oppressed everywhere saying
    No More!

      The sound of your power withering as the vibration of
      truth roars!

Your impotence being revealed for the world to see.

Your greatest fears are coming true as we begin to break free.

But what's underneath your thin skin?

Is it your pride, desire for power, and need to win?

No, it's the mountains of bones you stood on to sustain your place.

Now revealed, the skeletons lay bare in this open truth space.

Keep looking away if you must but we all can see.

The crumbling of your world built on lies and hostility.

Now paving the way for truth and more harmony.

The rebirthing of a world that once was, as we rematriate a space for all to be.

Creating safety we so desperately crave, want, and need.

The space to be seen, heard and known.

Shared power, worth, and responsibility as we step into the unknown.

Co-creating for our children and generations to come, a world and life that sustains us all, not just some.

Built on renewable resources of love, empathy, compassion, and truthful integrity.

Creating a world that reflects the parts and the whole.

A place where we are known, body, mind, heart and soul.

A place that for so long only existed in our dreams.

Hope now stitches us back together as we heal collectively at the seams.

Adrianne Vangool

FAIRY WINGS AND GOSSAMER: THE FORCED STERILIZATION OF INDIGENOUS WOMEN IN CANADA

Yvonne Boyer

To my Grandchildren,

> *I am truly gifted to be able to say those words – "TO MY GRANDCHILDREN". Many cannot – the Indigenous women in Canada who have been sterilized without their consent or were tricked into consenting – which is not consent at all – the 200,000 plus Indigenous women in Peru that were forcibly sterilized under the Fujimori regime –the Ecuadorian women – the women in Vietnam – the intersex, the disabled, the mentally ill, the trans, the men and on and on ...*

I am writing this letter, story, article, study, and opinion to place a trail marker in the years 2015, 2016, 2017, 2018, and 2019. The marker denotes the "pulling off of the blankets" of a health care practice that seems to be ingrained in our health system – obviously since the early days and it brutally continues today. The wound we uncover is called forced or coerced sterilization.

Sterilization is a surgical procedure for the permanent prevention of conception of a baby. Tubal ligation is the surgical sterilization of women by burning or cutting and tying of the fallopian tubes. The fallopian tubes are the delicate tubes (like the hollow stem of a flower) that live inside a woman that provide a route to carry the eggs she produces to the uterus (the nest). Sometimes women who are now being sterilized, and those who underwent this procedure before believed it was reversible because they were told it was. In reality it really is considered a permanent procedure. Forced sterilization happens when someone is sterilized even after saying they do not want to be sterilized. Coerced sterilization happens when someone is tricked or lied to, to sign a consent form. Both ways are wrong, harmful, and go against Canadian, International and Indigenous laws.

A Little History of Your Grandmothers

Your grandmothers and great grandmothers commanded the highest respect in our communities as the givers of life. They were the keepers of our traditions, practices, and the customs of our nation. They were the tellers of stories and gave wise Teepee Teachings to us as children. It was well understood that all women held a sacred status as they brought new life into the world. Women were revered for their capacity not only to create new life but also by providing a new connection with Creator. The babies that were born were given the law of the Creator and were given the responsibility to enter into new relationships in a balanced and good way.

The grandmothers, mothers, and women made important decisions about family, property, and education. Underlying principles of balance between men and women and the roles they played within society formed the basis for a good life. This way of life was very different from the Europeans who came to our nations in the old days with their hierarchical laws (Indian Act) and residential schools, religions, and patriarchy (meaning the male is superior).[1]

The laws of our nation, our grandmothers, and great grandmothers have always been to respect the laws and relationships that teach us connection with each other and nature – not separateness – no one is better than the other. Each of us have our own roles and responsibilities – together we make one. Men are not more important than women and women are not more important than men – together we are spiritually balanced.

So, now you can understand how important it is that we view birthing as a valuable contribution to the family and community, but also as a strengthening of the relationships to the land, nature, and our cultural relationships. It is also a way to teach and transfer knowledge to you – my grandchildren who are involved and serving at the ceremony of our sacred birthings. Forced and coerced sterilization is the shattering of these important relationships, which ends the ability of a woman to give birth and thus harms the individual, the family, the whole community, and the nation.

A Little Western History on the Practice of Sterilization

In Canada (and elsewhere) the term "survival of the fittest" referred to levels of intelligence and a "scientific," criteria and standard for determining if a person was simply fit for survival or not. A related notion of those times (and today) is that those who are most mentally fit are threatened and facing depopulation, because the "mentally unfit" were reproducing at a faster rate. The unfit were labelled as "mentally retarded persons, alcoholics, epileptics, schizophrenics, criminals, prostitutes, and others whose physical and behavioral characterizations were considered to be genetically determined and inherited."[2] The term Eugenics refers to the science of controlling the breeding of people to "improve" a human population. It became associated with Nazis (WWII) and the "Master race" and genocide.[3] It has not been kind to our grandmothers.

In Canada, both Alberta (1928) and British Columbia (1933) enacted Eugenics legislation. Between 1929 and 1972, 2,800 people were sterilized under Alberta's Sexual Sterilization Act.[4] Although many provinces considered passing similar laws (including Saskatchewan), British Columbia and Alberta were the only provinces that actually passed these Eugenics laws. Alberta sterilized far more people than British Columbia. About 400 people were sterilized under the British Columbia law.[5]

Though neither the Alberta nor the British Columbia Sterilization Acts directly discriminated against women and/or Métis, First Nations or Inuit people by naming them in the language and words in their legislation – their implementation had devastating effects on women and Indigenous Peoples, since both provinces have always had high Indigenous populations. Because of their social placement and economic status, a disproportionately high number of women and Indigenous Peoples were sterilized.[6] These laws have now been changed, but the basis for our health policies have still been influenced by this and other legislation and laws.[7]

In fact, it may be surprising for many readers and for you my grandchildren to learn that Indigenous women have been coerced into sterilization during routine care in our health system as recently as 2018. I believe it is happening right now, this instant – even as I speak to you.

I will now give you a little background on why I think this is worthy of telling you about it in this little story or monograph – why I am telling you – my children and grandchildren and great grandchildren. I hope and pray to the Creator that when you read this, it is a practice that has been eradicated forever.

Our Auntie Lucy

Grandpa, Lucy, & Grandma

The story goes that I have always had an interest in addressing atrocities on behalf of vulnerable people and particularly our family. As a little girl I lived with my aunt (your great Aunt Lucy – who gave her name to at least one of you) and I heard the bedtime stories of what it was like to live in a tuberculosis sanatorium. I have a bright and clear vision of her being a tiny little brown girl in a big metal hospital bed with starched crisp white sheets. She was quiet and obedient and scared, at least in the early days. Here is a photograph of her at age fourteen getting dropped off at Fort San by her parents. She was very sick and said she didn't think she would live:

Tuberculosis in those days was a deadly disease. She was the only child to get it in the family of thirteen children. She got it from a cow. It was called bovine tuberculosis, and it lodged in her spine. I think she acquired tuberculosis of the lungs when she was a patient at Fort San. She had experiments done by the doctors on her lungs and her ribs.

Auntie had a thirst for knowledge and would read a book a day. She had to use those funny looking prism glasses that allowed her to read a book while she held it in her hands propped on her little chest and the mirrors in the glasses would reflect the words from her chest to the glasses to her eyes to allow her to read.

She couldn't get out of bed; she was on bed rest. It was called "Chasing the Cure." She spent ten years in bed in Fort San and five of those years were in a body cast. Although she made many friends, many friends died. She talked to me about what it was like to be treated differently because of skin colour and what it was like not to be able to see your family. She saw her family once in ten years. She talked of experiments done on children and that sometimes monsters walked the halls in human form.

I do think it was because of her and my dear mother that I got grounded in this sense of the importance of standing up for what was right and speaking on behalf of people that could not, those who had their tongues cut out in one form or another. It also helped that I was born into a family of brothers and I was never afraid of a good fight. I guess that is why I chose to be a lawyer. I became a lawyer many years ago and have continued to use my voice and my skills to speak for and fight for people that would not and could not fight. I want to continue my story about fighting to stop the practice of sterilization when someone does not want to be sterilized or does not know that it is permanent. Auntie never had any children. I believe she was sterilized in the tuberculosis sanatorium. I now think of Aunt Lucy in the spirit world and I think of my mother in the spirit world and I believe we as women are connected by something so ethereal, so deep and spiritual, that it cannot be named in our languages, but it can be aptly described as looking like fairy wings. Fairy wings are made of gossamer. When you spread them and look at them through the sun, you can see their vital energies and vessels throughout – they sparkle with life and they shine and glisten. Inside each woman there is a pulsing, radiating, living ball of delicate, fairy wing gossamer; it connects the generations and it pulses with the spiritual power of connection of women. When one woman is sterilized, the other women know and they offer the living light of gossamer, so she is never alone and has the strength to hold tight to the blankets.

Grandchildren, the point of telling you the stories of your ancestors, and their relationships with all life, is for you to know the sacredness of birthing, which ensures our survival.

As I reflect, I visualize this holy intimate connection between my aunt, and mother, and I, and indeed, all the ancestors – the women who came before us who make us who we are – they stand with me, and your ancestors stand with you – my grandchildren. I am with you and you are with me. We are one so we are never alone.

And we continue the fight… .

January 29, 2024

PULLING OFF THE BLANKETS

In *Sacred Bundles Unborn* I had a message from the grandmothers to the grandchildren. While I have been concerned with telling the grandchildren about the plague of forced and coerced sterilizations – another unsuspecting force of energy has entered my life that has convinced me to share some thoughts from my heart and the voices of the ancestors.

A few days ago, I carefully unwrapped a brown box that came to me in the mail a few months ago. I had put the box away with my "family treasures" to be opened later. The box had been mailed to me by my Godmother. I had put it away and forgotten about it. It is interesting how the spirits guide you and the ancestors wake you up when it is time.

While sorting through various things tucked away in the "family treasure" corner I noticed a box and realized that I had not opened it when it arrived. In the box was a note from my Godmother saying that she was now passing this treasure down to me. In it was a beautiful quilt with a pattern of little squares and "x's" or "boxes" or "tracks" or "stairs". The quilt was not fancy like the star blankets we see today, but this quilt was very practical and reminiscent of the quilts I grew up with – this one was similar in that it was squares sewn together in a simple and useful pattern.

This quilt had been given to my grandparents (Louis Amable Boyer and Mary Rosalie LaRocque) on their wedding day in 1899. It was made by Louis's grandmother – her name was Elise Allard (daughter of Marguerite Saulteaux), and she was born in 1821, she was from Red Lake Minnesota.[8] Here is a photo of the quilt laying on my carpeted floor. You can see the tiny stitches it took to piece it all together – the stitches are perfectly the same in length and width. The quilt is worn and well used since Louis and Mary had 12 living children. It is bigger than a child's quilt though – I believe it was made for the bed of Louis and Mary and maybe used for the many children too. There are a few holes in the fabric where it is worn through – but for a 200-year-old quilt – it is remarkable. As I held it in my hands, I could feel it rhythmically and gently pulsing with life.

When I first opened the parcel, I sat back and with a huge gasp of a breath I said "here it is" - here is the physical connection to the grandmothers. I closed my eyes and breathed slowly. I knew I had to take time to really understand what this meant while I held the quilt close to my heart, cheeks and nose. It smelled like it had been put away for a long time, it smelled like my history, my family, it smelled and felt like the old people.[9] It was soft and the cotton was well worn, it was stuffed with little rolls of cotton too.

I carried the quilt to my favorite chair, and I wrapped it around my shoulders and before long I was lulled into a soft gentle sleep. When I woke, I felt I had been joined by company and that the ancestors were awakened and were with me. The feeling held me close all day.

When I went to bed that night I slept soundly, the quilt was in another room. From a deep sleep, I was awakened, electrified, and startled by a loud booming male voice. A man's voice yelled "**HEL-LOOOO**" – I jumped up with my heart pounding and racing thinking someone was in my room – or outside my door or more likely flittering outside my window (on 2nd floor) – and whoever it was, wanted me to awake **NOW.** I grabbed the light switch and looked around. I shakily gasped (maybe from relief) because I couldn't see anyone – the house was quiet. I inspected the rooms. The cats and dogs slept soundly – I was the only one awake – it was only me that heard the voice.

Puzzled. I laid back down, assessing what just happened.

I sometimes have dreams of ancestors, I sometimes have dreams that tell me things, or sometimes I get feelings, I sometimes feel danger and often feel love. I sometimes see glimpses of a light or movement out of the corner of my eye. You might say I am sensitive to some things – Aunt Lucy was also sensitive, her and I used to talk about the things we couldn't see but only feel. I know others in the family were sensitive as well and I do know on the other side that the spirits gather their strength and powers to do these things. It is okay when they happen for me. Rather than being afraid, I feel more love because I am sure it was not an easy feat for that ancestor to contact me. My dreams are often of the family on the other side.

As I wondered "What were they trying to tell me?" "What am I supposed to do?" The voice may have been my grandfather Louis – it was not my father's voice. On reflection about what happened – I think it was simply what it was "wake up Yvonne" – we are awake too. I am still thinking about this message and what it meant but for now…

The quilt remains wrapped around my favorite chair in my favourite room with a loving presence. It is the ancestors that have called me. I am now calling my grandchildren – our descendants – and we are waking with love and gratitude as I write this and continue to literally and figuratively "pull the blankets off" the issue of forced and coerced sterilization of our children and grandchildren.

Today

I think that while I have been speaking to my grandchildren in *Sacred Bundles Unborn* the generation of young, teen, and preteen Indigenous women continue to be high risk – simply by being born Indigenous – they are at risk of being sterilized against their will, at risk of going missing, and at risk of being murdered.

In Canada we are on the precipice of making change. There are several initiatives moving forward to eradicate forced and coerced sterilization. These initiatives must be supported by everyone – all Canadians, all people worldwide. It is up to every person to plant the seeds of change.

There are many papers and reports written on this topic – for years the people involved in the eradication of forced sterilization have been talking, writing, and taking action.[10] Journalists have been researching and writing – from all over the world.[11] As a Senator it is our responsibility to sit on committees of the Senate (there are 18).

I have been a member of the Senate Standing Committee on Human Rights where we studied the issue of forced and coerced sterilization and produced two reports. In June 2021, *Forced and Coerced Sterilization of Persons in Canada* was tabled and in July 2022 *The Scars that We Carry: Forced and Coerced Sterilization of Persons in Canada Part II* (Scars We Carry) was tabled in the Senate of Canada. The Recommendations in the *Scars We Carry* provide a comprehensive framework to eradicate the issue of forced and coerced sterilization. Have a look at these.

Additionally, the Survivors Circle for Reproductive Justice (SC4RJ) was incorporated in 2023. The existence of this organization gives the government (and others) the ability to work with survivors directly – rather than political organizations that claim to represent them.

The SC4RJ consists of a professional governing board of matriarchs who are mothers, grandmothers, and survivors who possess the knowledge and skill to effectively carry out the objectives of the survivors to ensure that forced sterilization is eradicated. There are approximately 200 member survivors. A Registry has been established to ensure all the women who are survivors are duly represented.

The objectives of the corporation are:

- to speak with one unified voice.
- have legal standing that recognizes the collectivist of women who have been sterilized and other Indigenous women who have experienced reproductive injustice.
- to seek fundraising opportunities for the operation of the Survivors Society.
- to create a registry that registers and collects data on all who have been sterilized against their will in Canada.
- to create a research arm that reviews all aspects of reproductive justice for Indigenous women, as directed.
- to be a well-recognized and respected global entity that is representative of all survivors of reproductive injustice in Canada.
- to create and administer healing and wellness programs for members; to advocate and liaise with private donors, colleges, the health care system, and government entities to advocate for reproductive reform in law.
- to be the authority with respect to impacts of reproductive injustice; and to advocate for the implementation of preventative measures.

This is a comprehensive list to help eradicate forced and coerced sterilization. We will watch in the future as the membership grows and the objectives are realized.

In *Sacred Bundles Unborn* we hear from Nathalie Pambrun and Cherylee Bourgeois on Indigenous midwifery and how important it is. I agree, this is one more important initiative to help eradicate forced and coerced sterilization. If you haven't read that chapter – please do – it is critically important.

We also heard from First Nations lawyer Alisa Lombard. She initiated and is still leading the Saskatchewan Class Action on behalf of the women who had been coerced or forced into sterilization. As far as I know there are five other class actions occurring across Canada. Support these legal actions – they also are important.

I introduced Bill S-250 and it is in the Senate right now – it is expected to move to the House of Commons quickly and become law. Bill S-250 adds a section to the Criminal Code of Canada that will criminalize the act of coercing or forcing anyone into sterilization. The proposed penalty is up to 14 years in prison.

This topic brings me to the Case Study of Andrew Kotaska. Andrew Kotaska is a doctor who might be seen "at the top of the doctor food chain." He has served as president of the Northwest Territories Medical Association. He has years of practicing medicine as well as professorships at the Department of Obstetrics and Gynecology at the University of Toronto, University of Manitoba, and at UBC School of Population and Public Health. He has published articles on caring for Indigenous patients and surprisingly – informed consent and ethics (yes... ethics). Andrew Kotaska is a former clinical director of obstetrics at Stanton Territorial Hospital in Yellowknife. Andrew Kotaska may be emulated by some as a "leader" and a "role model" at the successes of his career.

In July 2019, through a remote ultrasound he diagnosed a 37-year-old Inuk woman with pelvic pain. He performed surgery to address a painful cyst on her right ovary at the Stanton Territorial Hospital in Yellowknife in November 2019. She only consented to the removal of her right fallopian tube and ovary, if necessary. Andrew Kotaska removed her right fallopian tube and right ovary and before he **ALSO** removed her left ovary and fallopian tube, testimony heard by the Inquiry Board claims that he stated, "Lets see if I can find a reason to take the left tube." This vicious quick slice of the scalpel left her sterile forever.

A civil suit was launched in April 2021 against Kotaska and the NWT Health Authority for 6.5 million dollars. Both Kotaska and the NWT Health Authority filed Statements of Defence and Andrew Kotaska denied sterilizing her without consent (A year later he publicly apologized). In his defence he stated that his medical student heard the Inuk patient say she did not want any more children. Andrew Kotaska seems to think that if the organ was not being used – it shouldn't be a problem if it was removed, particularly without consent.

An official complaint was launched against Andrew Kotaska with the NWT Department of Health and Social Services (who licenses physicians in NWT), and a virtual hearing was held on Feb 10 and 11, 2022. The board of Inquiry found that he violated the Canadian Medical Association's Code of Ethics and Professional Responsibilities. They suspended his medical license for 5 months (already served). He was ordered to pay $20,000 in costs related to the hearing and he had to complete an ethics course at his own expense. The board considered a letter signed by his colleagues as "an accomplished thoughtful surgeon who is capable of excellent decision making" when making their recommendations.

Obviously, besides the obvious heinous act of sterilizing this woman without consent, the cultural significance of Andrew Kotaska's act of sterilizing the Inuk patient was not considered. There does not appear to have been an Inuk on the Board of Inquiry. It is unlikely an Inuk colleague penned their support for Kotaska for his "excellent decision making"? The high rates of forced and coerced sterilization of Indigenous women and considering 26% of all Inuit women in Igloolik were sterilized – this factor might be a very important one that was obviously ignored.[12]

In addition, Andrew Kotaska should be charged under the aggravated assault provisions in the Criminal Code of Canada. The RCMP stated they will not pursue charges because the survivor has not filed a criminal complaint. As a lawyer, I believe that there is no requirement for a victim to participate if there is compelling evidence. There were several professionals in the operating room who can testify that there was no consent to remove the left ovary and fallopian tube.

Despite all this, Andrew Kotaska currently practices medicine in a hospital in the interior of British Columbia, He is fully registered with the Society for Physicians and Surgeons of British Columbia.

What the Kotaska Case Study shows us is that he would be subject to the criminal sanctions in Bill S-250, had Bill S-250 been passed into law – would that threat have prevented him from "finding a reason to take the left tube?" Although a precedent was set with the NWT Department of Health and Social Services who held the Inquiry – it isn't enough. This Inuk woman was in a vulnerable position surgically. There are many more who have not been in the news. My office continues to receive calls of distress of women (and men) who have not consented to sterilization. The health care structure must change to stop this crime. The generations of grandchildren will benefit from an intersectional line of structural change.[13] We hear them and feel them and honour the spirits before us, and we honour the spirits to come. The ancestors walk with us all. It is time to act.

A WARRIOR'S UNSUNG HONOR SONG (SPOKEN WORD)

Standing, crawling, carrying, creating, praying, birthing, fighting, speaking out against tyranny thru daily life, living monuments of immense strength, no statue could justly portray the enormity of your SPIRIT, ceaseless, relentless, ruthless in defiance of discrimination projected unto you, me, us, our whole spectrum of universal LOVE, rising sage sisters smudging, paying homage to mothers who carry on their backs generations of genocide, peeling off skins of discolored bruises beaten unto you, me, us, our whole being of liberated LOVE, rinsing paternal sins saturated with rape upon torture, defying death to birth another baby, preparing her/him to restore humanity, you are our mercy, a song sung so long ago in ceremony, encircled serenely enshrouded by ancestral shadows who dance around you, enraptured child, this world is yours, your life is ours to adorn in laughter and protection against prosecution of your gender, she will teach him to be tender, he will taste her breast milk to nurture his Spirit, he does not know, yet, how sacred his walk is with his mother, sister, daughter, he will learn to defy a deliberate attack against Women of all Nations, Global Girls United, Unified beyond Flags of Countries. We will never lay down to die. We cannot. We are life. We are Women. Our shades of skin color is mute to our force of life, our bodies birth life, our blood bleeds as pure as innocence is born, our birth right is beyond benevolence and beauty for servitude, for truth is as tasteless as the air is to breathe as water is to life, women weep in joy, pain, horror, happiness, the depth of her emotion is eternal, whether loved or scorned, she will cry for the mercy of her children, sometimes her cry is resurrected from a distance so lost, no sound can remotely resonate her resistance so raw, so real, she can only walk miles upon miles in her skin, skin that knows no limits, not even those limits imposed on her can break her SPIRIT… she stands in honor. Honor her. This is not a request. This is not a task. This is the right of every woman ever born. For in her quietest moments, silence screams for her sacred bundles unborn, her right to birth taken, yet she rises, every day, until she draws her last breath, she wonders…do they know, these ancestors unborn, how sacred they are, how loved. NO. ONE. KNOWS. Only those whose lives were taken from them scream silently, generations, their cries now a warrior's unsung honor song.

Morningstar Mercredi

SURVIVORS OF STERILIZATIONS

Survivors of sterilizations who gave their testimonies, whether through interviews with media, print, radio, television, or with a therapist, partner, friend, elder, family member, whomever their confidant is, whether months, or decades later; each and every time a survivor retells and shares their experience, it comes at a great cost. From personal experience, I am aware of the inability to verbalize that which the body is unable to articulate, some women cannot even speak of being sterilized, which is understandable and respected. The mental, emotional, physical, and spiritual toll on a woman (or man) who has been sterilized is in itself enough to survive. Many of us who have survived sterilization and were asked to willingly evoke memories so deeply embedded in our psyche, body, and hearts, memories of such profound trauma that even the word 'trauma' fails to describe the indescribable, have done so with a depth of vulnerability comparable to the innocence of a baby, a baby whose life depends on the care of her/his mother/father, and caregivers. Feeling and being inexplicably exposed and vulnerable in order to retell, over and over and over, being sterilized. Layers are peeled back, tearing open wounds which will never heal, and every time the memory is spoken, the heart breaks, again and again. Until silence is a reprieve, a kind, loving respite from loss. Loss of life. Loss of the ability to give life. Loss which knows no bounds in the heart. Only silence.

It is from this place I hold in the highest regard these women who bravely reopened these wounds, over and over and over, in hopes of preventing sterilizations from occurring with malice contempt for a woman's right to conceive because of the color of her skin, her race, ethnicity, based on her being born First Nations, Métis, Inuit or women of color in Canada. (And indeed, throughout Turtle Island).

Morningstar Mercredi

REFLECTIONS ON THE COERCED STERILIZATION OF INDIGENOUS WOMEN: TOWARD SEEING THE HUMANITY OF INDIGENOUS PEOPLES[1]

Karen Stote

Who Am I?

I'm a settler of Irish, Scottish and English descent who was born and raised on the sovereign territories of the Wəlastəkwiyik (Maliseet) and L'nu (Mi'kmaq). You may think my submission in this collection of writings by Indigenous women is out of place. Maybe you're right. Maybe I've always been out of place...

I grew up in one of only a couple English speaking families in a French Acadian village in rural New Brunswick. As some of the first settlers on Mi'kmaq lands that were being claimed as a French colony, Acadians were subsequently displaced by the British. Many later returned to the area where I grew up, long before my family and I moved to town. The Mi'kmaq never did though, having been placed on reserves more than an hour away.

I don't really know in any significant detail about my historical origins. On my mother's side, I have ancestors who came from Ireland after the colonization of these lands by the British, and a

34

potato famine that resulted in the mass starvation and migration of many to North America. Her mother, with part Scottish origins, is somehow distantly related to Sean Connery, the Hollywood actor. My father's father was a white, Anglo Saxon, Protestant Minister. He and his wife, my grandmother, had seven children. These are stories told about my history.

I am not unlike many other White settlers who find themselves living on Indigenous lands and are no longer able to remember histories or ways of life prior to the current one. And without wanting to be, I am now part of a society that continues to impose itself on Indigenous peoples, lands, and bodies in an effort to divorce them from their own histories and ways of life.

Growing up, I always knew I was queer, but living in an environment where Christianity was the norm, queerness was sinful and transgressive. There was no place for me to exist as I am. This could be why, when I first met a Cree-Saulteaux woman who became my partner for much of my twenties, I understood a small something about what she meant when she told me colonialism had left no room for her to exist either, even though our experiences were different.

Feeling out of place may also be why I've always taken great comfort in the power of my internal life – of thoughts and feelings, and how to dream these into being. This must be what informed my love of books. Books connected me with ideas, people, and worlds outside of the small one I lived in growing up.

My love of books is likely what led me to write one. I understood very early the power of words to tell stories, or to silence them, depending on the author's purpose, all with the stroke of a pen. I currently work within the academic industrial complex, where books are written, but where competition, expert knowledge, and so-called objectivity are valued.

I am not a competitive person. I always feel guilty playing games where winning takes place at the expense of others. I still don't know what an expert is or how anyone can speak of injustices without stopping to think about the people who experience them. I've also noticed there is very little space in academia for dreaming.

I now think the uncomfortability and fear White settlers experience from being out of place is what leads too many of us to remain committed to racism against Indigenous peoples. If we give up our claim to Indigenous territory and the lies we tell ourselves to justify this, what do we tell ourselves instead? Where do we belong?

How Did I Get Here?

I spend so much time each day thinking about the coerced sterilization of Indigenous women. I've been doing this for almost twenty years. But Indigenous women have been experiencing this violence for much longer than this.

Nearly one-hundred-years.

My work on this issue came out of relationships with Indigenous people. Professional and personal relationships, some intimate, most loving.

I often say that other than my mother, Indigenous people have taught me the most important things in life. I say this because it's true.

These relationships continue to teach me about who I am, where I come from, and how to live in a better way. That the way society is organized is denying all of us our humanity. And that there are alternatives to this based on respect for all of life's diversity and the natural world.

There are many alternatives...

None of this was the responsibility of Indigenous people, but they have done it anyway. Thank you for this. As much as this piece is centered on acts of violence, it is a story guided by love and the knowledge that things can be different. Things need to be different. And that there is an urgency to this need. I hope the reader can see this.

Indigenous people had to tell me coerced sterilization was something happening to them. I didn't know. Engaging in this work was a way for me to take responsibility, to do something, to be accountable. I wanted to write something that was useful to Indigenous people, but without speaking for them. The Indigenous women I know are quite capable of speaking for themselves. I did want to speak to non-Indigenous Canadians, to push them to learn their history and take responsibility for it, today.

I never imagined so many Indigenous women would come forward publicly with their experiences of coerced sterilization. I want to acknowledge these women. I recognize the decision to share these details is a difficult one to make, and I know this decision is not without consequence for you. I also know some of you may never come forward. Still others are no longer here to tell their stories.

I want you to know that I know you exist. I hear you. The violence you've experienced is not your fault.

I offer these words knowing they aren't enough. They aren't much of anything really. I offer them anyway, if only so you know that some of us do not consent to your dehumanization.

Since beginning this work, I've realized that Indigenous women beyond Canadian borders have also faced coerced sterilization. I want to acknowledge these women too. The social relations operating in Canada are linked to those affecting women elsewhere. The details of your experiences may look different, but there are also remarkable similarities.

The reasons for this violence are connected through relations of global imperialism, colonialism, capitalism, and white supremacy. The desire to exploit Indigenous lands and resources is a worldwide phenomenon, as is the violence Indigenous peoples face.

And though not the focus of this piece, some non-Indigenous people have also been considered disposable to those in positions of power, and problematic to the social relations being imposed, and they too have sometimes experienced coerced sterilization. Gender diverse people, those labelled mentally or physically disabled, those racialized, criminalized or living in poverty. I want to acknowledge you too.

Documenting (His)Story?

Much of the research I do is in federal and provincial archives. These are quiet places, almost peaceful. But only if you overlook the violence found in the thousands of documents that take up these empty spaces. Documents that tell the minutia of a genocide actively being carried out. Stories of infants dying from mostly preventable conditions. Of parents wanting to know where their child has gone. Of government officials meticulously accounting for life and death in Indigenous communities while justifying why it is not them who are financially responsible for addressing the mess they've created.

I'm often struck by the ability of those in decision making positions to reduce Indigenous lives to concerns with budgets and cost efficiency. Meetings. Minutes. Memoranda. Denial. Blame. Repeat.

The stories I read sometimes cause me to speak out loud in the quiet of the room. To cry. There is very little humanity in the archives. It's easy to overlook the fact that it is human lives that are being discussed. It's from this starting point that I offer this reflection.

Eugenic Sterilization

Some Indigenous women experienced coerced sterilization under eugenic legislation in Alberta and British Columbia. Eugenics, or the idea that some people are unfit to reproduce, is only one form of racism – Indigenous peoples have experienced many. As a theory of population control, eugenics helped to justify coercive interventions in the lives of those suffering the most negative effects of social relations of exploitation.

The documentary record shows that Indigenous women were often declared mentally defective and disproportionately targeted for sterilization under Alberta's Sexual Sterilization Act, from the late 1930s until its repeal in 1972.[2]

There is much unknown about British Columbia's Sterilization Act, which operated from the 1930s to 1973. However, some Indigenous women were sterilized under this legislation.[3] One Indigenous woman, described by those mandated to *care for her* as "incorrigible, wild, undisciplined and promiscuous," was recommended for sterilization to prevent her from having "illegitimate children" that the community would need to support, and for whom it would be difficult to find foster homes.[4] Indigenous women have so often been considered unfit mothers.

Sterilizations in Indian Hospitals

Sterilizations also took place outside of eugenic legislation. In my first book, *An Act of Genocide*, I examined archival documents which show that more than 1,000 Indigenous women and over 100 Indigenous men were sterilized over a 10-year period, in the late 1960s and early 1970s, sometimes in federally-operated Indian hospitals across Canada.

These documents do not tell the experiences of each individual who was sterilized. They do show that decision makers loosened guidelines on when sterilizations could be performed, that consent forms were known to be inadequate, and that qualified interpreters were not always used. All this while government officials were being questioned about the possibility that coercion was taking place.

Other documents tell of violent abortions and birth control promoted to address poverty and reduce the Indigenous birth rate. And they show arrogance, racism, and paternalism on the part of government officials, policy makers, and medical doctors – bureaucrats and professionals who purported to know what was best for Indigenous women.[5]

History is Repeating Itself (But Indigenous Women are not Laughing)

More than 100 Indigenous women from across Canada have come forward with their experiences of being coercively sterilized – since the 1970s and as recently as 2019.

These more recent examples have taken place under the banner of family planning. In my second book, *The Genocide Continues*, I show how federal officials, guided by population planners and their theories of overpopulation, hoped that by decriminalizing birth control, in 1969, which made sterilization more acceptable, this would help address poverty and other social problems in Indigenous communities while containing their reproduction to keep lands safely in the hands of the foreign invaders.

In Saskatchewan, where many women who have been coercively sterilized have come forward, provincial officials said Indigenous people were "breeding like rabbits" and viewed the Indigenous population, purportedly "mounting in leaps and bounds," as a "serious threat to peace."[6] I say purportedly, because even with all the talk of overpopulation, the Indigenous birth rate had taken a "sharp nose dive" by the late 1960s.[7] Indigenous women have on average only one more child than the Canadian average.

Despite this, family planning policy has regularly approached Indigenous reproduction as something needing to be curbed. Government officials, and health and welfare professionals have sometimes continued to portray Indigenous women, particularly young mothers, as a threat to their children, communities, and society.

Since the 1970s, and up to 2018, more than 10,000 sterilizations have been performed on Registered Indian women in Saskatchewan. The term "Registered Indian," a category imposed by the federal government to bureaucratically eliminate Indigenous peoples, obfuscates the humanity of those to whom it refers and does not account for "Non-Status Indians," Métis, or Inuit. And while not all these sterilizations were necessarily coerced, the data shows that Registered Indian women were disproportionately sterilized, and more likely to have abortions, especially in northern parts of the province, as compared to other Saskatchewan residents.[8]

In 2017, an external review conducted by Yvonne Boyer and Judith Bartlett documented some women's experiences of systemic racism and coercion while giving birth in the Saskatoon Health Region.[9] They concluded that all the women they interviewed either were coerced, felt coerced, or felt an attempt to be coerced into sterilization by health and welfare workers.

Through a series of federal and provincial actions and inactions, health and welfare professionals have been allowed to act more freely in pressuring Indigenous women to consent to sterilization. This, coupled with the longstanding relations of colonialism and systemic racism, continues to inform a context in which Indigenous women experience coercion in their reproductive lives.

In response to this history, some still doubt whether Indigenous women have been coercively sterilized. Women wanted to be sterilized, they say. It was for their own good, others say. Where is the evidence of coercion anyway?

Indigenous women are as capable as anyone else of choosing sterilization. But sometimes I think the continued refusal of some to believe that Indigenous women are coercively sterilized comes from not knowing any Indigenous people. When you know Indigenous people who live the realities of colonialism every day, to believe they may be coercively sterilized is not a far stretch at all.

Maybe the real problem is that some of us still refuse to listen...

Colonialism (is) Violence

There is a direct connection between the multiple and layered forms of violence committed against Indigenous peoples, and colonialism – or the theft of Indigenous lands and resources to the benefit of settler colonial society (capitalism and capitalist interests). The desire to ensure access to lands and resources on the part of the Canadian state, private corporations, and non-Indigenous Canadians, and the idea that land exists to be owned and exploited for profit, is central to the violence committed against Indigenous peoples. And land needs to be part of any discussion of justice. But colonialism is much more than land. It is also personal. Its impacts are worn on Indigenous bodies every day.

I don't want to define Indigenous people by their experiences of colonialism. They are so much more than this. They have lived and thrived on these lands without the help of non-Indigenous people forever. And the Indigenous women I know continue to assert themselves in an uncompromising way despite the centuries long attack waged against them and their peoples.

But to be born Indigenous today often means a shorter life span, higher death rates from preventable diseases, and an increased likelihood of suicide.[10] It means being more likely to live in poverty, lack clean drinking water, and face polluted environments.[11] To be murdered, raped, or abused.[12] It also means people close and dear to you have likely suffered these realities too. And it can mean you are disconnected from family and community, unable to speak your language.[13]

Living under colonialism affects self-worth, intimate relationships, and the willingness to trust. It often means being criminalized and subject to surveillance while your legitimate needs and concerns go unaddressed.[14] And it means facing the risk of being coercively sterilized.

Coerced sterilization is only one of many forms of violence experienced by Indigenous women, but it is such an intimate form of violence – a violation of bodily integrity and theft of humanity – the humanness of bearing children. There is no getting over this. Most especially when the reasons for this violence continue.

Colonialism shapes every interaction Indigenous women have with the Canadian state and its institutions, and non-Indigenous Canadians. It is what gives rise to the systemic racism that impacts the everyday lives of Indigenous people, and this systemic racism is violence.

We increasingly hear talk of systemic racism out of the mouths of government officials. To say Indigenous experiences of violence are systemic means they are found all throughout the system, but it also means the system itself is based on violence. This violence began when settler colonists first started exploiting Indigenous lands and resources. Years later, it persists in order to conceal this *continuing* dispossession and exploitation.

Systemic racism shows itself in the unequal treatment of Indigenous people under law, and the imposition of discriminatory policies and practices while Indigenous ways of life are undermined. It is the sexist and racist stereotypes people hold about Indigenous women. It is the failure of non-Indigenous people to live up to treaties and other responsibilities that come from living on Indigenous lands. To have compassion or empathy. To see and treat Indigenous people as human beings. To listen to Indigenous voices when they speak. It is thinking and acting as if Indigenous consent over what happens to their lands, communities, children, and bodies does not matter. And it is our failure to do what is required to stop coerced sterilization.

What is the Weight of 500 Hundred Years of Violence?

The impacts of coerced sterilization do not exist in isolation from other manifestations of colonialism and systemic racism. The harms that individuals experience as a result of coerced sterilization intersect with these other, multiple forms of violence. *The harms are cumulative.*

Coerced sterilization permanently denies Indigenous women the ability to have children, and to care for and socialize their children based on Indigenous ways of living and knowing. It works to destroy the connection between them and their peoples while reducing the number of those to whom the federal government has moral and legal obligations.

The practice is linked to explicit policies stemming from the Indian Act which have also attempted to reduce the number of Indigenous people by displacing the power of women and two spirit people in Indigenous societies. Though not all Indigenous women can or chose to give life, policies under the Indian Act have undermined their role as life givers, decision makers, and link creators between generations. And these policies have made them more likely to be subject to systemic and individually-perpetrated forms of violence within and outside their communities.

Residential schools and the sixties scoop forcibly transferred children out of Indigenous communities and into state-run institutions and non-Indigenous families. Indigenous children continue to be overrepresented in the child welfare system, and Indigenous women and men are over-incarcerated in prisons. To remove people from their communities promotes assimilation while simultaneously criminalizing Indigenous people. And it continues to reinforce the stereotype that Indigenous women are unfit mothers, unable to care for their children.

To coercively sterilize Indigenous women allows the Canadian state to deny responsibility for, and avoid doing something about, the social, economic, and health conditions in many communities – caused by dispossession and the attempted destruction of Indigenous forms of life. It becomes more cost effective to limit the ability of Indigenous women to reproduce than to improve the conditions into which children are born. And in failing to do what is required to effectively address these conditions, which lead to higher infant mortality rates and premature deaths, Canada is effectively reducing Indigenous populations by consequence, if not by intention. This "natural death control" is also a form of population control, after all.[15]

To undermine the ability of women to consent to what happens to their bodies is consistent with other ways western medicine has been offered to Indigenous peoples which have sometimes amounted to increased control, the undermining of Indigenous health and wellness, and the criminalization of Indigenous reproductive practices.

Children are highly valued in Indigenous communities, but this doesn't mean Indigenous women didn't control or limit their fertility.[16] They also generally had healthy pregnancies and babies, assisted by women, midwives.[17] The impacts of colonialism and the continued removal of some pregnant women from their communities to give birth in western hospitals undermines Indigenous reproductive sovereignty.[18]

But there is a finality to the practice of coerced sterilization. The break that comes from robbing Indigenous women of the ability to reproduce cannot be undone – it effectively terminates the line of descendants who hold histories, relationships, responsibilities, and legal title to land. This has always been the goal of Indian policy.[19]

When understood within the longstanding and continuing history of colonialism – as one of many policies and practices imposed on Indigenous peoples in order to undermine their ability

to exist under conditions of their own choosing – coerced sterilization is not only a human rights violation, it is an act of genocide.[20]

Coerced Sterilization (is) Genocide

Genocide is defined as any of the following acts committed with
the intent to destroy in whole or in part a national, ethnic, racial, or
religious group as such:

    a. Killing members of the group;
    b. Causing serious bodily or mental harm to members of
        the group;
    c. Deliberately inflicting on the group conditions of life cal-
        culated to bring about its physical destruction in whole or
        in part;
    d. Imposing measures to prevent births within the group;
    e. Forcibly transferring children from one group to another.[21]

Article II (d) was broadly conceived to include sterilization or
compulsory abortion, the segregation of the sexes, and the imposition of obstacles to marriage.[22]

How should one respond to accusations of genocide? The Canadian government initially responded, in part, by limiting how we
define the term. When it incorporated the first definition of genocide into the Criminal Code, it simply left out "imposing measures
intended to prevent births."[23] Canadian law now includes a full definition of genocide, but this crime continues to be associated largely
with instances of mass killing.[24]

Canadians themselves often argue about whether this is the
proper term to represent hundreds of years of violence against Indigenous peoples. It is as if the genocide against Indigenous peoples is
up for debate.

When accused of enabling coerced sterilization, governments
have often minimized allegations of coercion and sought to avoid

accountability rather than approach the issue with the openness and honesty it requires. This denial and defensiveness sometimes shows itself in the reactions of the general populations as well.

Where is the accountability for these crimes? Where are those criminally responsible, directly or indirectly? Why have governments failed to act up until now? Why has no one been held accountable?

How difficult is it to make sure no woman is sterilized without consent? Each year, we manage to do many things. Surely this year, we could do what is required to stop this practice.

Some Possible Ways Forward?

There is a fundamental tension that exists in how to respond to women's experiences of coerced sterilization – a tension between the absolute need to do something, anything (?), in the immediate, to stop the practice and care for those affected, and the need to address why it's happening in the first place.

Certainly, women who have experienced coerced sterilization require all possible support to assist them in sharing their experiences if they chose, and in dealing with the continued impact of this violence in their lives. These women require justice and accountability.

Those working in health and welfare need to be challenged on their knowledge and understanding of colonialism, systemic racism, and poverty, and any associated stereotypes they hold. They need to know that coercion of any kind in the delivery of services is unethical, immoral, and criminal, and clear consequences need to follow if coercion takes place. And Indigenous women need to be given the time and information necessary to make fully informed decisions about what happens to their bodies.

Meeting the threshold of informed consent is important, but this alone isn't enough. Indigenous peoples have always had their own ways of health and healing, and of regulating fertility and giving birth. For women to be able to freely choose western medical options, fully-funded and supported Indigenous options created by, and under the control of Indigenous peoples, and embedded in Indigenous forms of life, need to be restored as viable alternatives wherever they are wanted.

For the corporate interests who were so instrumental in funding its expansion, western medicine was always intended as a tool of colonialism. The year before offering a first investment in western medical education in Canada, former Rockefeller Foundation president George Vincent stated, for the purpose of "peacefully penetrating" colonies and "placating primitive and suspicious peoples," western medicine had some "advantages over machine guns."[25] Medical professionals and others who participate in this system need to grapple with how they may be promoting imperialism through their work, whether this is consciously intended to or not.[26]

As a broader collective, we too need to grapple with the ways that western medicine, in its focus on the bio-individual rather than social origins of illness, functions as a tool of capitalism by mitigating the costliest consequences of exploitation on our health and wellbeing, to ensure our continued value and contributions as productive workers, *not as human beings*. We have much to learn from Indigenous peoples, whose forms of life, based on respectful, reciprocal, and responsible relationships with the land, have helped ensure healthier bodies and communities – the ultimate form of preventative medicine.

So much of what I see happening in response to the coerced sterilization of Indigenous women runs the risk of leading down paths that Indigenous peoples have not laid out, in directions I'm increasingly unsure any of us should desire to walk. The courts and the criminal justice system, even human rights mechanisms as they currently exist, have histories embedded in colonialism, capitalism, and global imperialism, and the undermining of collective responsibilities and relationships to land and peoples.

I would never purport to tell anyone else how to survive hundreds of years of oppression. But I do wonder if systems and approaches which have functioned to enable continued dispossession and exploitation can be relied on to achieve any modicum of justice. Or whether it is up to us, as collectives, to right our relationships and build alternatives to what is being offered, to save ourselves and each other...

Before heading too quickly and too far down roads already paved, perhaps we would do well to consider "towards what justice" we are headed – what are the "lodestars" guiding our course and how do we ensure they will be reached by walking the paths we are on?[27]

To fully address systemic violence, systemic change is needed – to the relations that lead to the possibility of coercion in the first place. If they are to be of any use, those in government must respond with the humility and fortitude required to end relations of colonialism. This needs to include a respect for Indigenous peoples and their inherent and sovereign relationships with their lands, to meet their own needs in their own ways – without stipulations.

No matter what the cost.

Anything less is falling short of what is required to ensure this and the many other injustices experienced by Indigenous women and their peoples are stopped.

Systemic change requires the participation of all non-Indigenous Canadians. The coerced sterilization of Indigenous women isn't only a dark chapter in our collective history, it's ongoing, here and now – today. As are the many other injustices Indigenous peoples face.

Are we able to recognize our complicity in genocide – that our way of life, our standard of living, and our means of supporting ourselves and relating to the lands upon which we all depend are what give rise to the violence committed against Indigenous peoples?

We all benefit from this violence. *We are all responsible.*

What are we prepared to do, and to give up, to ensure this violence stops?

I often resist giving in to impatience. Some of us are acting, but not nearly enough of us and not fast enough.

If the ultimate goal is justice and dignity for Indigenous women and their peoples, then humanity must be centered in the process of achieving it.

Too often, violence committed against Indigenous people is viewed in isolation, as if one injustice is not connected to another. The (act) of acknowledging injustice is sometimes taken as an opportunity to do nothing. To apologize without stopping what you are doing. To deny blame or limit liability. To create divisions. Or to allow private interests to continue enriching themselves while those who suffer are offered such meager compensation it is insulting.

I hope justice will look different this time.

Christi Belcourt writes that the harms of colonialism have been thrown at Indigenous peoples intentionally – to wipe them off the earth as recognizable, sovereign, and distinct nations.[28] Yet still, Indigenous peoples remain willing to sit down and talk about reconciliation. A problematic term, yes, as a self-interest in exploiting Indigenous lands and resources is what motivated us to seek out Indigenous peoples in the first place. *It was never about peace and friendship*. But, Belcourt states, how peaceful, dignified, and beautiful Indigenous peoples are that they have endured all of this and are still willing to share.

When I reflect on my life, I think of my mother when I was growing up who, despite being dedicated to the Church and its views of queerness as sinful, *loved me, her relations*. She chose love instead of remaining committed to ideologies that were meant to divide us. Her making that choice is what allowed us the opportunity to find our way back to each other.

And I think of how love taught me about that longing for a space to exist. A longing that is still shared by the white girl from rural New Brunswick and a Cree-Saulteaux woman from Saskatchewan, even though our experiences are still different.

As everything does, this relationship has changed over the years, though it remains one of the most important relationships in my life. But I now realize the act of loving is what allows us to take on each other's burdens. In doing so, we also carry each other's dreams. So much so that these dreams can sometimes become our own.

My Question to You

What are non-Indigenous Canadians prepared to do to recognize the beauty, dignity, and humanity of Indigenous peoples?

Do you know that it is only by recognizing the humanity of Indigenous peoples that you will have any hope of restoring your own?

MENTAL HEALTH: LIVING WITHIN SYSTEMIC RACISM

(Trigger warning: Intergenerational trauma-
rape-sexual exploitation-sterilization)

Morningstar Mercredi

Considering all the generational trauma I've experienced as an Indigenous woman, I've adapted and created my own Feng Shui psyche, compartmentalizing childhood, adolescence, and adulthood trauma in order to move forward with the ebb and flow of life in the obstacle course of systemic racism. It's a marathon.

My essence is in a constant spiral of processing, healing, and being present, which is more complicated and spontaneous than it sounds. I understand "healing" will not remove past trauma, nor will "acceptance" of the things I cannot change – change the past.

I live with PTSD. Therein lay a problematic culmination of triggers and ensuing impulsive reactions, until I became aware of how I navigated through life making "trigger" choices. I lived in fight, or flight, wreaking havoc in nomadic chaos without a map.

Nonetheless, I have an insatiable free spirit that has led me on numerous journeys globally, where I've experienced joy, enlightenment, awe and disappointment. Such is life. PTSD hasn't entirely ruled the roost and my passion for life is not quenched, despite moments where I stared into the abyss until I was consumed by it.

Healing, for me, is like a vehicle breaking down, metaphorically speaking. I understand the need to process trauma, maintenance so to speak. I otherwise spin out and remain "stuck" in past trauma, and not by choice. This is the conundrum of PTSD. The flashbacks I experience "in the now" place my response in a time warp. Once I am triggered, I relive the trauma, and my nervous system escalates from coasting at 2 skyrocketing to 60.

My therapist, Terri Bailey, continues to guide me through my awareness of my PTSD responses through Somatic Experiencing Trauma Resolution.

Terri is an angel in my eyes.

I've often referred to my nervous system as being reconfigured, rebooted, with the understanding that I have a default system I need to recalibrate. I was unaware of how hardwired PTSD and trauma affected me in all aspects of my life, work, home, family, and relationships.

My solace is my sobriety, thirty-five years clean and sober, and throughout the years I've sat in more than one chair, or couch, in the company of a therapist, unravelling intergenerational impact of genocide, colonialism, and systemic racism, as well as my share of #MeToo.

I've exercised my "Treaty" right to access therapy through mental health practitioners, as well as paid out of my own pocket. The "Indian Act" medical manual doesn't authorize all mental health practitioners within its policy and framework, nor does the "Indian Act" manual recognize "Indigenous" methods of "ceremony" or "protocol" for healing. This is a good thing. Otherwise, I'm certain the government would try to commodify the spirit realm, prayers, ceremony, and protocol.

Let's just say, I put tobacco down often, and made my offerings.

These words are offerings – a continuum of prayers for those suffering, ceremonial songs sung in honor of those who passed, feasts, celebration, and compassion for those among us who survived intergenerational impact of genocide.

It's been my experience that 'healing' is not a one-way street.

For me, healing became a synergy of mental, emotional, physical, and spiritual - survival mechanisms over a lifetime of varying degrees of bodily assaults. Rape, child sexual exploitation, and in my case, as well as thousands of unknown women and girls who survived sterilization, whether forced or coerced. And those who did not survive are not forgotten. I too have relatives and friends who are Missing and Murdered Indigenous women, girls and men. I'm related to survivors of the 60's Scoop.

I recognize the majority of First Nations, Métis, and Inuit people experience generational systemic trauma. Period. Full Stop. This is Canadian history.

Yet, we rise, stronger, aware, and empowered. One generation at a time.

PTSD is not a conscious state of mind, or being, until one becomes aware of PTSD symptoms. As I became aware of my mental health, and the impact of colonialism and generational genocide, I began peeling off projectile prejudice of systemic racism. A snake peels layers of skin, my desquamation was a painful process of shedding layers and layers of societal dogma and stereotypes onto my beautiful-bronze-brown skin.

No one wakes up to say to themselves, "Today, I will focus on 'healing' from systemic racism and intergenerational genocide with the intent to *kill the Indian in the child*."

It took years for me to recognize the complexities of how, I/we, are affected by systematic, intergenerational-genocide over the last two centuries.

Genocide.

A strong word, evoking the seemingly impossible connotation that genocide is occurring in Canada. The denial and minimizing of ongoing genocide are real, and problematic, especially when spewing out plight sentiments such as Truth and Reconciliation.

The right hand admits there needs to be reconciliation, while the left-hand hides two crossed fingers, promising to clean up the mess and do better. But; the bureaucratic bullshit gets piled higher and higher, especially during Provincial and Federal elections. Politicians shamelessly, and disrespectfully make promises on their smorgasbord platforms, spewing rhetorical platitudes for votes, and term after term, decade after decade, the parliamentary party flavor of the day disregards the mess in their backyard. Yet, always managing to create an empire of decadent budgets, presumably to purge Canada's past inequities as their promises remain a diffidence of hypocrisy regarding Truth and Reconciliation.

Fortunately, First Nations, Métis, and Inuit, aunties, grandmothers, mothers, daughters, and men in our communities, generationally, take a stand to do our part in the dismantling of systemic racism; albeit, this overhauling, metaphorically, requires a wrecking ball and a few bulldozers to dispose of the rhetoric and bullshit of generational white supremacy amongst the patriarchal dynasties of the party's old guard proliferate Canadian apartheid systems; established with the intent to wipe out Indigenous peoples.

Though unsuccessful in their efforts.

We are still here, growing stronger with each generation, and as with most people; life carries on, and so does earning a living, raising a family, and functioning in some semblance of responsibility.

My ability to adapt is my wild card.

I come from a strong line of Denésoliné-Cree-Mi'kmag-Saull-teaux-Annishinabe-French-Irish-Scottish women, and ancestors. I know my bloodline on Turtle Island, and beyond its shores.

To say I'm nomadic by nature is an understatement.

Throughout the years my mode of travel varied. I've owned a couple of Harleys, and I'm a Class 1A driver. Learning to drive semitrucks, tandems, and roll off bins, or coach buses came naturally. Driving became easy seasonal work. Bread and butter employment in between gigs and other pursuits in the arts, media, writing, and producing.

My eclectic background is summarized in three separate curricular vitae. Frontline human rights activism, the service sector, media and the arts. Or, broke, surviving, and garnering funds for a project, ensuing work contingent on how passionate I am? Being an artist requires creativity, tenacity, and an attitude of gratitude for the creative process.

In 2013, I produced a documentary, *Sacred Spirit of Water*, which led to driving a coach bus to earn a living after I invested everything into producing this documentary. Then one day I paused. Albeit, it felt more like I crashed. Burnt-out and stress landed me on my ass in the small town of Osoyoos in southern British Columbia.

It took over six months before I felt like myself again, whilst unwinding and exerting the bare minimum of energy. I rode and relaxed in the Okanagan Valley, surrounded by mountains in Canada's only desert terrain. Occupied in my ethereal realm, writing, hiking, hanging out and enjoying my slumber.

Riding my motorcycle through winding mountainous roads, or on the flat prairies of Alberta, or Saskatchewan, clears my head and lightens my heart. Rain or sun, doesn't matter. Ride it out, without a destination, free to just be. The wind on my face embracing the wide-open space of roaring rumble and road.

I affectionately named my Harley Davidson Dyna Street Bob, 'Bobbie Jo', after what would have been my name, had it not been for my mom. Dad wanted to name their three eldest daughters after the characters of Petticoat Junction, a 1960's sitcom. We would have been Betty Jo, Bobbie Jo, and Billy Jo. I'm so grateful to my mom for winning that argument, much to dad's dismay and his wry sense of humor.

Bobbie Jo was better suited for my Harley, spunky, hard core and intense enough to calm my wild spirit. I became acquainted with a few people in this quaint southern community, but nothing too intimate or strenuous, and for the first time in years I laid back and took in the sights, enjoying my cozy nest in the hot sunny valley.

My touchstone in the valley was a close friend, Randy Williams, known as Silleattsa7 – his traditional Shuswap name. The grandfathers placed him on my path when I was driving a coach bus to Kelowna, BC, from Kearl Lake, AB. I enjoyed the solitaire journey along highway 5 via Kamloops, BC, or highway 1 via Revelstoke, BC, through to Alberta via Banff. The buses I drove to Kelowna were being refurbished.

It was a good gig, until one hot afternoon the bus stalled midway on a bridge. Thankfully, I managed to coast the bus off the bridge, pulled over and parked off road just as Randy rode past on his Harley. All he saw was the back end of me in my daisy dukes, steel toed work boots and a worn-out t-shirt, holding onto the door at the rear end of the coach bus talking to my supervisor on my cell phone.

Randy turned around and when he pulled up, I stepped off the back end of the bus, the conversation with my supervisor escalated to yelling before I hung up. In my fury, I sarcastically asked Randy if he was my 'guardian angel'.

He asked if I was okay, and if there was anything he could do to help after he introduced himself.

I vented, swearing like a trucker, pissed off with my boss for allowing this heap of junk for a bus on the road. I could have been killed, or worse, someone else if I hadn't coasted off the bridge in time.

Randy watched me with amusement and a twinkle in his eye as I cussed out my supervisor again on my cell.

Arrangements were made for the bus to be hauled to Revelstoke, which was an hour away. Randy sat with me in the bus as I waited for the semi tow truck to arrive, as well as my ride, I phoned a girlfriend to pick me up. Randy and I visited for hours before the tow truck arrived.

Since then, our friendship was cemented in good humour, good stories, respect and an ease in one another's company like we'd always known each other.

In retrospect, I smile at the lighter side of the 'grandfathers' bringing us together. Randy was the 'west door keeper', sent to welcome me in a good way. Unbeknownst to me at the time, I would soon be a resident among the Okanagan peoples' traditional territory.

It was a good day.

Months later, Randy often dropped by for a visit in Osoyoos, and then we'd ride off on our Harleys. Now and again, I rode with him just to take it all in. These were the days of sweet bliss. No worries, lotsa laughter and stories, so many stories. Then he'd ride off on his motorcycle until the next time. Our friendship remains strong, until we see each other again.

He's my Bro, I got him – he got me. Nuff said.

Living in the Okanagan Valley, I often returned to Alberta or Saskatchewan to visit family and friends for a few days, enjoying the journey before returning to BC.

On one particular return trip from Saskatchewan in 2016, I was introspectively taken on a detour that irreversibly altered my life. Coming full circle is uncanny in unpredictable ways; a shadow chasing me throughout my life catapulted me into a realm I hadn't been conscious of for more than four decades, and I couldn't run anymore.

I was driving through southern Saskatchewan, tuned to CBC Radio, when an Indigenous woman was being interviewed on herstory of forced sterilization, her right to conceive taken from her without her consent. As she described how being sterilized, against her will, affected her in life, I robotically turned off the radio.

The feeling started in my gut. Anxiety gripped me as I held my breath and then began hyperventilating. A knot in my stomach loosened, stirring nausea, then rage. Scenes flashed from my psyche. A trap door opened that I couldn't close as I gripped the steering wheel, speeding down the highway, focused on staying between blurred lines, engaged in fight or flight.

The speedometer read 145 km when I forced myself to slow down, fighting the urge to swerve into the ditch and run as fast as I could with all the force of my body to stop the terror of a memory revealing itself.

I felt betrayed by my senses as I screamed until my throat was hoarse and my tears came. I slammed on the brakes and pulled over on the side of the highway, turned on the radio, changing the station to hard rock blasting the volume all the way up, struggling to silence my racing mind. Angrily wiping tears off my face, I cried until I was numb.

I drove in a dissociative state for hours. I didn't want to stop driving and I couldn't stop my nervous system from setting off an internal alarm. I felt separated from my body as flashbacks once fused in my psyche assaulted my consciousness like glitches of strobe lights disorienting me. I zoned out on the highway in front of me with the radio on full volume, driving in methodical autopilot.

This wasn't the first time I had been jarred with these flashbacks over the course of forty years.

Every year, I slowly unraveled in depression during the months of November, December, and January. I never understood why. The despair escalated in my late thirties after I decided to explore in vitro fertilization. I wanted to have more children, so I found a gynecologist in Edmonton. Optimistic and hopeful, I scheduled an appointment with him. During our initial interview, he asked whether I had children. I said I have one son, explaining I had an ectopic pregnancy when I was nineteen and have not been able to conceive since.

The specialist told me when to return for an examination in a few weeks. The date arrived, and I went back to the medical clinic. As I was being prepped, the nurse explained what was involved in the examination and procedure. "The doctor will be using a scope to examine your uterus. You will be given a general anesthetic before surgery."

When it was over, I woke up with some discomfort in my uterus, but I was more concerned about the effects of the anesthesia than anything else. Taking drugs made me anxious, so I avoided taking any. I fell back asleep until the specialist came to see me, wasting no time to explain the results of his examination.

He asked, "What happened?" He then explained to me, "You have scar tissue damage in your uterus, and your left ovary and fallopian tube have been removed."

"What do you mean?" I asked.

The specialist spoke candidly, in anger and disgust, "In my professional opinion, there is no medical reason you should have the scar tissue damage you have in your uterus. You were mutilated. Your left ovary and fallopian tube were removed...you were very young, based on the scar tissue, and your right fallopian tube was severed from the ectopic pregnancy when you were nineteen and is irreparable. You are not a candidate for in vitro."

I asked again what he meant regarding scar tissue damage. He repeated, surprising me with his candor as he dropped the f-bomb.

"I've never seen scar tissue damage like this in my professional career, and there is no fucking medical reason for it!" He calmly asked again, "What happened?"

Silence.

I am numb...unable to talk.

"What happened to you?"

I am sitting on a table. I'm wearing a green hospital gown. The gynecologist is looking at me. I wandered off in my memory when I was fourteen years old.

I had been examined by a doctor in Blaine Lake, Saskatchewan; he wanted to know what my abdominal incision was from. It was several weeks after I had been released from Saskatoon City Hospital.

I am sitting on a table. I'm wearing a green hospital gown. The doctor and nurse are staring at me. Silence.

He also said there is no medical reason for such a haphazard, blunt incision in his professional opinion. I sat numb on the examining table as he spoke to me with glossy tears of empathy and concern. A nurse watched me with as much sympathy as the doctor.

Silence.

The doctor then explained to me I had a nervous breakdown and asked again, "What happened?"

Silence.

I whispered, "I was born. Can I leave now?"

I sat in numb reflection of that doctor in Blaine Lake, Saskatchewan asking me the same question over forty years ago.

I heard the gynecologist speaking as I held myself back from passing out from the effects of the anesthesia. He gave me his card and told me to contact him anytime. I left the clinic fading into a familiar abyss of nothingness, jared from too much information, too much recall, too many flashbacks, my nervous system couldn't handle. In both situations I was unable to articulate "what happened."

I never talked about it, and I wouldn't be able to talk about it until I was in my fifties. I moved back to Saskatoon, SK, from Osoyoos, BC, to be closer to family, and then I travelled to Edmonton two to three times a month to care for my late dad.

In October of 2017, I made a phone call to an attorney, Alisa Lombard. I had read about her in an online article. She was representing Indigenous women who survived forced coerced sterilizations.

I felt like I was losing my mind as I attempted to articulate to Alisa "what happened" over forty years ago. I don't know if I made sense; nothing made sense. In October, I turned fourteen. A month later, in November, I went into a catatonic state followed by a nervous breakdown after being discharged from Saskatoon City hospital.

She then told me she had hoped she would never receive a phone call like this but that she was prepared for anything, and yes, we could talk.

For the following three years, PTSD and suicidal depression held me in its death grip in the midst of an extremely painful, stressful family crisis. I did the only thing I knew, fight or flight.

I moved back to Alberta from Saskatchewan and hit rock bottom mentally and, for the first time in over thirty years, I thought about drinking, or ending my life; it would take everything in me to not give up.

Once again, I sought therapy in Edmonton, where I met Terri Bailey. And for the first time in my life, I started unraveling the events that led to "what happened" over forty years past, on the verge of another nervous breakdown, I dug into the darkest recesses of my subconsciousness and when I felt safe enough to talk about it openly with Terri, I returned to memories I compartmentalized.

I was fourteen years old when I admitted myself into Saskatoon City Hospital in November because I slipped and fell and then I had started spotting and cramping. I was six months or more pregnant from being raped when I was thirteen. I did not consent to the surgery that the doctor was adamant I should have. When I asked "why?" I was ignored. I was alone, underage, and there was no one I could contact.

The doctor's only concern was getting parental or guardianship consent for surgery. He was unable to contact my parents for consent, and for whatever reason, social services weren't contacted either.

My only concern was for my baby, and it aggravates me to no end to state the obvious: I was not drinking or using drugs. I was pregnant. Drinking or using drugs was not a priority.

Two days later, I was released from the hospital with an incision from my panty line to my belly button and without my baby. I went into a catatonic state and had a nervous breakdown. Six months later, I attempted to take my life. This was the beginning of my PTSD suicidal depression.

NOTE: *Through ongoing sessions with my therapist, to date, I was able to recall being in the hospital for several days, in and out of consciousness. I lost a lot of blood and I was being heavily medicated, leaving me incoherent. I doubt I would have survived the bodily assault if not for the ability to disassociate.*

When I was finally able to talk about "what happened" – forty years later – I was the personal directive and caregiver of my late dad. Life's responsibilities didn't permit me to be engaged in PTSD 24/7, yet there were days a menial task like doing the dishes was a triumph. Most days, I crawled out of bed and escaped reality by binge-watching Netflix.

Over time, I recognized the need to honour my spirit by taking time to grieve the losses of my two babies. I turned to our ancestral ways and held a naming ceremony for both of them, and then I cried like I've never cried; I wailed. I grieved my inability to conceive. Part of me died on that operating table when I was fourteen, and then losing my third baby at nineteen. I wept, releasing pent-up rage and pain until I was spent.

There is no closure for these losses.

I took what comfort I could from naming both of them: "Thunder Cloud" and "Morning Mist Star Woman." I began the process of letting go.

VOID

Fluid silence Ebbs and flows
From my blood
Unto yours
Our bloodline
Our connective tissue
Forming our umbilical cord

We share more than dreams I had of you
Of holding you
Of loving you
Of knowing you
Ours is
Life

Is it you
Or I?
Does the Goddess
Determine your eye colour
The shade of your hair follicles
Your skin tone
Do the Gods
And Celestial Star relations
Determine your chart

Your destiny
Born of me
You inherent fire
Passion
Insatiable curiosity
A quest verging on hunger
For universal unknowns

Forged by an innocence
A longing to return
Somewhere
An unquenchable
Quest
Such as I weep

I now live for
Justice
Retribution
Answers
Though none will
Bring you back

My womb was crucified
My bloodline
Denied
Unto you
My child
Forever severing
Our umbilical cord
Breaking my heart
Not my spirit

Fury
Rage
Bittersweet anguish
Replaced
Birthing
Twisting me
Internally

Until I named you
Decades after you were taken
Against my will
Without my consent
When I was gutted
When you were
Ripped from my uterus

As a sage
I held ceremony
Then and only then I wailed!
Releasing
A sound
For generations unborn

My human right to conceive
Stolen from me
From you
Us
Inhumanely
Disguised as human
A doctor

Defiled my ovary
Sliced my fallopian tube
I was meant to bleed out
But I survived
To honour those who had not
Forced coerced sterilization
Incognito mutilation…

The greatest blessing and miracle in my life was being able to conceive my son when I was sixteen. I turned seventeen during my healthy pregnancy, weighing over 200 lbs. I was three weeks overdue when I went into labour. Midway through eighteen hours of hard labour the doctor suggested I have a Caesarean, which terrified me. I told my husband not to allow them to "cut me." I gave birth to a healthy 10 pound 13-ounce baby boy. As soon as I was able to, I nursed him.

When I was brought to my bed on the maternity ward, I couldn't sleep as I listened to babies crying, upsetting me because I wanted my baby with me to breastfeed him, but the nurses wouldn't allow my baby in my room with me.

They insisted my baby had to remain in the nursery, so I phoned my husband and told him I was leaving the hospital that night with our baby because the nurses wouldn't allow me to see, or hold our son.

When my husband arrived, we were given our baby.

A couple years later, I had an ectopic pregnancy and bled internally. I flat-lined and was revived. I was nineteen then. We divorced a few years later, and I never remarried.

Throughout my adult life, I wanted nothing more than to have more children, and it wasn't until in my thirties that I accepted what the gynecologist in Edmonton confirmed. I would never have more children.

I lay to rest my dream, my longing to give birth, to feel life grow within my womb. The wonderment that chases the mind's eye and fills the heart with expectation in celebration of a tiny being born into my life. To feel my baby suckle, safely feeding her/himself. The purity of a newborn's tiny fingers reaching for me as he/she grasps for his/her needs to be met by me, her/his mother, I lay to rest my pining of wonderment of who she/he would be.

Sacred Bundle

All that is earth, stars, celestial ancestral realm
I call upon you and those before you, and those before you
Praying until my tongue is dry and pasty
Like a pleading preacher
Studiously
Pissing yesterday's wine at the podium
Drowning their pedophiliac preferences
Begging for absolution
Saintly
Atonement
Penance
Shame
A sinister sin
Casting my soul to hell
I'm told I'm "Damaged goods"
After I refused to die
Under the scalpel and forceps
Is this my pass at Saint Peter's feet?
Pretending to be perfectly
Fucking angelically unfazed
By the legion of demons ascending
On their paternalistic altar
Physicians' clamouring claws
Sanitizing
My brown skin
Taking all that is
Sacred
From my womb
Birthed by an unwanted
Caesarean
Slicing

My fallopian tube and ovary
Sacrificially
Tossed into a bedpan
Societal
Dogma righteously in support of surgeons
Segregating
Indigenous girls and boys, women and men
In not-so-sterile ESP experiments
Shock therapy
Scientifically
Slicing anatomy
Forced coerced Sterilizations
Pseudoscience mythology
Permitted to sanctimoniously murder within
Sanatoriums
Established to execute genocide

"Did they wrap my sacred bundle?"

In our Indigenous cultures, children are valued and sacred. Unlike the systemic commodification of Indigenous children within Canada, where bureaucracies have been established since the founding of Canada, capitalizing on Indigenous babies and children in residential schools, child welfare, the scoop and forced coerced sterilizations.

Numerous studies and inquiries created interim currency, branches within the ivory towers of parliament, justifying a slow-drip transfusion of money unto itself. Studies, surveys, inquiries and commissions with calls to action that are not followed up, much like Treaty promises.

Indigenous experts-scholars have provided Ottawa with the answers. These answers and calls to action fall on deaf ears. This trend of inaction on the part of Ottawa is in keeping with our historical treaty relations. Each government presents a platform of promises, yet each government has not followed up on these.

Ballad of Prime Ministerial Bullshit

Square dancing with shadows during an Indian Act masquerade, a promenade of enactment, do-si-do laws of the land, "take your Indian by the hand" slip reel em through policies until they are too dizzy to stand, face the two-faced moniyaw, flip em around, sit em down, spin em round, make him reinstate Truth and Reconciliation, for real this time, hurry up before he cashes in, again, on your Indian Status, that two-faced moniyaw.

I am accountable to myself for my mental-emotional-spiritual-physical health and well-being, despite the ongoing systemic genocide of Indigenous Peoples in Canada. Nonetheless, sun spirit shines on a new dawn fortifying creation, grandmother moon heals, grandfather sky blesses earth with cleansing rain, snow and air. A vibrant life force and energy from our star-celestial relations reigns over each night. "Kiyam, it's a good day to be alive for our children's children, for our-selves." We rise and grow, this is who we are, besides, manure nurtures soil, so don't let the BS weigh you down. We are still here, generations of all our relations - born of all races – rooted on Turtle Island, our homeland on mother earth.

I honour the matriarchal medicine of my grannies, aunties, and my late mom. Strong women who have overcome generational genocide, yet until coerced sterilization is criminalized, Indigenous women and girls remain at risk within the health care system in Canada.

Star Children Descendants – Ascended

Life givers
Your womb
Carries generations
Of our
Sacred Bundles Unborn
And those
Born
Light fuses with eternal synergy
Placed unto-into
Your womb
Carries generations
Of spiraling
DNA Passage
Of
Life
Life givers
Chosen
To incubate
Embryos
Generation upon generation
Commune
Unto-into
Your womb
Life force
Floats in fluidity
Forming
Your son
Or

Your daughter
Your legacy
Born of generations
Before you
Linked
Molecular
Mapping
Intrinsic
Manifestation
Of dreams
In spirit realm
Physicality
A foundation
Of
Who we are
Star beings
Being
Human
Tobacco offered
Prayers
Honouring
The
Descendants
Living
Having survived
Ongoing
Colonial-paternal-systemic
Genocide
And to

Our
Relations
Ascended Among
Star Celestial relations

Marsi Cho – Hiy Hiy
For your Earth Walk

All my relations

Turtle Island and beyond her shores...

Void imprints cast on earth
Lonely shadows lingering o'er barren
Empty desert dry mirages reflected
In a mother's tears
Grieving for her uterus
Fallopian tubes
Womb
Babies
Not conceived
Generations
Past
Present
Future
Wishes and dreams blown
In the four directions
Across
Mother earth
Barren Babies
Never will they lay
In her arms
Nor
Walk on earth
They eclipse
Faded silhouettes unto ancestral
Shimmering northern lights
Watching o'er among ancient ones…
Reunited

In spirit
Only to be unearthed in dreamtime...
Descendance denied
Descent from embryonic
Existence
Into earthly realms
Of fluidity
Nestled within
A mother's Womb
There is no return from this place of grief for her
unborn child/children
Not on earth
Nor in spirit

Morningstar Mercredi

"WHY DO THIS WORK?: A HISTORY OF SOLIDARITY THROUGH ROOTS AND RHIZOMES"

Lucia Stavig

I remember when I learned of the forced sterilization of over 300,000 people (almost all Indigenous women) in the 1990s in my mother's home country of Perú. It was the run-up to the 2011 presidential elections in Perú, and many Peruvians had taken to the streets to protest the candidacy of Keiko Fujimori, the daughter of the ex-dictator. I had just begun a PhD in Justice and Social Inquiry at Arizona State and was starting to put together my plan of research. I knew I wanted to work in Perú to be closer to family, but I also wanted to do work that connected my two countries. I grew up with a very clear sense of the U.S.'s imperial projects in Latin America: coups undertaken by the CIA; death squads trained at the School of the Americans at Fort Benning, Georgia; the extractive, colonial economic relations that left Latin America poor and made the U.S. (and Europe, and now China) rich. The history is more complicated than I have just painted it, but the truth of the U.S. 's continued colonial relations with Latin America cannot not be denied. Never, though, did I imagine what I would come across in my research design class, nor the next decade of work, grief, pain, and healing it would bring.

I don't remember what I Googled that brought The Image before my eyes: four women marching in the streets of Lima, lifting their *polleras* (layered skirts worn by Indigenous Andean women) to reveal pictures of cut and bloodied uterus, red paint streaming down their legs. I had no idea what they were referencing. I read the article accompanying the Image and felt my blood run cold.

Hundreds of thousands of Indigenous women were forcibly sterilized from 1996 to 2001. Government Quotas. Doctors paid. Women kidnapped. Trapped. Abandoned. Sickened. Dead. I couldn't breathe.

I was no stranger to horror. For the previous few years, I had researched the after effects of a massacre of Tzotzil Maya peoples in the small mountain town of Acteal. I had gone to the town in the southernmost Mexican state of Chiapas, traced the holes in the side of its wooden church. Those who couldn't run from the bullets screaming through the town—pregnant women, children, and elders—had taken refuge in the church.

The paramilitaries then turned on the sanctuary. Survivors recalled soldiers yelling "Kill the seed! Kill the seed!" as they shot and disemboweled pregnant women. The massacre was intended as a message to the zapatistas, the Indigenous social movement that, in 1994, had declared itself in rebellion against the Mexican state and neoliberal economic policy more generally. This horrific scene was a punctuated moment in the centuries-long genocide of Mexico's Indigenous peoples.

I crossed the church's threshold in 2007, ten years after the massacre. A statue of the Virgin Mary dressed in Tzotzil Maya *traje* presided over the church from the altar. A ray of sunshine peeking through a bullet hole shone upon her. I stopped the dusty light coming through the wall with my finger. How could something so small wreak so much havoc? Light and dark, life and death, triggered by a finger.

My thoughts were interrupted by a member of our group telling me we had been invited into the crypt where the fallen were buried. I couldn't go into the tomb that first time. I had lost my dad unexpectedly two years prior, and the weight of my grief anchored my feet to the sun-filled patio. Our griefs were not comparable; none are. I hadn't lost my dad in a massacre; we weren't persecuted peoples, and the United States (my dad's home country) had trained the paramilitaries who stole their loved ones' lives. But we did share the void of grief, an emptiness full of questions, anger, and pain—and the knowledge that if you don't keep moving you will also die in spirit if not in body.

I entered the tomb the following year. With more time to process my loss, I began to see how the community was doing the same. In the decade since the massacre, Acteal had transformed its sorrow into a social movement. They built their new community space above the tomb, making it not just a place of mourning but of remembrance— even re-membrance, a space to put its shattered pieces back together, to move forward toward a new wholeness.

The universe does not abide destruction alone. All that falls apart reorganizes, reshapes, remembers. Lands that have been destroyed eventually sprout ferns, then bushes, then trees. The insects and animals return. Nothing remains a wasteland, not even the human heart. We are resilient beings, us earthlings, all of us—plants, animals, earth beings, the Earth herself. We were made to regenerate, to start anew. We just have to remember how to grow.

& & &

I was born in Lima, Perú in 1986 at the height of the civil war that rocked the country from 1980 to 1992. My parents drove to the hospital with a white flag out their window to signal they were civilians seeking medical attention. But though I was born in Lima, it's not where my story starts. My parents met in Cusco in the early 80s while they were doing research, my mom as an anthropologist for the International Potato Center, and my dad for his dissertation on the 18th century Indigenous rebel, Tupac Amaru II, Tupac Shakur's namesake.

Both my parents were oddities in their families. My dad, from California, was the first in his family of farmers, fishermen, and lumbermen to go to college, and joined the hippie movement in San Francisco. My mom was the first woman in her family to go to college and to break with the PLU (People Like Us) mentality of Lima's upper class. Both sought to tell the human stories of Runa (Quechua) peoples, to uplift the knowledge and struggles that most Peruvians disdained or were completely ignorant of.

Because of my parents' work I often joke that I owe my life to the humble potato, but it's truer than not. For thousands of years, Runa peoples of the southern Andes have cultivated this tenacious tuber. They've kept each other alive through unthinkable loss, but have also accompanied each other in festivals, carnival, and every celebration in-between. Potatoes grow better at higher altitudes and cooler weather. Too hot, and the pests get them; too cold, and they freeze in the ground. The lands must be just right. Runa leader, ex-congressperson, and my friend, Hilaria Supa Huaman, says that the process of colonization is like being uprooted from the place you grow best and being dumped somewhere else: sometimes the new soil is fertile, and roots can take hold, but not usually. At best, the new land is unfamiliar; at worst she is unable to support life. Some people die trying to root in this new place; others run away in search of better lands; and yet others do the best they can in their new location, their roots always reaching for home.

I come from settler families. Both my mom and dad's families had a place to settle because of colonization and the dispossession of Indigenous peoples. But I often also think about the forces that led my families to move: a constant denial of place kept my mom's German-Jewish family moving, eventually to Perú in the 1850s; poverty, crop failure, and promises of land impelled my Norwegian farmer family to migrate to the U.S. in the 18th century. All these histories, those of Indigenous peoples, of my ancestors, are tightly knit together in an imperialist capitalist system that demands more resources, more labor, more profit, more poverty, more misery: more, more, more, and never enough.

In my family's histories of movement (both compelled and chosen) are stories of resilience. I am inheritor of these histories, constantly transplanting, constantly re-rooting, re-membering myself back together. My life is built on networks of roots and rhizomes, each reaching toward the other: delightful, unforeseen connections. Personally, I grew up going between the U.S. and Perú. My family later moved to Bolivia, and we also spent time in central Mexico. For my studies I moved from Florida to Arizona to Alberta to North Carolina, with stops in Nicaragua and Ecuador between. I am a child of Abya Yala, the Americas. In each place, I have had the privilege of learning and growing with First Peoples, all of whom, amidst continued violence and loss, continue to value radical care and reciprocity. My experiences have carved me deeply, shaped how I move through the world, even how I love. My history allows me to see the deep connections between seemingly disparate places and events. I love all the places I've lived, and they have all made me; but there are certain places where I grow more-lush, flower more beautifully. I call these taproots home. I am a potato at heart.

So, Cusco is where my story starts—and not just Cusco, but the connected worlds of Runa peoples.

These are worlds based in reciprocity; worlds where plants, animals, mountains, rivers, lakes are regarded by humans as kin; where love and affection are shown in friends asking how "our" parents are doing; in shop keepers calling their clients "mami" (little mother) and "papi" (little father); in "what's wrong?" becoming a question of mutual interest: (like it or not) we're in this together. As Mary Oliver might say, the soft animal of my body recognizes and relaxes in this love. Is this world perfect? Not in the slightest. Violence, sexism, alcoholism, and political corruption exist alongside mutual care, veneration of Mother Earth, radical joy, and communal ethos. It's not even a contradiction. It's life.

When I saw The Image that fateful day in 2011, I knew this story was also part of mine. As I caught my breath The Image had sucked out, a question began to form: How could anyone want to hurt these women?

These gorgeous, hardworking, and loving women? My heartbreak was not intellectual, it was visceral. I felt the outrage in my bones. These were the women who had helped raise me, whose worlds and histories had shaped my own. That's when I knew I had to do something.

I began my work by trying to understand what had happened. Over the next six years, two grad programs, and two international moves, I learned about the history of population control and its role in U.S. foreign policy. I learned more about Perú's history of internal and settler colonialism, "social hygiene," its love of Indigenous cultures and its disdain for Indigenous peoples. I learned about the sterilization program itself.

Promised as Peru's first publicly funded family planning program, the ex-dictator, Alberto Fujimori, stood in front of the world at the United Nations Fourth World Women's Conference in Beijing in 1995. There, he lauded the program as a means of giving women control over their bodies and futures. Later that year, however, it became clear that's not what the National Program of Reproductive Health and Family Planning 1996-2000 (PNSRPF 1996-2000) was about. Between 1995 and 2001, approximately 314,000 people were sterilized, 95% of which were Indigenous women living in the Andes, Amazon, or as urban migrants in Lima. Documents later revealed that this genocide had been planned by a civico-military junta in 1989 during the internal armed conflict to curb the "terrorist" threat.

To stop population growth, we [the Peruvian government] must *urgently address existing excesses* using widespread sterilization in culturally backward and economically poor social groups... Permanent birth control methods should only be experimental, but tubal ligation should be the norm in health posts...We must discriminate... against these social sectors given their incorrigible character and lack of resource...the only thing left is their total extermination (*Plan por un Gobierno de la Reconstrucción National 1989*/The Plan for the Government of National Reconstruction 1989, quoted in Getgen 2009, 28, her translation).

In the department of Cusco alone (like a U.S. state or Canadian province), 10,000 people were sterilized.

The stories are harrowing, and while "the world needs to know" might be a good enough reason for some to share, I have become more sensitive to the effects of collecting and telling these stories. Years of wading through the sorrow led to too much weed and too much alcohol. The shocked faces of my audiences also give me pause. There must be a better way to tell this story. People need to know, yes, but there must be a way to do so without sucking the life out of them. We need them whole to fight The Good Fight, not curled up in a ball at the horrors of the world. Anthropology also seems to thrive off a good horror story—as if telling the horror were the same as doing something about it; it's not. So, I didn't want, as Tuck and Yang put it, to serve up pain stories on a silver platter for the academy either.

It was clear to me: if I wanted to escape from the images, stories, how must the women themselves feel?

I wanted to learn from them, but how to do it without having them relive their trauma—especially if I could offer nothing to ease their suffering in return? There were plenty of documentaries and news pieces recounting the horror, and I did not want to make these beautiful women cry just to get "my" research done. So instead, I spent 2015 to 2017 doing research on the Peruvian feminist movement's reaction to Fujimori's policy and reports of abuse.

How had it come to pass that a women's rights program had become the vehicle of the violation of Indigenous women's rights? Asking this question helped me learn about the context of 1990s Peru and the aftermath of the sterilizations; about why women's legal cases were going so slowly; about what kinds of legal and human rights violations had been committed by the state; and how Indigenous peoples consistently fall (or are pushed) outside the protection of the law. A small but committed group of academics, lawyers, and social activists have devoted their energies to making the state accountable for the atrocities it's committed—a frightening prospect given the persecution of human rights workers in the wake of the civil war. They march, write letters, and stage protests on the steps of the Supreme Court, but justice seems far away and affected women are still sick.

During my stay in 2015, I met Hilaria Supa Huamán, the first person to denounce forced sterilizations in Peru. A Runa leader from the Anta province of the state of Cusco, she helped organize women's federations to help combat sexism, domestic abuse, alcoholism, child malnutrition, and illiteracy in Runa communities in the early 1990s. Until 1969, Indigenous peoples attached to *haciendas,* plantation-like agricultural ventures, were not allowed to go to school. Twenty years later, the struggle was for women's education. To this day, many women over forty do not speak, read, or write Spanish. Their world is completely in Runasimi (Quechua), their husbands and children are their go-betweens. As part of this work Hilaria and her fellow leaders organized women's soccer tournaments in the mid 1990s to show that women were just as capable as men. These tournaments were also spaces for women to have fun and to forget their worries for a while. So, when several of Hilaria's players no longer wanted to participate citing illness, she became suspicious.

At first, these women didn't want to tell her what had happened. But finally, they told her: they had been taken to the health posts and sterilized without their consent. Because she was sent to work as a maid in the city at the age of seven, Hilaria spoke Spanish, and because of this outrage in her life, she was later able to contact lawyers in Lima and denounce what was happening.

Her leadership eventually propelled her into a congressional seat in 2006. She spent a decade deflecting racist attacks on her person and advocating for sterilized women and Indigenous peoples more generally. She helped pass laws on gender parity; laws protecting and revitalizing Indigenous languages; laws around prior consent and consultation; and laws working toward intercultural healthcare. In her capacity as a congressperson, she was also able to help impell president Ollanta Humala to sign a presidential decree in 2015 creating a program (REVIEFSO) to help sterilized women access medical and psychological care.

Affected women have many ailments that would be relieved with proper medical attention, but this care is hard to come by. To this day, many doctors say affected women are lying about their steril-ization or exaggerating the pain it is causing them. Other doctors, while sympathetic, simply can't find anything physically wrong with them. I know one woman who, with Hilaria's help, traveled to Lima, the capital, seven times. After all the blood tests, x-rays, sonograms, MRIs the doctors' answers were always the same: *no te pasa nada.* There is nothing wrong with you, the most frustrating diagnosis of all.

From the beginning, Hilaria knew that the law and biomedicine were not going to be enough to heal these women beset by headaches, dizziness, nausea, insomnia, anxiety, pain throughout their body and a deep, deep sadness. Many sterilized women were abandoned by their families, and in communities across Perú, silence reigns over this genocide. No one wants to talk about it, or believe it happened. It just hurts too much, I think. This silence leaves affected women in even more precarious positions, even more sick.

Hilaria got the idea to build a healing center for sterilized women while in hiding. She awakened one morning in early 2002 to find a bloody knife in her door. The powers that be regularly harassed Hilaria and sterilized women advocating for their rights. Police would come out to their communities, pick them up as if arrest them, only to leave them in the middle of nowhere. The bloody knife was a new level of intimidation, so Hilaria went into hiding, supported by a German woman who had married into her family. Together, they applied for funds from a German NGO, and when she came out in 2003, Hilaria began building the healing center. She called it *Mosoq Pakari,* or a New Dawn.

For several years women came To Mosoq Pakari for healing. A medical doctor treated their physical maladies, incorporating medicinal plants, acupuncture, and massage. *Paqos,* or medicine people, performed ceremonies, and *curanderas* (healers) called their spirits home. But the most potent medicine of all was the medicine of being together. For these women, many still in shock, being with women who had suffered the same fate was a balm: *I'm not crazy. This happened to you, too. This happened to us.* Together, women began to build memory and strength for their search for justice.

Women from Anta, Cusco had been fighting for justice since the late 1990s, coming to Lima in 2001 for the first press conference led by affected women. In 2003, the movement won a major victory at the Inter-American Court: Perú signed a "friendly accord" in the case of Mamérita Mestanza, a Runa woman who died from complications of her tubal ligation. Following the court's findings, Perú's government agreed to investigate and prosecute those culpable. A case of crimes against humanity committed by the state was filed within Perú against the state in 2003 on behalf of 1,300 forcibly sterilized women; it only entered the courts in 2021. The legal case has been at the heart of sterilized women's political activism, but coming home to heal on the land was something else entirely. Unfortunately, when Hilaria was elected to congress in 2006, there was no one to keep the center going, so it closed for a decade.

You may be asking where I fit into this story, dear reader. The paths Creator opens for us are often unclear and meandering, but never without reason, without purpose. We are sent where we are meant to be, and as it turns out, I was meant to be by Hilaria's side, as her *masi,* or friend. The kind of work that Hilaria does is not popular, at best not well understood by her community. As in many Indigenous communities across the Americas, colonization, economic changes, and everything in-between has led Indigenous women to be oppressed not only by wider society, but within their own communities as well. Things viewed as "women's issues" don't get much attention. Though well-regarded in Cusco more generally, Hilaria's own community is less supportive. We have a saying in Spanish, *nadie es profeta en su propia tierra.* No one is a prophet in their own lands. So, to get the center back up and running she needed outside help.

As mentioned, I first met Hilaria in 2015 at a conference announcing the creation of REVIEFSO, the registry for sterilized people that came with promises of medical and psychological care. The program was funded for a year, but detractors made sure its funding was not extended. So, when Hilaria's term in the Andean parliament ended in 2016, she moved back to her community in Anta and began work to reopen the healing center.

In 2017, a colleague and I invited Hilaria to present on a panel at the Latin American Studies Association conference taking place in Lima. She, along with two *presidentas* of associations of affected women, activists, and journalists, came to Lima to present the case to a new generation of university students and activists (this is part of what us academics can do to support our collaborator's work). The day after our panel, Hilaria and I ran into each other in the hustle and bustle of the conference corridors; we decided to retreat from the din and go for some tea. As we talked, I realized we shared a common concern: the health of sterilized women, most of whom remained very sick even twenty years after the fact.

Hilaria has suffered from severe rheumatoid arthritis since her early 20s. She knows what it's like to be a Runa woman who cannot work in the fields, care for her children, partake in *ayni,* reciprocal labor, or *minka,* community work. You're left to the side; pitied at best, reviled, and abandoned at worst. This experience has connected her deeply to sterilized women and their plight. It's a solidarity borne of empathy.

Lawyers speak of women's experiences in terms of human rights violations and, as I mentioned, doctors seem to be at a loss. For my part, I knew the harms of sterilization went beyond any legal or medical definition. I had enough knowledge of Runa worlds to know that this harm was not just being felt by individual women, their families, or even their human communities. I had a hunch that the harms reverberated into women's relations with the very Earth herself. I spoke of my intuition, and something about my words led to the invitation that would change the course of my life: "come visit me in Anta," Hilaria said.

That first visit in 2017 was short but felt like going home—not any easy home, mind you. The Andes are a harsh environment, as cold and unforgiving as they are beautiful and awe inspiring. While I was there, we sorted potato for seed, washed quinoa, fed *cuyes* or guinea pigs that are a staple of celebratory feasts in Runa communities. We peeled lima beans (two skins!) by the *q'uncha* or fire stove, the heart of Runa homes. Though they pegged me as a *huaylaca* (a woman who doesn't know how to do women's work, which includes killing and dressing animals, sorting potato seed, and dexterously flinging heavy bundles wrapped in *lliclla* or woven cloths onto your back), they saw something in me and asked me back.

I returned in 2018 with my mom, and Hilaria took us to the healing center for the first time. It is unusual for anthropologists to be taken to the field by their moms, but mine had worked in the same region forty years earlier. She knew it was important for people to know I wasn't *q'ala,* or socially naked: I had people. Relations are everything in Runa worlds, and my mom wanted the community to know I wasn't a random person who might prove dangerous to them. So, we walked through the community all together, up the hill to the healing center, admiring the hawks floating on the morning thermals along the way. Hilaria unlocked the center's tall metal gate, opening a new world to me. The center's buildings were a little worse for wear. Plaster fell from the ceremonial roundhouse's adobe walls and parts of the *ichu* or feathergrass thatch were sliding off its conical roof. The other buildings were also in a state, but still beautiful. Hilaria had big plans. But first, lunch.

Hilaria and her nephew took us to eat *chicharron,* fried pork, served with raw, salt-soaked onions, mint, fried potato rounds, and boiled hominy. As we rolled our way home across the prairie of Anta held in the arms of towering snow-capped mountains, I thought about the morning at the healing center, about the women who were still so sick. I leaned forward, sticking my head between the front seats to better see Hilaria. I asked, "Hilaria, the symptoms that women have: nervousness, lack of appetite, not being able to sleep... do you think they have PTSD?"

"Of course they do!" She answered incredulously from under her tall hat. "But what you call psychology we call spirituality. Affected women would like access to psychologists. They have the right to see one through the SIS [Public Insurance] because of REVIEFSO, but no psychologist comes out here. They had psychologists for a little bit right after REVIEFSO was put in, but one or two sessions is not enough, and it was hard for women to get to a town. In any case, the doctors and psychologists don't understand this spiritual part. They only want to treat *una partecita*, just a part of you, *no más.* These women have *susto.* Can you imagine waking up on the floor with women screaming and children crying all around you, not knowing what happened to you? That is a big *susto.*"

In Runa medicine, you can receive a fright so big that your spirit leaves your body. This spirit fright is called *susto* in Spanish or *mancharisqa* in Runasimi (Quechua). Susto is an *enfermedad de la tierra,* an "illness of the land," a class of illness that stems from breakdowns in social relations among humans and between humans and their other-than-human kin. Along with susto, these include illnesses like *wayrasqa* (getting hit by a bad wind sent by the Old Places or Old Ones); *llapachasqa* or *pacha qapin* (when you fall asleep on the ground, and the Earth grabs your heart, taking your energy) or *soq'a* (when you are seduced by spirits who take the form of people, making you sick and eventually killing you). These are distinct from "illnesses from God," that come from bacteria, viruses, or fungi. Those the doctor can take care of. But medical doctors cannot see or treat illnesses of the land: to heal susto, for instance, you must seek the aid of a *paqo*, a medicine person, or a *curandera*, a healer. This is what the center could offer women. We agreed that I would return the following year to support the rehabilitation of the center (decolonization=land back, resources back) and to do research on what forced sterilization had harmed by looking at what was being healed and how. Healing, not trauma, would be the focus of our work.

I spent ten months with Hilaria between 2019 and 2020, and together, we watched the healing center come back to life. I observed how the center had been built on three terraces following the Andeans three-world cosmos; I learned that the octagonal shape of the of the guest house had come to Hilaria in a dream; I helped make adobe bricks and harvest highlands feathergrass to repair the roundhouse's roof, and was struck that only one man knew how to re thatch the roof, though forty years ago, most the roofs were grass; I watched as each worker offered a little *chicha* (corn bear) to the earth and mountains before drinking it him or herself: the pachamama, *mother earth*, and the *apus,* mountains beings, were as much a part of the rebuilding as any human. I also learned that the location of the center had been chosen by the ancestors: they came to the medicine people during a ceremony.[1] Even the hawks circling overhead signaled Hilaria that this was a sacred place for sacred work. When the roof on the guest house was finished, we had a big party, and Hilaria rechristened the center *Mosoq Pakari Sumaq Kawsay:* A New Dawn for Good Living. Before we were able to invite women back, though, COVID hit, shutting all our work down. The center would remain closed for another three years.

I was finally able to return in the summer of 2023. In my absence, Hilaria had continued working. The center now had infrastructure for a sauna, a new bathroom and guest quarters, and boasted adobe chicken and guinea pig houses and a big garden. The healing center is a space reminiscent of prior Runa households. While Runa today still raise cuys and pigs, many no longer have chickens or home gardens and depend on buying and selling at market to procure staple foods. This is fine when there is money, but COVID revealed just how fragile Peru's (and the world's) food system was.

Moreover, most households now use *materia noble* or "noble materials" like rebar and cement block (instead of adobe) to build their homes, as these materials signal economic success. But cement block is a terrible material for homes in the frigid climes of the Andes. Unlike adobe which holds in heat and stays dry, cement holds in cold and moisture, leading to upper respiratory infections. Likewise, roofs made of metal sheeting are not as warm as those made of highlands grasses or terracotta tile. New technology is not always the best technology. So, alongside serving as a healing center for sterilized women, the center is something of a model house, a reminder of the importance of process, reciprocity, and passing along traditional knowledge that have kept Runa alive and healthy all this time.

As I settled into the rhythm of daily farm life, Hilaria and I started planning a two-day healing workshop for affected women. Having worked closely with her for years, I had an idea of what Hilaria wanted to achieve: a workshop that could contribute to women's healing in several dimensions and on their terms, on their lands and in their language. Affected women hadn't received detailed information about their case since before COVID, so we invited Quechua-speaking lawyers well familiar with the case. The land hosts an abundance of medicinal plants, but some of the more technical knowledge regarding plants and their varied uses has been dispersed (not lost), so we invited a bilingual expert in plant medicine. Affected women remain traumatized, so we invited Quechua-speaking trauma informed psychologists. The women are spiritually sick, so we also invited a healer to *pasar huevo* or pass eggs over the bodies of the women to diagnose their illness, as well as a medicine man to do a ceremony to feed the Earth and beseech the mountains and land for their support in women's healing; food is medicine, so we chose the menu with care: the day of the *despacho,* or ceremonial feeding of the Earth, we would eat and offer pachamama cuy soup, a meal to please human and earth-being participants alike.

Eight women arrived early on the first morning, bringing wood, vegetables—anything they could spare—to share. In the Andes, you never arrive empty-handed, nor do you rest on your laurels. And our guests immediately went to work. A small group sat outside in the early morning sun peeling potatoes, the *ssschrk, ssschrk, ssschrk,* of their knives cutting potato skins setting the rhythm of their words, punctuated by the *plop!* of potatoes hitting water. The women's conversations ranged from how to take care of sick chickens to ornery husbands and wayward children. Runa are very funny people, and these women were no exception, making each other laugh in the middle of stories that might otherwise break your heart. I was reminded that, for these women, just being together was a tonic. They didn't have to prove to anyone that what they said happened in fact did. They all carried the scars on their bodies and their spirits.

Around 9:30 a.m., the lawyers from Human Rights Without Borders arrived. We planned to have everyone sit in a circle on stools, but the eight women decided to sit directly on the grass instead, and the lawyers joined them in this horizontal communication. Time runs differently in rural and agrarian life. Though distances have been compacted due to the presence of cars and phones, activities like planting, weeding, fertilizing, caring for animals, cooking on wood stoves, and coming to community decisions through consensus, all continue to take the time they take, no more and no less. You can't rush a plant to grow.

For the next two hours—an eternity in legal time—affected women were able to get an update on their legal cases and, for the first time, have the process explained in their own language. The women were able to ask questions and get clarification to finally understand why their cases were taking so long (answer: government strategy, legal corruption). They were able to lodge complaints: Why were their notices for giving testimony not arriving? Or if they arrived, why were they being given to community authorities (not always sympathetic) instead of directly to the individual it was addressed to, or at least the leaders of their organization? The notices for testimony were themselves intimidating: a full page of Spanish legalese that even I, *Doctora Luci,* had trouble understanding.

The women also wanted to know why they didn't have lawyers. Of the 1300 women listed in the class-action, only two hundred or so currently have legal representation. What could they do to assure their representation? Even though some problems remained intractable, at least the women now knew what they were. With knowledge, action becomes possible.

After our lunch of chicken and quinoa soup, Profe Justo, a Runa-simi-speaking plant biologist, arrived to reinforce women's knowledge of medicinal plants. (He recalled meeting Hilaria thirty years earlier when she was a young *dirigenta* (community leader), and he a recently graduated biologist. A relationship renewed!) Profe Justo's lessons were important as during the forced sterilization campaign, government health officials also persecuted midwives.

Health officials' justification was that too many women were dying in childbirth and that if there were no midwives, women would have to go to the hospital, which would save their lives. Runa women know better than this. While they may not die, the abuse they receive at the hands of medical professionals is such that, even in 2019, one pregnant woman told me that she would rather die than give birth in a hospital. At first, I was shocked by her statement. But being with sterilized women, seeing how they suffered, and listening to other women's stories of obstetric violence, I came to understand that there are, in fact, fates worse than death—especially in worlds where having your abdomen cut is akin to cutting your life force and not being able to have children is personally tragic and socially punishable.

Importantly, midwives, *parteras,* don't only deliver babies; they're also expert herbalists. When parteras went underground, so did a lot of their knowledge. Most households continue to have a working knowledge of common medicinal plants for stomach ailments and pain (plants like *muña, ruda, llantén, ch'iri ch'iri, yawar ch'unka, malba, tarwi tarwi, molle*), but vast amounts of plant knowledge has been dispersed through years of violence, out-migration, and cultural shame. During his lively presentation, Profe Justo went over the various plants that could help women cure their inflammations, infections, insomnia, and other ailments, making them laugh, answering their questions, and dialoguing with them as equals—all in Runasimi.

The day's final presenter was Nely, a young Runa psychologist from Hilaria's *comunidad campesina,* or peasant community. She led a workshop on trauma, family dynamics, and relaxation—the usual psychological suspects. Nely was also trained, though, in psychology based on the Runa cosmovision. This was the first time she had been exposed to the sterilizations in depth, but through her training and lived experience Nely had intimate knowledge of the personal devastation that Runa women might experience if they could not have children, work in the fields, or reproduce their family's and community's social, spiritual, and biological lives.

She began with somatic exercises, getting the women on their feet to shake out their bodies. Nely explained that trauma lives as tension in the body and that getting it out makes you feel better. She likened ruminating thoughts to *gusanos*, worms digging through your body just as worms eat through potatoes: "You have to take them out, look at them, throw them to the ground, and watch them wriggle away—or else eat them! Grind them up with your teeth!" The women roared with laughter.

They also talked about problems they were having in their families, with their husbands, with their children, and how to handle those conflicts. First and foremost, it was important to remember

---

that their sterilizations *weren't their fault* and to stand firm in that knowledge. Guilt ate at these women, often leaving them unable to fend off psychological attacks.

Importantly, the women did this work of processing feelings *together*. So often, psychology emphasizes one-on-one therapy. This approach isn't always effective in Western contexts where people's ideas of selfhood are already more individual, so it's especially ineffective in more communal or collective contexts. Everyone needs privacy and time to themselves to process. But when it comes to healing, reconnecting to your community after trauma (which destroys bonds by its very nature) is part and parcel to the process. We don't heal by ourselves, just as we don't get sick by ourselves.

The next morning, we began the process of spiritual healing. Mama Hilaria (not my friend Hilaria), a curandera came to *pasar huevo* or pass eggs over the women to diagnose what ailed them. She was called to her healing work by lightning: among Runa, those who get hit by lightning (and survive) are called to work with the energies of the earth, to mediate among the human nations, the plant nations, and the earth-being nations, and to connect this world (*kay pacha*), with those of the sky world (*hanan pacha*), and the underworld of regeneration (*ukhu pacha*).

When they encounter spiritual illness, healers use eggs or guinea pigs to diagnose what is wrong. In the case of the eggs, the healer passes two all over the patient's body, invoking the mountain beings, earth beings, the pachamama, and Jesus Christ to pull malevolent energies out of the patient. Most traditional healers are also Catholic and invoke the healing power of all spiritual beings to heal their patients. Both eggs are then cracked into separate glasses of water. The healer raises this glass against the light to read the egg and find out what negative energies are hurting the patient to prescribe treatment.

Having Mama Hilaria there to do the pasada de huevo was particularly significant as she herself is a survivor of sterilization. She knows intimately the struggles of her fellow survivors. Mama Hilaria had us set up a table in the middle of the center's yard and cover it with a *lliclla* or woven cloth. The women sat in a crescent in front of the table, waiting to take their turns. One by one, each woman sat at the table, taking off her hat and sweater. The morning sun was strong, and the women closed their eyes as Mama Hilaria took the eggs in her right hand, passing them over the women's heads and necks, under their shirts, around their backs, down their legs and feet. As she did this, Mama Hilaria invoked the earth beings around us: *"Pachamamita, ayuda a nuestra hermana. Apucitos, papitos, Jesu*

Cristo, te suplicamos, cura a tu hija/ Pachamamita, (Mother Earth) (-ita is the diminutive, expressing closeness and care), help our sister. Apus (mountain beings), little fathers, Jesus Christ, we beseech you, heal your daughter." When she finished passing the eggs over the woman's body, Mama Hilaria had her blow *haaa, haaa, haaa* onto each egg to pass a bit of her *aliento* (literally breath, but also breath of life) into this being.

Everyone watched closely as Mama Hilaria cracked each egg into the water. Some yolks sank to the bottom. Others floated near the middle or sat at the top (not good news). Some eggs whites remained clear, while others sent wisps of slightly cooked egg to the top of the water—also not good news. She diagnosed something physically wrong with each woman, usually inflammations in their legs, arms, or abdomen, but all had one illness in common: they all had susto. Some had it stronger than others, but they all had it.

Having anticipated this, at the same time that she passed the eggs, Mama Hilaria also called each woman's spirit home. As she brushed their bodies, she would say "Natividad,[2] where are you? Natividad, come back." Cupping her hands around the crown of Natividad's head Mama Hilaria breathed her spirit, *haaaa, haaa, haaaa,* back into her. If a woman had family there with her, Mama Hilaria would say, "María,[3] come back! Your granddaughter is here waiting for you."

As I commented in my dissertation on healing from susto in the Andes:

> In Runa theories of health and wellness, *el espíritu* (Spa., spirit), is the part of one's being that connects one to others. It makes social relations possible (Mujica Bermúdez 2020). Mancharisqa [susto] is a dangerous illness because the spirit is a discrete bodily entity that can become dislodged from the body through fright, which affects the sufferer's

ability to relate to their world (Cáceres Chalco 2008). If left untreated, the initial damage to the body done by susto penetrates deeper and deeper (Mujica Bermúdez 2020, 71; see also Yánez de Pozo 2005). This inward progression can continue into the person's absolute interiority until their *ukusunqu* (inner heart), the "space of resistance, critique [as thinking-feeling], and mindful watching," is weakened (Mujica Bermúdez 2020, 73). Over time, this weakening can result in the loss of their "spiritual reserve," their will to self-protect and to protect relationships. If this progression goes untreated and their relationships with themselves and others fall away, eventually, the person with susto ceases to be *gente*/human, ceases to be Runa (Mujica Bermúdez 2020, 73). In other words, the death of relation with oneself and with others is the death of a person recognizable as a human: without a sociality that is collectively oriented, that thinks in terms of relations, that person is no longer Runa, no longer a "real human" (Stavig 2022, 142).

People who have experienced deep depression might recognize this inability to connect or this loss of spiritual reserve, self-regard, and self-protection. Rarely, though, in modern Western medicine is depression connected to the spirit. But Runa and other Indigenous medicines (as well as mystics and devotees of the great spiritual traditions) remember what biomedicine has forgotten: we are more than flesh and bone; we are spirits having earthly experiences, and sometimes, for many different reasons, we are plunged into the "dark night of the soul."

A diagnosis, susto is different from clinical depression or PTSD because it centers the loss of spiritual connection with themself and community as the main source of illness. Its treatment, then, is based on attenuating the source of fright and reconnecting the patients to themselves and their communities — human and beyond.

I have intimate knowledge of this process as Mama Hilaria treated me for susto in 2019. Years of work on forced sterilization and other horrors, multiple moves, eight years of grad school, and a failing long-distance relationship had taken their toll. I was extremely sick. Unable to sleep well, I awoke terrified. Mornings had set me gagging since mid-2018. I had seen doctors, therapists, and psychiatrists, but no one took my illness seriously. I was too "high functioning" for anyone to believe something was seriously wrong, even as my mind began suggesting that death was a good solution. I wanted the terror and pain to end, but these suicidal thoughts scared me.

I felt guilty going to Hilaria's in such a state. I couldn't eat well, and not being able to eat in a society in which relations are built through food didn't seem wise. But I didn't see another choice given the demands of my program, funding cycles, and my own compulsion. So when, months into research, Hilaria and I were taking a family member to see Mama Hilaria, I took the opportunity to finally state the obvious.

"Mantay (elder mother), I think I have susto."

"I'd believe it," she said matter-of-factly. It's true I hadn't been at my best. Even though I was able to work and put on a brave face, I was still quick to cry, slow to eat, and losing weight at an alarming rate. I knew Hilaria was worried. "Let's see what Mama Hilaria says." I hadn't said anything because I didn't want to be a bother or take up precious resources. (Was this research ethics or depression talking?). But it was becoming clear that my illness wasn't mine alone. It affected other people, Hilaria included. I had already been scolded for trying to hide a stomach infection.

I started to throw up after several days of feeling sicker than usual, and Hilaria worried that I had been hit by a bad wind. When there is social conflict and the Old Places or Old Ones send a *mal viento* or bad wind, it doesn't always hit the people directly involved. Sometimes it strikes someone tangential to the conflicting parties, particularly if that person is already vulnerable due to illness. Needless to say, I was a sitting duck. So, when I started throwing up, Hilaria feared the worst. However, the timeline of my illness didn't match up with wayrasqa or wind sickness—especially once I told them I had been sick for a while. "You can't say you are an honest person and not tell us when you are sick!" Hilaria admonished me. But I still felt uneasy. How could I possibly have the same illness as sterilized women? They had gone through something so terrible. How could I be suffering from the same illness? I finally conceded the possibility the more I read and learned about susto. Susto is a spectrum illness. Kids get it when they fall, and it's easily treatable. Adults get it for many different reasons, from the mundane (family conflict) to the horrifically exceptional (forced sterilization). Soul fright is just a fact of life. I wasn't comparing our illnesses; I was being human in a frightening world.

Mama Hilaria treated my susto in the same way she treated the women at the healing center: passing eggs, lighting incense, brushing my body, calling my spirit. I wasn't immediately healed, and neither were the women at the center. But very importantly, someone finally validated the sickness—and could even tell us what was wrong. We weren't crazy! Our paths to healing are, of course, very different, but they started in the same place: reconnecting with ourselves.

After my treatment, I felt anger for the first time in months. Anger can be, among many other things, an indication of self-regard, a recognition that your boundaries have been crossed. I finally started to feel like I was worth protecting. In the case of sterilized women, they were literally cut from themselves and their more-than-human communities. No one can heal that physical cut. But the susto this cut caused can be treated. As mentioned, healing from susto takes many different forms, but at their core they all involve reconnection, being brought back into the fold. No one does this work alone. Trauma and illness reverberate throughout the shared body of a community, and this is why the work of the healing center is so important: helping one person heal brings the community one step closer to healing, too.

As Mama Hilaria finished the *pasada de huevo* with the eight women at the healing center, Tayta Hipólito and his family arrived to perform a ceremony that included a *despacho,* or ritual feeding of the Places and Beings: mountain beings (*apus*), water beings (*q'ochas*), the lands we were on (*pachamamas*), Mother Earth (*Pachamama*), the ancestors (*machus*), and many more. There are parts of the ceremony I can't discuss according to protocol, but the Tayta (*father,* an honorific used for *yachaqs,* "people who know," or those who mediate between the human and spirit worlds) told me it was it was appropriate to share the despacho.

In the days prior to the workshop, Hilaria and I ran all over Cusco buying the necessary ingredients for the despacho, including carnations, roses, incense, *coca* leaves, quinoa, perfume, sweet wine, and liquor. As we set these things up on the offering table, Tayta Hipólito, his two sons, and his wife put on colorful ponchos and *chullos* (woven toques with ear flaps). Their chullos were beaded according to their advancement along the spiritual path, and Tayta Hipólito's was covered in so many tiny white beads you could barely see its rainbow colors beneath.

He laid a piece of white butcher paper on the table. He began to talk and drink pisco (Peruvian brandy) as he prepared the despacho. One by one, he invited us to add *quintu,* offerings of three coca leaves, asking for our health, the health of our families, success in economic endeavors or children's and grandchildren's studies— anything for which we needed support. Tayta Hipólito arranged our quintus in a ring, surrounded them with flowers, incense and candies. He sprinkled wine and liquor over the despacho and then passed us the libations so we could drink alongside the Places and Beings. Once finished, he folded the paper into a packet and wrapped it in a beautiful woven cloth. He then came to each of us and, one by one, passed the packet over our bodies.

We followed Tayta Hipólito and his sons out onto the mountain to find a place to burn the despacho. His sons opened a small hole in the side of the mountain, offering libations and incense to the Place. They started a small fire and when it was burning hot, Tayta Hipólito had us turn away before placing the packet on the flames. When the packet burns, the Places and Beings come to eat the despacho. The fire becomes the conduit of reconnection. The women stood by, facing away from the fire, looking at the lake. My god children and several women's grandchildren ran around the mountain, but Tayta

Hipólito's wife, a recently retired schoolteacher, drew their attention to the lake to make sure they didn't look at the flames and risk spiritual harm. Once the fire had consumed the packet, we all hugged and made our way back down the mountain to a sumptuous meal of cuy soup. After two days of being away, the women were anxious to get home to their families and animals. Farm life never stops. So, as we finished up lunch, the women started packing their things and left one by one and hugged as they went.

A week after the healing workshop, Hilaria and I went to Natividad's house to buy grass for our guinea pigs. One of Natividad's neighbors was also sterilized and attended the workshop, so we talked to both for a while. They said that for the first time in years, their bodies didn't hurt, and they were sleeping through the night. They looked lighter, more rested, healthier. Hilaria's face lit up at this news, and I could feel her energy lift. She herself has good and bad days because of her illness, and seeing the women feel better, with strength, energized Hilaria, too. Hilaria and the women who came have been walking together for justice (*justiciapaqmi purishanchis*) for almost thirty years, but this was one of the first times they had gotten to heal together on the land since the early 2000s. "We need to keep going, Luci," Hilaria told me as we drove home. "See how happy they are? That is what this is all about."

Hilaria and I are now in the middle of planning further healing workshops to keep the momentum going, to bring more women, and involve more community members. We also want to expand the center's work to help meet the climate crisis, which will further affect the community's food sovereignty. We've partnered with a U.S. Indigenous foundation to support the community's efforts to harvest and store water. The hope is that, over time, this partnership can support other efforts toward climate resilience like reforestation of native trees, reestablishment of family gardens, and whatever else the community decides it wants and needs. The future is not certain, but hemispheric solidarities among Indigenous peoples certainly make it brighter.

Healing goes beyond the individual. Just as sickness does not stay with the sick, neither does healing. We all benefit from each other's wellness, so let us take care of ourselves and each other the best we can. It is my great honor to share this story with you, dear reader. I hope these pages serve as a reminder that even in the midst of horror, there is great hope—and not the hope of wishful thinking, but the hope borne of action, of Indigenous women's and allies' fights for a more just and loving future. *Añay, sulpay, urpillay sunqullay.* Thank you from the bottom of my heart.

JIJAQEMIJ[1]
(SPIRIT OR SHADOW WOMEN)

Alisa R. Lombard

Sharing is Medicine

Giving birth is a private, intimate experience for many women. Sometimes, mom is unaccompanied. Other times, a gathering of people await the arrival of new life. Sharing the experience is uncomfortable and gives rise to a sentiment of vulnerability for me.

Life givers have engaged in this process since literal time immemorial, human, animal, fish and plants alike, in their own ways. Birth is the essence of human existence. Birth stories are rarely, if ever, shared lightly with strangers, caregivers, or even family members. Many people believe that birthing stories are a gift. I think I do too.

However, relating to the lived experiences of the people we represent, as lawyers and advocates, strengthens the bond of understanding and compassion. For those reasons, and on Morningstar's respectful request, I will share, for they say sharing is medicine. I too believe this.

When I was approximately seven months pregnant, I attended a prenatal visit accompanied by my husband. In the habitual manner, the attending resident went through a series of questions and cautions – all familiar to us. We sat patiently in the examination room and answered in turn. I was dressed in a suit, having left work to go to the appointment, and my husband sat beside me in casual attire, his t-shirt showing the tapestry of tattoos he confidently adorns on his arms. Like a lightning bolt, the resident asked, "Oh, I don't have this on the chart. What's your nationality?" We both responded in unison, "Native," and looked at each other perplexed. The resident promptly followed up with, "You know you're not supposed to drink when you're pregnant, right?" My jaw dropped, my husband erupted into laughter, and all I could muster was, "Yes, of course I know that." Immediately after, I said, "You know, if you had buffered the nationality question and that statement with other questions or statements, I may not have noticed that our race appears to be what provoked you to say what you did. That's not okay." He scurried out of the room, and we never saw him again.

I went through my first pregnancy braving the pain of an auto-immune disease that affects the joints in my spine and hips. Anky-losing spondylitis is a very painful condition made more challenging by weight bearing on the person's front end. If treatment is not administered early on in the progression of the disease, one's back may curve forward irreparably. I was diagnosed with this condition after years of mysterious pain, and in the beginning of my first preg-nancy. The medication I was taking to treat the disease and its pain had to cease before the third trimester; otherwise, the baby's heart may suffer defects. This was not a risk I was willing to take, and so the third trimester was a harrowing time toward the end of which I was not able to walk very well and was in a lot of pain. Although my rheumatologist was confident that I would need a Caesarian section due to a fusion of my sacroiliac joint, I was induced three days before my due date and gave birth naturally somehow.

After three days of attempted induction using less invasive mea-sures; baby did not respond. I was exhausted for those three days, in pain and mostly immobile. On the morning of the fourth day of induction attempts, I was admitted to the hospital, where my water was broken and I was administered drugs to bring about labour. Committed to a birth without an epidural for reasons that now seem generally masochistic, I braved 8 centimetres with only gas for the pain. At that point, an epidural was offered and I desperately accepted. Despite our birthing plan to go without, my husband wisely said absolutely nothing when I accepted it without reservation. I had been seriously concerned about possible contra-indications with my auto-immune disease. Despite the risks, I jumped into the idea without hesitation.

The anesthesiologist attended with a resident because I birthed in a teaching hospital. He took what felt like forever to run through the risks, benefits, and alternative options as I continued contractions and pleaded for relief. He explained that my consent was important, and that he was professionally and legally required to run through all this information before administering the epidural. During contractions, he would pause the carefully prepared script, and commence once again when the contraction waned and I was able to semi-focus. Once the epidural was inserted, and the medication (including fentanyl) ran through my body, I felt warm, relieved, and gleefully numb in places in my body where I had felt I was on fire moments prior. I'll never forget Dr. Feelgood. After the feelgood medicine, I rested and even slept for 30 minutes. When I woke, I was checked, and informed that it was time to get to work – my body was ready.

With only a nurse and my husband, I began to push and appeared to be better at it than the nurse had anticipated as she frantically called for the physician. He arrived just in time to deliver our first sacred bundle, who came into this world screaming so loud our family in the waiting room heard her loud and clear.

They placed my little chubby bundle on my chest soon thereafter, and my husband and I cried tears of joy as we studied every little part, fingers, toes, nose, and those big cheeks. Bald as could be, she was adorned with a little hat to keep her warm and a blanket that we have kept and cherished to this very day. All the while, my husband reports being shocked and troubled by the amount of blood and injuries I sustained in the process. The doctors dutifully stitched me up while I took in the first moments of motherhood, completely unaware that I had sustained a second-degree tear due in part to the speed of the baby's birth. I didn't feel it at the time, but in a few hours, I began to be wholly aware.

For me, giving life was life-altering. It felt like an eclipse of time in which I faced the awesomeness of my own strength, and the endless limits of my physical, emotional, mental, and spiritual resilience. Unconditional love at first sight and its long-awaited anticipation pushed me well beyond every limit. My singular concern was my baby – my own well-being, a distant, fleeting non-thought. Lay it on me, Dr. Feelgood. I'll deal with whatever happens. Just pause this pain, please! I didn't even care that I was getting a needle in my spine because any pain associated with it was nothing compared to the pain of labour, I felt.

In the moments following each birth of my two daughters', my eyes closed to embrace each and every note of my daughters' sweet scent. The sounds in the delivery room faded into quiet blurred mutters by the intensity of the moment. My fingers touched their plump-fleshy faces, which I'd only been able to imagine while they were in my belly all those months. My dear sister-friend, Waneek Horn-Miller, braved pregnancy with me and gave birth to a beautiful baby girl six days after me.

Birth was also traumatic. I laid awake at night before the birth of my first daughter, thinking about the coming pain, my baby's well-being, recovery and the sleepless nights ahead. Birth may result in vaginal tears or cuts, incisions to a woman's stomach and stomach muscles, loss of blood, permanent injuries, and even death. I could not stop thinking about what was coming, and the fact that there was no way to stop it. As a first-time mom, the anticipation was anxiety-provoking, to say the least. Women risk their lives in child birth. I did without hesitation, twice, and may do so again; we're not sure yet.

In my experience, the combination of horror, fear, wonder, and respect on a partner's face as they witness that which they cannot do, and, for some; can barely watch. My strong, tattooed *Nehiyewak* husband paced, prayed, winced, covered his face, held my hand, and looked away. The proud and dedicated father of our girls clutched his medicine pouch, which had been carefully prepared for the purposes of housing our daughter's belly button. He waited, hour after hour after hour. They arrived. He cried, overjoyed, overwhelmed, falling in love in the deepest way with his baby girls. Relieved, grateful and exhausted. We both could think only as far as making sure our babies were healthy and getting them home to our family's safe space, to protect them, to introduce them to their relations, to watch closely, and take in every moment, as they already began to change before our eyes.

Despite the agonizing pain of labour and delivery in 2016, I somehow enthusiastically and eagerly repeated the experience in early 2019. Adrenaline rushed through my body again in what now feels like the distant past. I knew what would generally happen this time, though I could not be absolutely sure. It didn't matter. I could only think as far as holding my second baby girl in my arms and getting to know her, take care of her, love her, and to see her grow into kind, strong and grounded women, close to her big sister who was beyond excited to make her little sister's acquaintance.

My second term pregnancy was much more bearable as I was, and continue, to take biologics to manage my auto-immune disease. Nonetheless, the end of pregnancy was filled with sleepless nights, discomfort, and equal parts excitement and glee. When I was eight months pregnant, our eldest took ill with respiratory syncytial virus (RSV) and was hospitalized. As she underwent tests, I was in the maternity ward with oxygen levels lower than they should have been. Diagnosed with pneumonia, I stayed by my ill daughter's bedside, answering work emails when I had the strength, and taking a puffer ritually to assist my breathing. We recovered, but I still struggled with shortness of breath for some time.

Our second daughter commenced her debut at 1 a.m. on the morning of my own birthdate, a full week after her due date. I advised my husband that the familiar labour pains had started, and, having timed them before waking him, I reported that they were now three minutes apart. With my niece, her fiancé, and my big sister at our home for the weeks preceding her birth, we all juggle work, my niece's law school, her fiancé's university obligations, my husband's work, my own work, and our first-born's day-care attendance and general care.

It was a busy time. Without our family's dutiful support, I don't know how we would have managed. My husband flew out of bed and alerted my niece and her fiancé of the show's commencement. He helped me down the stairs, our first-born quietly sleeping, and packed our pre-prepared necessaries in the vehicle to start toward the hospital. The ride was faster than usual, angst fuelling my expert driver husband's conduct on the highway that early winter morning. My husband made some phone calls, the first to his mom, Kokum, but I wasn't focused on what he was doing as I tried to cushion the bumps on the road.

We arrived at the hospital, I was checked in, and it was determined that I would need to breach four centimetres cervical dilation before I was admitted to the birthing ward. I wasn't far off already, and a little walking did the trick. I was quick to express my wish for an early epidural, which was the plan all along and honoured. The anesthesiologist and attending nurse praised my husband and I for the hypnotic way in which we came together during the spinal's administration.

What I didn't know, but learned after, was that to keep the pace of labour after the administration of an early epidural, induction medication must be administered consistently to ensure that contractions keep the pace. This had not been done, and my contractions fell to 14 minutes apart. The nurse in charge of the floor came in and reminded the attending nurse that the baby had to come out soon, that she was in distress, and that meconium was in the water. Unable to crank up the induction medicine in a single dial motion, it became urgent for baby to be born. Although she was not as far down as she needed to be for me to start pushing, I was asked to anyway, so I did what I was told. After an hour of creative positioning and pushing, baby was born, lethargic and purple, without a single sound. No sooner did they place her on my chest, than the head nurse said, "I don't like the colour of this baby" as she swooped her up, my husband on her heels. As I was being repaired and feeling the greatest degree of anxiety ever known to me despite the drugs, I heard baby scream and felt instant relief. They returned her to me, bundled and regaining colour. My husband and I rejoiced and studied her intense stares into our souls.

About an hour later, I answered an email or a text (I can't remember which) from my former work colleague, who was astonished that I had been so communicative while still lying on the birthing table.

Mothers around the world brave the exhaustion, the pain, the bewilderment of pregnancy and childbirth. Mothers experience the roller coaster rides of hormonal fluctuations, sometimes severe and plagued with unsettling impacts on mental health. A mother can be up night after night after night, tending to her precious sacred bundle, with bags under her eyes and a tired smile on her face. Sometimes, tears for no reason – just happiness, exhaustion, wonder, and emotions with no names.

We experienced early parenthood, pregnancy, miscarriage, and viable childbirth while I represented Indigenous women who had been, and continue to be, robbed of their reproductive autonomy. I miscarried on March 31, 2018 and carried on. I feel that my husband carried much of the pain and agony of our loss, as I soldiered on. Thankfully, we became pregnant a few months later. I carried on with my pregnancy, working obscene hours, travelling for work one out of every two to three weeks, while trying my best to be a good mom to my first born, and a wife to my super-dad husband. As I carried on my pregnancy, I did not pull back my advocacy as my family had asked that I do. Rather, I increased it, and spoke frequently about the experiences of my clients, on their instructions, for the purposes of raising public awareness.

I thought of the women constantly and saw my first-born daughter in them. I had to keep doing it, no matter how tired and emotionally drained, because my daughters, and all our daughters, have a right that was callously denied to a disproportionate number of Indigenous women and girls. I did not accept the potential of this lot for her, which means we cannot accept this lot for Indigenous women and girls, period.

Equality under the terms of the Constitution does not exist in columns or casts. Substantive equality, to which Indigenous women and girls are entitled at law, is not a guideline, it is not a recommendation, and it is not a privilege. It is a right, which Canada has constitutional, international and morally binding obligations to fulfill. There are no exceptions when it comes to bodily-autonomy, self-determination and the right to receive health care free from racism and discrimination. Indigenous peoples are the collective survivors of delayed personhood. The humanhood of Indigenous women and girls, once unlawfully denied, is not subject to any measure of debate.

Story after story after horrible story drove me to fly over the pond in November 2018. At the time, I was into my third trimester and needed the permission of my doctor to travel, which she granted after a serious discussion about whether or not it was necessary as I was considered high risk. I explained that a Committee of the United Nations was meeting and willing to hear from my clients on the issue of very important human rights violations. Unbeknownst to me, she had been aware of my advocacy on the issue of the forced sterilization of Indigenous women and girls.

I will never forget her expression as she smiled and said solemnly, "That is important," as any concern seemed to leave her expression. She said, "I know what you've been working on, and I support it. I can't imagine what those women went through, and are going through. But let me tell you, medicine is full of men who think they know what's best for mothers." At the time I thought, *What could possibly be going on in the culture of medicine that my own obstetrician would say this to someone she knew was trying to bring systemic change on behalf of her clients, before discussions about systemic racism dominated public conscience?* I understood that she supported the efforts, and I cringe at the thought of why and what she may have heard or seen in her career.

When my second daughter was about to arrive, I percolated in the vicarious trauma, a distant second to the pain, devastation and harms my clients experience because of unwanted sterility. Guilt was a dominant sentiment at that time. To comprehend I could conceive, be pregnant, give birth, that which is a human right every woman should be able to trust blindly is that which had been taken from them. To be clear, my clients were nothing short of gracious and genuinely happy about my pregnancy and my daughters, but I couldn't help but feel incredibly sad, while also feeling incredibly fortunate.

The complexity of those emotions came to a head five weeks after my second daughter was born. As the weeks had worn on, without skipping a beat of work, sleep deprived and recovering from childbirth, I torpedoed into a deep hole of inconsolable sadness, anxiety, and irrational fears about the well-being of my family, the future of my daughters, and their rights to choose what happened to their own bodies in their most vulnerable states.

I went from thinking about what would happen to them if I wasn't there to protect them, to change the tide, to rid health systems of systemic racism, to coming to terms with and accepting that I would not be there for them much longer. I held them both tightly in my bedroom, blinds closed, in the middle of the day, as I agonized over the irrational, yet strongly held, belief that someone was about to take my girls away. I catapulted into a not-so-distant future where I saw my spirit's return to Mother Earth and planned how I would cause my release from the physical world. At the time, I deeply felt, and firmly believed, that there was no other way. I could not readily distinguish between mental construction and actual fact.

At the epicenter of a mental health crisis, my loving husband had the wherewithal to insist that I go to the hospital, and so we did. My mother-in-law left work, and met us at the emergency room, and advised her work that she would likely be taking a month off to care for our newborn. We brought the baby to the hospital as I was exclusively breastfeeding and carefully left our eldest in the care of family in the comfort of our home.

When we arrived at the hospital, I was unable to speak. My husband spoke on my behalf at triage and explained what had been happening. They beckoned a social worker who brought me to a room off of the emergency room and repeatedly asked whether I was sure that I wanted my husband to be present. Of course, I could not fathom the thought of being without him at that time. We entered the room as Kokum cared for and caressed our newborn. Without my knowledge, she had called her daughter to come and bring every variation of formula on the shelf because she was unsure as to which formula baby might take.

As the social worker began asking questions, one of the first was my race. She asked me questions about my childhood, and whether I'd experienced any abuse. There, she asked again whether I wanted my husband present, and I nodded yes. As she sat before me, a pregnant Black woman, I was hesitant to share any information I thought might cause her any measure of anguish. I was taught in my pregnancies that a pregnant woman was to be treated with the kindest of words, the softest of tones, and the gentlest of dispositions to ensure that no negativity passes on to the baby she carries in her womb.

I struggled with that teaching, and the questions she asked me. I answered them factually and briefly, as my husband sat by, learning more than he ever had about my makeup of lived experience. He wept as he sat silently. When the interview was done, we left the room. As the door was opened, we were faced with a lineup of standing police officers. I looked around to see whether they were attending to someone who had been injured in an accident. A fight, maybe? Perhaps an inmate needed emergency medical attention? My brief observations resulted in no conclusions as to why they stood before us. I passed through their human chain, uttering "Excuse me," and followed the social worker, my husband trailing close behind me.

We walked to the back of the treatment portion of the emergency room. I was seated to wait for a physician. My husband left for a short time to attend to business matters. During that time, the physician entered and began her questions with "Is everything ok at home?" to which I answered, "What do you mean? Clearly not. I'm here." She then clarified and said, "Do you feel safe at home?" to which I responded, "No, I am having panic attacks, irrational and suicidal thoughts." She pressed on, "Do you think any of that has to do with your marriage? How are you treated at home?

I felt confused, though in hindsight, I appreciate that women who live with family violence would benefit from these questions without their husband present. Also, in hindsight, I now understand why police had been called – they suspected family violence and that I was a victim of the same. I am grateful for their efforts to rule that possibility out, but still sore about their emphasis on that issue over the more likely situation, given what I had shared, that I was experiencing a mental health crisis. Nonetheless, as the session came to an end, my husband arrived, and I was told that I would need to attend at the back to see a psychiatrist. My husband advised Kokum, who was holding our newborn, and I heard him say, "If they keep her, I'm staying there with her." As a health professional, she understood. I did not know what he meant at the time, and I didn't have the mental and emotional wherewithal to enquire.

I walked in the direction that I was instructed, in a numb pain that only those who have experienced like situations can understand, while my husband softly caressed me, walking by my side to the opening of a unit with two doors. They mechanically opened, and we entered.

As we breached the doors, we heard screams and saw a bustling nurse, cleaning up what appeared to be blood. I looked at my husband and said, "What is this place?" As a trained social worker, he calmly told me that it was the psychiatric unit. We sat where we were told. I observed the room. The television, placed high on the wall in a box, had a thick plexiglass face. I saw a woman down the hall speaking to what appeared to be a health professional, sharing a lot of personal information with the door wide open. I asked my husband why the door wasn't shut, as it appeared to be a consult. He explained that the doors are kept open for the safety and security of all involved in the consultation. My mind still failed to grasp where we were, and why.

As we waited for what seemed like an eternity, my husband received a text message from Kokum, who, five hours into the visit, shared that our newborn was crying and needed to feed. She reports that she paced the halls the entire time, contemplating what she needed to do to keep her little family safe. Although I had fed my daughter here and there throughout our time at the hospital, she was, and remains, a very healthy eater. I beckoned the nurse and asked to excuse myself for the time it would take to fill the baby's belly. She refused. I asked if I could bring the baby in so I could feed her, and she dismissively rejected the proposition, indicating that the ward was not a safe place for babies. I turned to my husband and said, "Well, I'll just go through the doors, feed her, and come back."

Then, my husband informed me that the doors were locked, and that there was no way out until they let us out.

My eyes grew wide. My stomach turned. I felt hot and cold at the same time, and panic overtook my every fibre. *I need to feed my baby*, I thought. *How am I going to do that?* My mind, as though a geared machine, shifted into a state of pragmatism. "We need to get out of here," I told him. He explained that the psychiatrist would be the one to decide if I could leave, and that Kokum and Aunty had the baby and our eldest under control in all respects. This did not loosen the knots in my chest, though. She's my baby, and it was my duty and responsibility to feed her when she needed to be fed, not when I was ready, not when I had finished dealing with this strange cloud of whatever-it-was but now, right now, when she needed it.

Soon after, a very tall, svelte, and soft-spoken man, with salt and pepper hair, and some flair, summoned us to his small, intimidating, jarring grey office. I sat down in a chair, my husband already trying to explain to the doctor what I'd been feeling, and saying, through a trembling voice – just barely holding it together himself. I could tell the doctor was troubled by my husband's consumption of space, and so I waved him off and said, "It's ok love, I can speak." He stopped talking immediately, and said, "Ok, thank God." At that moment, I could tell that the good doctor's perception of the situation may have shifted some – he looked at my husband with a baseline of curiosity, and an edge of surprise. Turning his attention back to me, we talked. I laid out the facts of what I had been experiencing for the past few days with the precision I was used to. The cloud lifted, I focused, and I got what I needed to get across so that the doctor had enough information to do the work required to help me lift this wet blanket of an existence from my shoulders.

I was diagnosed and treated. With time, my perception of the world, and my family in it, brightened. We carry on.

In the face of reproductive injustice, women will stand by one another until things are made right, as they must – for the ancestors, for the little spirits, and for the betterment of all systems conceived upon colonial bedrocks to perpetrate the continuum of Turtle Island's *ongoing* genocide.

Our sacred bundles, and women – their earth – have natural rights. Some of those rights are protected in Canadian law. Morningstar strongly believes that it is important that life givers know about them. Further to her wishes, I shared my experiences above, and will honour her specific requests below.

Reports of and Investigations into the Forced and Coerced Sterilization of Indigenous Women in Saskatoon

In 2015, women in Saskatchewan came forward to the media to disclose that they had been sterilized against their will, and without their consent, in Saskatoon. The Saskatoon Health Authority (now the Saskatchewan Health Authority[2]) commissioned an independent investigation, which I am informed was in large measure due to MRLP's pressure to both have an independent investigation conducted, and that the investigators be Indigenous women. Dr Yvonne Boyer (now Honourable Senator) and Dr. Judith Bartlett found that "…interviews revealed both covert and overt racism in the hospital environment."[3]Addressing the "spectrum and Continuum of Ignorance, Bias, Racism & Discrimination," the Report said:

> Another health care provider felt severe racism first hand: "One resident on labour and delivery said, "I fucking hate you people more than any other race on this entire earth." There is an unrecognized power differential that is not perceived by some health providers. One provider indicated that, "I don't see us as a paternalistic department…it's not something I've perceived to be an issue."

Another provider, in attempting to understand why some Aboriginal women might not hear the whole explanation of tubal ligation, indicated, "And so when you talk to them [about tubal ligation], bring those long discussions to them, I'm sure they're not attentive and you know, patients they are quite stressed and this is a stressful time for them, childbirth and like especially if they are coming away from home, they have other family there and kids..." Another health-care provider knowingly stated, "If a person has always had power, they don't know what it is like to be powerless."[4]

In addressing "Implicit Bias," the Report found:

[S]ome health providers felt that there could be subtle bias toward Aboriginal women relative to tubal ligation. One provider stated, "I do think there may be coercion, but I don't think it's in your face type of, 'have a tubal ligation or else.'" Another stated that "staff – and it may well be that the physicians involved as well – sit around the desk and talk about women having five children, and four have been apprehended – 'it's time to stop.'" All health practitioners interviewed made observations and had concerns about what may be happening to Aboriginal women in their care. One provider stated, "I want them to have the opportunities they need to manage their lives the way they feel it should [be] without being coerced." Another reflected that "if I heard they felt pressured, I'd have acted as a mediator." One health provider was concerned that "apprehensions – it's another state sanctioned ... We think we're doing it for the right reasons, but it's entirely wrong."

Significantly, the report found that "the discrimination visited daily on Indigenous people so robs them of their dignity and self-respect, that some begin to believe they deserve no better."[5] The Report further emphasizes a "disconnect because pervasive structural discrimination and racism in the health care system in general (despite attempts to remedy these) remains unmistakable."[6] Relying on the information shared during the Report's interview process, the Report adopted the words of a specific health-care provider who had been interviewed: "If it had been a non-indigenous woman coming forward, someone might have lost their job. Racism needs harsh consequences."[7]

Without consequences, racism operates with impunity. Without consequences, there is no mechanism by which to operationalize institutional accountability. This is the work of systemic racism.

The Absolute Right to Bodily Autonomy and Self-Determination: Patient is the Boss[8]

None of the words that I will share in this section resonate as dearly, nearly, and clearly as our own. I don't know all the words, but I know some, and asked speakers of other Indigenous languages how to express the concept in some Indigenous languages.

In L'nu (*Mikmaq*): Bodily autonomy can be understood with two terms: *Alsomsin [al-soom-sin]*: You exude great control of yourself and self-autonomy; and *Keskelumsin [guess-ge-loom-sin]*: You exude great self-preservation and protection of yourself.

Nehiyew (*Cree*): *Tipeyimisiw – She is free and independent.*

(Credit for Cree translation: Darlene Johnson)

Mohawk: *Sathataweh* – Independent/in control. *Aionthatawe* – in control of all of you, body included.

(Credit for translation: Kahn-Tineta Horn, Kaniekahaka Nation)

Inuktitut: ᓂᒻᒥᓂᒃ ᐃᓱᒪᖅᓲᑎᖃᕐᓂᖅ – Timiminik isumaqsuutiqarniq – Bodily autonomy

(Credit for Inuktitut translation: Jeannie Arreak-Kullualik)

Chipewyan *(Denesuline)*:

Dëne denı ʔųɫį betth'ı ts'ën k'aldhër -u, denı ʔedeghą k'aldhër: T'ą patient helį s´ı denı k'áldhër ʔat'e.

Ts'ékuı dálį betth'ı t'aldhën s´ı denı ʔųɫį bets'ën halı.

Translation:

A person, he/she is the only one who is the boss of their body and he/she is boss of themselves: The one who is the patient; he/she is the boss.

The women, what is done to their body, that is their sole right/responsibility.

(Credit for Denesuline translation: Elizabet (Sabet) Bisaye)

Women have the absolute right to decide what happens to their body. This is called the right to "bodily autonomy" and "self-determination," and means that doctors, nurses and anyone touching a woman's body, proposing medical treatments, or performing procedures on your body, must respect your rights and decisions. This inalienable right is protected by section 7 of the *Canadian Charter of Rights and Freedoms*.[9]

It is legal for a woman who wants to be sterilized, for a medical procedure to be performed on her body, as long as she provides valid consent.[10] Valid consent means that all the legal elements of consent have been satisfied.

It is perfectly legal for sterilization to be performed where the patient provides valid consent.[11] The notion of fundamental personal choices is entrenched in section 7 of the *Charter*, including protection against State-induced serious psychological stress,[12] as well as freedom from endurance of intolerable stress.[13]

The Supreme Court of Canada in *E. (Mrs.) v. Eve*[14] established that *Parens Patriae*[15] prohibits the authorization of procedures that are non-therapeutic. The Court found that sterilization was non-therapeutic because it was not sought to treat any medical condition.[16] The Court found that physical integrity, and its maintenance, is of utmost consideration as a social value. These principles stand in stark contrast to the ideology of eugenics – a thundering clash in the reproductive experiences of Indigenous women.

Sterilization in Law

The legal elements of consent[17] are tied to section 7 of the *Charter*. They are amplified where a non-essential, non-emergent procedure is at issue. Consent is established through a series of legal cumulative requirements. Where a procedure is non-essential, non-emergent, and/or non-therapeutic, such as a permanent form of birth control, the requirements of consent are amplified.

It is incumbent on the doctor who is obtaining consent to prove that a patient's consent is legitimate. Legitimate consent must be: voluntary, and free from coercion or undue influence; provided by a patient with capacity; referable to both the specific procedure and operating surgeon; and, informed. The onus is incumbent on the doctor to prove that all the elements of consent have been met.[18]

Mallette v Shulman provides further support that even where a procedure may be life-saving, treatments may not be administered in circumstances where the nature of such treatment is in contravention of a person's conscience and religious beliefs, where such beliefs are known to the physician to be going against the will of the patient. Where a patient has expressed their wishes, known to the physician, and such wishes operate to endanger the patient, or secure the patient's fatality, a physician is powerless to overlook those wishes.

Consent Must be Voluntary

Voluntary consent means it cannot be given by: force or threat of force; and/or while you are sedated or under the influence of drugs.[19] Consent must be voluntary, free from coercion and undue influence,[20] and misrepresentations. Consent is vitiated if obtained in any of the aforementioned circumstances. Where there is a power imbalance such that persuasion and influence of a third party on a patient is so extensive that genuine consent cannot be verily deemed as voluntarily and freely given, the physician should discuss the matter with the patient alone.[21] English Courts have upheld the refusal of consent as subject to being vitiated by undue influence.[22]

The authenticity of consent was at issue in *Norberg v Wynrib*.[23] The patient's Indigeneity was not mentioned in the decision and did not factor into the Court's analysis of vulnerability and voluntariness. Gerald B. Robertson & Ellen J. Picard summarize the Supreme Court of Canada:

> [I]n view of the inequality of power between the parties, the exploitative nature of that relationship, and the patient's vulnerability as a result of drug dependence, her consent to sexual activity was not voluntary and accordingly the physician was liable in battery.[24]

Every effort must be made by doctors to acquire consent from a patient whose judgment is not affected by medication in an environment free from coercion.[25] There ought to be a presumption, subject to rebuttal, that consent was not voluntarily provided.[26] Fraudulent misrepresentation by the doctor with respect to the nature of the procedure vitiates consent,[27] but only where the doctor has intentionally misled the patient.[28]

Voluntary consent also requires that you need to be given the opportunity to think about the information that the doctor has shared with you, in the right place, at the right time, and in a state of mind where you have the capacity to decide what's best for you and your family.

Capacity to Consent is Necessary

Consent must be provided by a patient who has capacity. If the patient has capacity, the consent of other persons is not required. While shared decision making between spouses is ideal, a patient has the legal right to make decisions for themselves as a function of bodily autonomy.

A functional assessment, as is required, of capacity involves whether the patient is, first, capable of understanding the nature of the procedure, and second, whether the patient actually understands the nature of the procedure. The former criterion is the dominant factor,[29] while the latter assists in answering the former. Although each is subject to its own body of law, the concept of voluntary consent and capacity are linked with respect to a birthing Indigenous woman.

A patient who refuses consent to a procedure that others may view as beneficial or necessary is not an indication of incapacity. Rather:

> [p]atients have a fundamental right to make their own treatment decisions. As Justice Robins noted in *Malette v. Shulman,* for this freedom to be meaningful, "people must have the right to make choices that accord with their own values regardless

125

of how unwise or foolish those choices may appear to others." Focusing on the apparent unreason-ableness of the patient's decision as evidence of incapacity, where the "refusal of consent is seen not as an assertion of will but rather as a symptom of unsoundness of mind" undermines the patient's right to medical self-determination.[30]

The British Columbia Court of Appeal in *Smith v. Tweedale*[31] dismissed the appeal of a physician who had been found negligent in the sterilization of a birthing woman on the basis that the requisite standard of care, in the circumstances of birth, had not been satisfied. The Court of Appeal recognized that the state of labour and delivery required more than a routine explanation of the procedure. This nudges the element of informed consent, examined below, but is also relevant to capacity. The Trial Court was:

> persuaded that Dr. Tweedale could have been much clearer in his presentation. He could have said, "Are you sure you understand that this procedure is permanent?" or any number of other simple things that would make someone lying on a delivery table understand clearly that there was no turning back. He did not. By his choice of language, he left [the patient] open to whatever preconceived ideas she might have.[32]

Diminished capacity associated with labour and child birth is typically ephemeral. It is not the subject of mental illness or uncon-sciousness, but rather the pain, stress, trauma, and for some, eupho-ria, associated with the process of giving life that diminishes capacity to consider matters other than those immediately requiring atten-tion. It is cruel and unusual treatment to sterilize a woman while she is in the throes of labour and post-partum. Her concerns are often laser focused on her baby, her own recovery and their mutual well-being and bonding.

Capacity means that you are able to appreciate the consequences of a decision.[33] To have capacity, you must be able to understand the nature, purpose and consequences of a medical treatment. Your actual ability to understand the likely benefits and risks of the treatment or procedure, other options if available, and the possible consequences of refusing the proposed treatment, are also part of a doctor's job to decide if you have capacity to consent.[34]

Consent is Specific to a Doctor and a Procedure

The Supreme Court of Canada states that a doctor's liability for battery arises if "emergency situations aside, surgery or treatment has been performed or given beyond that to which there was consent."[35] In *Kanis v Sinclair*,[36] the patient requested that her sterilization be done by clipping instead of cauterization because she felt that clipping had a better chance of successful reversal if she decided she wanted more children. The doctor cauterized the patient's fallopian tubes because he was experiencing challenges inserting the clips. The Court found the doctor liable in battery because the method he used was explicitly contrary to the patient's specific request, and there was no emergency to justify a deviation from the patient's wishes.

Murray v McMurchy[37] establishes that a patient undergoing surgery with respect to her reproductive organs has the right to consent to all procedures associated with the same. In the instant case, a patient underwent an operation to have a cyst removed from one of her ovaries. The physician, while operating, discovered additional fibroids and took the liberty of tying both her fallopian tubes on the basis of his justification that there was an increased risk for an ectopic pregnancy. This had not been discussed with the patient. The Court determined that the patient, by virtue of her inalienable right to bodily autonomy, had the right not to be subjected to the

Morningstar Mercredi & Fire Keepers

secondary procedure without her consent. Convenience to the physician did not operate to cure the battery that the court ultimately found had been inflicted upon the patient.

A Patient Has the Right to Correct, Complete and Honest Information

When you see a doctor about birth control, or a doctor' talks to you about birth control, including around the time you are having a baby, you have the right to be informed. That right comes from your autonomy and your right to bodily integrity.[38] Being informed means that the doctor has to make sure that you understand the nature of the treatments, the risks and benefits associated with them, and the availability of other treatments. This information must be provided to you *before* you make a decision about what treatment, if any, you want.[39]

If the doctor misrepresents the medical treatment of a procedure in any way – which includes not explaining the risks to you on purpose or lying about them – any consent given by you is cancelled out.[40]

Doctors have a duty to inform the patient of material risks, and other important information, prior to obtaining consent.[41] The doctrine of informed consent contains layered principles, housed within the general doctrine of consent, and ought not to be conflated with invalid consent. Where the patient is not informed, battery is likely to arise.[42] Where a patient is inadequately informed, negligence is at issue. In *Smith v. Tweedale*, the Court of Appeal opined that two conclusions underpin the propriety of the trial Judge's decision that the doctor was negligent:

> The first was that by requesting to have her "tubes tied," the plaintiff essentially conveyed to the defendant her own preconceived notion that the

procedure in question was reversible and thus the defendant was placed on notice that more than his usual presentation was required. The evidence established that the expression "tubal ligation" is a general term which covers a number of different procedures which have different consequences, ranging all the way from complete irreversibility to reversibility with a 50% chance of future pregnancy. The second conclusion was that in the circumstances in which the plaintiff found herself, after thirteen hours of difficult labour and lying on the delivery table, more than just a routine explanation of the procedure was needed.[43]

The conclusions relate to the applicable standard of care, which the Court found had been breached by the physician's failure to explain the procedure he was undertaking, alternative methods of "tubal ligations," and because he failed to ensure the patient understood the information disclosed. The Court found the information shared to be insufficiently clear in the circumstances of thirteen hours of active labour.

Tubal Ligation is Never an Emergency

There is a big difference between what a doctor needs to do to get consent in an emergency situation, compared to a situation where there is no emergency or risk of immediate harm or death to you. Convenience to either you or the doctor of doing two different procedures during a single operation is not a legally acceptable reason for there to be an emergency.[44] If this happens, it is the responsibility of the doctors acting without your consent to show that the operation was needed to preserve your health or life.[45] Even then there are limits to what can be done without your consent.

Tubal ligation is an elective procedure, which means that the doctor's legal duty to explain the risks, consequences, and options connected to tying your tubes may be more demanding. That means that even small risks should be explained to you.[46]

A person can withdraw their consent at any time and the doctor is required to honour that choice unless there is a serious medical risk if they stop the procedure when you withdraw your consent.

Children in foster care under the age of 16 – some provinces allow a court to order treatment that it thinks is in the best interest of the child. If the child in foster care is 16 years or older, their consent is needed unless the Court believes the child does not have the capacity to consent.

Replacement Decision-Making

There are circumstances in which other people, including health care practitioners, can make health-care decisions for a patient. This is called replacement decision making and does not involve birth control decisions while in labour or at any other time.

If a patient has granted a power of attorney over personal care to another person, that person may make some decisions, as directed by the patient, about their health care. This type of arrangement is unlikely to arise in the context of a woman giving birth and tends to be used where a person is nearing the end of life or is incapacitated and cannot make health-care decisions for themselves about life-saving treatments – not birth control. It does not apply to treatments more conveniently carried out at a particular time. If a child cannot appreciate the consequences of health decisions, their parents or guardian may make them for them. If a child can appreciate the consequences of health treatment, the child may make the decision for themselves. If they cannot, and are wards of the state in the foster care system, a court order is necessary to subject them to invasive treatments with life-long repercussions.

If a person is unconscious or unresponsive and there is no next of kin or replacement decision maker available, attending physicians may make healthcare decisions of an urgent and life-saving nature for the benefit of the patient. In this regard, the physician's discretion does not extend to life saving procedures explicitly rejected by the patient and known, or where it ought to have been known to the attending healthcare provider. In our view, this extends to sterilization or abortion procedures.

Where doctors recommend a particular treatment, you have the right to take time to think about it, weigh your options, and ask questions. In law, what a health-care professional would do with their own body is inconsequential. What the patient genuinely wants to do is what determines the appropriate treatment, if any. Other people cannot make decisions for you while you are in labour and delivery about your future reproductive capacity.

Sterilization Without Proper and Informed Consent on the International Stage[47]

Forced sterilization violates numerous rights protected by regional and universal human rights instruments.[48] In this regard, we call your attention to the Inter-American Court of Human Rights' approach in the case of *I. V. v. Bolivia*,[49] in which it determined that sterilization performed without adequate respect for free, prior, informed consent may violate, *inter alia*, the human rights to physical integrity, humane treatment, personal liberty and security, respect for honor and dignity, respect for private and family life, freedom of expression, and to raise a family.

Since early 2018, we and others have raised the issue of forced sterilization of Indigenous women in Canada before regional and universal human rights oversight bodies, including the Inter-American Commission on Human Rights, the United Nations Committee against Torture, Universal Periodic Review, and United Nations special procedure mandate holders, including the Special Rapporteur on Violence Against Women and the Special Rapporteur on Health.[50] These human rights bodies have responded with alarm and with concrete recommendations for Canada. The government has thus so far failed to commit to, let alone implement, any of the proposed actions or reforms.

In February 2018, Canada appeared before the Inter-American Commission on Human Rights and acknowledged its responsibility for the forced sterilization of Indigenous women, through its administration of the public health-care system, and pledged to make available the data in its possession.

In April 2018, the United Nations Special Rapporteur on violence against women visited Canada and urged authorities to address systemic discrimination and violence against Indigenous women. At the end of that visit, she *called on Canada* to take "urgent action on systemic violence against indigenous women."[51] She noted that Indigenous women continue to "face intersectional discrimination and violence at a higher level than non-indigenous women, and therefore require specific attention and focus."[52] She recommended that the government create a separate, Indigenous-led national action plan on violence specifically against Indigenous women, First Nations, Inuit, and Métis, using both the Committee on the Elimination of Discrimination against Women (CEDAW) inquiry recommendations and other UN treaty bodies' specific recommendations on violence against women (VAW), violence against Indigenous women, and the United Nations Declaration on the Rights of Indigenous Peoples.[53] She further called for the urgent repeal of discriminatory provisions that remain in Canada's *Indian Act*.[54]

In May 2018, Canada's Universal Periodic Review yielded a recommendation, by Argentina, that Canada address forced sterilization, which Canada accepted.[55]

In November 2018, the UN Special Rapporteur on the right of everyone to the enjoyment of the highest attainable standard of physical and mental health, Dainius Pūras, visited Canada. He noted that health-care often remains difficult for Indigenous people in Canada to access as well as a lack of trust in health-care relationships, which may be the result of pervasive discriminatory attitudes toward Indigenous people. He mentioned specifically that he had received information on "remaining practices of obstetric violence and forced sterilization amongst Indigenous women," an issue that he noted he would be elaborating on further in his upcoming report.[56] He noted that these challenges are indicative of Canada's need to implement a human rights-based approach in health-care.[57]

In November 2018, Canada had its periodic review before the UN Committee against Torture (CAT), at its 65th session. Representatives and advocates for Indigenous women who survived forced sterilization in Canada contributed to the review by submitting an alternative report[58] and by participating in the in-person briefing with the Committee. In its concluding observations, the Committee directly raised its concerns regarding involuntary sterilization of Indigenous women.[59] Specifically, it stated:

> The Committee is concerned at reports of extensive forced or coerced sterilization of Indigenous women and girls dating back to the 1970s and including recent cases in the province of Saskatchewan between 2008 and 2012. According to the information before the Committee, at least fifty-five women have contacted lawyers representing Indigenous women who have filed a pending class action lawsuit against doctors and health officials at a Saskatchewan public hospital for undergoing tubal ligation procedures without proper consent. The Committee takes note of the information provided by the delegation on the external review on this matter launched by the Saskatchewan Health

Authority (formerly Saskatoon Health Region) in January 2017, but remains concerned at the lack of information regarding the implementation of the "calls of action" included in the final report, especially those related to reparations (arts. 2, 12, 13, 14 and 16).[60]

Therefore, the Committee called on Canada to:

a. Ensure that all allegations of forced or coerced sterilization are impartially investigated, that the persons responsible are held accountable, and that adequate redress is provided to the victims; [and]

b. Adopt legislative and policy measures to prevent and criminalize the forced or coerced involuntary sterilization of women, particularly by clearly defining the requirements of free, prior and informed consent with regard to sterilization and by raising awareness among Indigenous women and medical personnel of that requirement.[61]

The Committee identified this issue as one of four priority concerns, requesting that Canada report back within one year on its implementation of the Committee's recommendations.[62]

In January 2019, the Inter-American Commission on Human Rights endorsed and expanded upon the Committee against Torture's concluding observations, stating that it "has received, in a consistent and systemic manner, reports from indigenous women, girls and adolescents who claim to have been subjected to sterilizations without their full, free and informed consent in Canada."[63] After reiterating the Committee against Torture's recommendations, the Inter-American Commission urged Canada to:

adopt legislative and policy measures to prevent and criminalize the forced sterilization of women. In particular, the Commission urge[d] the State to clearly define the requirements of consent with regard to the procedure of sterilization, in line with the Inter-American standards on the matter; to maintain public and periodically updated records on reports of forced sterilizations, duly disaggregated by gender, ethnicity and other relevant criteria; to provide comprehensive training to health practitioners; and to raise awareness among Indigenous communities on their sexual and reproductive rights.[64]

On February 21, 2020, Canada submitted its interim report to the UNCAT. While it acknowledges the heinousness of the human rights violations associated with the abhorrent practice of forced and coerced sterilization in Canada, and its qualification as an aggravated assault in Criminal Law, its response fell far short of a meaningful response to the UNCAT's clear recommendations.

The report primarily put forward the paralyzing operation of shared jurisdiction in law enforcement and health-care administration; the need for "cultural competence, cultural safety and humility" by way of various education and funding initiatives; the responsibility of the medical profession and its regulatory bodies to enforce proper and informed consent; and its initiative to convene meetings with provincial and territorial partners, medical associations and Indigenous organizations. None of the State's so-called preventative and investigative initiatives has meaningfully engaged the survivors and their families. Further, Canada has failed, and refuses to, take measures to specifically criminalize forced sterilization on account of the practice being considered an aggravated assault. In our opinion, this flies in the face of its previous campaigns for specific criminalization, particularly in relation to its treatment of abortion and female genital mutilation and medically assisted dying.

In my view, if individuals may be investigated, charged, and found guilty of offences that violate the right to bodily autonomy as above, so too should be people in positions of authority, operating with relative regulatory impunity, and being paid by the State, who plead practical blindness, who are robbing marginalized and oppressed Indigenous women of their right to give life on their own terms and in their own time.

Support in Canada

The National Inquiry into Missing and Murdered Indigenous Women and Girls suggests in their final report on the specific subject of genocide that the State's intention, as understood in the UN Covenant, "suggests that the mere subjective tendency to prevent births suffices."[65] The Inquiry also found that coerced sterilizations "qualify as elements of the *actus reus*"[66] of genocide.

The Senate has undertaken and continues to work on a report addressing the forced and coerced sterilization of women. The House of Commons Permanent Committee on Health has studied the tragedy and made recommendations to the House of Commons on next steps.

The Native Women's Association of Canada, under former President Francyne Joe's leadership, was the first to pass a motion supporting Indigenous women who have been sterilized against their will. The Federation of Sovereign Indigenous Nations (FSIN) from Saskatchewan, through their women's council led by Vice-Chief Heather Bear, passed a motion in support of the women soon thereafter. The FSIN's Chiefs in Assembly passed a unanimous resolution supporting the women as well. The Assembly of Treaties 6, 7 and 8 Chiefs also passed a unanimous resolution in support of the survivors. The Assembly of First Nations (AFN) followed suit, and also passed a unanimous resolution in support of the women. Many conferences, symposiums and articles have since addressed the issue of the forced sterilization of Indigenous women. The Indigenous community stands beside and behind the survivors in the fight for prevention, punishment and reparations.

There is a difference between the existence of protective legal principles and their *actual* accessibility to marginalized groups of historically oppressed populations and genders, like Indigenous women. When the barriers attaching to access to justice, or legal protection, are two-fold, as they are with Indigenous women on account of race and gender, the chances of achieving a measure of justice are less likely for the group experiencing discrimination than they are for a person who is not part of a group that experiences discrimination. This results in systemic discrimination fueled by racism and sexism. I do not know of an instance where an attending male in a delivery room was approached with haste, indicating to him that a vasectomy was required on account of the number of children he has, his perceived ability to support them, or his perceived ability to parent them. Although I would say that this is unacceptable, it is even less acceptable for a woman in labour and delivery to be approached with a similar proposition without the benefit of the safeguards entrenched in the doctrine of consent. Ongoing State inaction, impunity, and lack of accountability exacerbates the problem and the sentiment of violation among survivors. Intersectionality is a necessary component to resolving the decade-long violations arising from forced and coerced sterilization.

THE STORY OF A RESEARCH STUDY ON FREE AND INFORMED CONSENT AND FORCED STERILIZATION OF FIRST NATIONS AND INUIT WOMEN IN QUEBEC

Suzy Basile

In February 2019, the publication of an open letter became the starting point for a project that is ongoing to this day. Its content denounced the silence of the Quebec government, which refused to participate in a federal working group on cultural competency in Indigenous women's health, where the topic of forced sterilization was on the agenda. Co-signed by seven Indigenous and non-Indigenous professors and activists, the letter highlighted the fact that no research or investigation had been carried out on the matter in Quebec, although the available information at the time suggested that such practices had taken place in Quebec during various periods in its history. The open letter stressed that:

> By refusing to participate in the work of the federal government's drawing board and to discuss this issue with health network stakeholders from other Canadian provinces and territories, the Quebec government is perpetuating a colonial attitude that characterizes government bodies that turn a blind

eye and a deaf ear to crucial health, well-being and
fundamental rights issues of these peoples, such as
the right to the enjoyment of the highest attainable standard of physical and mental health set out
in article 24(2) of the United Nations Declaration
on the Rights of Indigenous Peoples. Shedding
as much light as possible about forcibly sterilized
women in Canada and Quebec is an integral part
of this fundamental right.[1]

The day after it was published, the letter sent shockwaves through
both Indigenous and Quebec circles, as yet another sensitive issue
concerning Indigenous women was added to the social and political spectrum. At the same time, First Nations women were publicly
disclosing that they had been victims of these practices in Quebec,
in contemporary times. While talking about it, the professors and
activists who had signed the open letter realized that one question
remained: what to do and where to start?

In January 2020, at an Ottawa national conference on choice and
informed consent in health care, the speech of one of the speakers was very revealing and disturbing to me. She hypothesized that
women who once had contracted tuberculosis, an infectious and
fatal disease widespread among Indigenous peoples in the early 20th
century, may have been sterilized because of the mistaken belief that
the disease could be transmitted from a mother to her fetus. Some
Indigenous women could thus have been sterilized "preventively." As
we have no evidence to date that this practice took place in Quebec,
or in the rest of Canada, the possible differential medical treatment
for Indigenous women leads me to believe that my Atikamekw
kokom (grandmother) may have experienced this. Having contracted
tuberculosis a few years after her third pregnancy, she had her left
lung and five ribs removed in a Quebec City hospital before spend-
ing four years (1955 to 1959) at the Macamic sanatorium in Abitibi.

She was 27 years old at the time of her release and had no further children. This also seems to be the case for many other Indigenous women from various nations who have experienced the same thing, according to an informal survey I conducted.

In the weeks following this national conference, I began the process of obtaining my *kokom*'s medical records, hoping perhaps to find an answer to the question that has hovered in the family for decades. Under the *Privacy Act*, it is impossible to obtain the medical file of anyone other than yourself. As my *kokom* passed away in 2015, obtaining a power of attorney from her was also impossible. The hospital's archive centre, where the medical files of former residents of the Macamic sanatorium are stored, did confirm the existence of my grandmother's medical file. They also sent me a document stating the reason for her hospitalization and the dates of her stay. As a result, I found an error in her date of birth, but I didn't learn anything more about her health or her four-year stay. Today, I am a bit hopeful because of the potential revision of Bill 79, which would finally allow parents to obtain the medical file and any other relevant document concerning their child who has disappeared from the Quebec health care system.[2] As of this writing, over 156 missing children files have been opened and are being investigated. Would it be possible to extend this law to allow children to obtain, within a limited framework, the medical records of their parents who are now deceased? Unlocking the past would certainly allow other families to learn the truth, a truth that concerns them closely and could partially explain another aspect of the trauma—the medical and obstetrical parts in this case—experienced by Indigenous women and their families.

This attempt to find out the truth, following the eye-opening conference I attended, was one of the triggering events that led to the massive undertaking of researching free and informed consent and forced sterilization of First Nations and Inuit women in Quebec. In close collaboration with the First Nations of Quebec and Labrador

Health and Social Services Commission (FNQLHSSC), a regional committee bringing together several Indigenous organizations and experts in Quebec was created in 2020, in the wake of the reports of two inquiries[3] that shed light on the many obstacles Indigenous people face when trying to access public services in both Quebec and Canada.

The year 2020 got off to a frantic start with several anti-pipeline protests, notably supported by a good number of non-Indigenous individuals and organizations, which paralyzed rail transport in the country. The thirtieth anniversary of the Oka events, better known as the "Oka Crisis" of 1990, also brought back into the spotlight the sensitive question about the relationship between Indigenous people, Quebec, and Canadian society regarding territorial and colonial issues. At the time of planning a first regional committee meeting, the tragic death of Joyce Echaquan, a mother of seven from the Atikamekw community of Manawan, Quebec, occurred on September 28 2020. Mrs. Echaquan died at the age of 37, while enduring racist and sexist insults from members of the medical staff at the Joliette Hospital, cell phone in hand, broadcasting the events on *Facebook Live*. This caused a shockwave in Quebec society, and its government was once again called upon to review the quality of its public services. What was less well known until then but has come to light through family testimonies and documents filed at the coroner's inquest in 2021, is the fact that Mrs. Echaquan had previously suffered obstetrical violence, including forced abortions and tubal ligation, as a result of being under pressure by medical staff.[4] The youngest child of the family was only five months old when his mother died. This event obviously shook the members of the regional committee, which was beginning its research on free and informed consent and forced sterilization, while confirming the need to take a closer look at the experiences of Indigenous women in Quebec's health network.

The development of the communication strategy and the implementation of gathering testimony were adjusted to the health restrictions linked to the COVID-19 pandemic (2020–2022). First Nations communities and Inuit villages authorities were thus forced to restrict and control the access to their territory, often making it impossible for the research team to travel and visit. A lot of them had to be collected via digital ways like Zoom or by phone. The participants understood very well the health situation and were nonetheless keen to talk about their experiences.

The summer of 2021 was particularly difficult for Indigenous people in Canada, as hundreds of unmarked graves were discovered at the sites of several residential schools,[5] and because the aforementioned Bill 79 was passed in Quebec. Many people told the research team that they needed time to reflect before sharing their experiences of sterilization or obstetric violence. In September, in response to media reports denouncing the mistreatment of Indigenous women in Quebec's health network, the Quebec National Assembly unanimously adopted a motion calling for an end to all forms of obstetrical violence and sterilization imposed on Indigenous women and girls in Quebec. The following month, a class action was filed with the Quebec Superior Court, seeking compensation for the twelve Atikamekw women who have undergone sterilizing surgery at the Joliette Hospital since December 1971, without having given their free and informed consent.[6] At the time of writing these lines, the Superior Court of Quebec has just authorized the class action.[7] The gathering of testimonials therefore continued until spring 2022, so that we could listen to everyone who had come forward.

The year 2022 was marked by the Canadian Senate's progress on the matter, led specifically by Senator Yvonne Boyer, towards the adoption of Bill S-250, which proposes "the inclusion of a specific offence in the *Criminal Code* relating to forced and coerced sterilization."[8] Giving my testimony at the Senate hearings in April was particularly challenging, as we were at the beginning of the process of analyzing what we had gathered as part of our research, and several stories were racing through my head and my heart. Furthermore, the Pope's visit to Canada over the summer kept the delicate subject of the treatment of Indigenous people by the Canadian state in the headlines. The visit ended with a statement and an apology for the genocide perpetrated against Indigenous children who were sent to residential schools. It is worth reminding one of the five criteria defining genocide[9] is the act of preventing births in a human group. The 35 testimonials we had gathered were analyzed in this context. This has been the most challenging research exercise to date.

The report identifies cases of forced sterilization and obstetric violence against Indigenous women between 1980 and 2019. Five of Quebec's Indigenous nations are affected by this phenomenon, which, according to the data collected, has occurred in several regions of the province. Here's an excerpt from the report showing the types of intervention we underwent:

> Of the testimonies collected, nine involved imposed sterilization, 13 involved imposed sterilization and other obstetric violence, six involved obstetric violence without imposed sterilization, three involved forced abortion and four involved such acts being done on a family member or in a work context and being witnessed by the participant.[10]

The report highlights four points. The first observation concerns the undermining of patients' free and informed consent. Indeed, many of them learned years later that they had been sterilized without their consent. The second finding relates to mistrust, fear and avoidance of health services, as many testimonies relate the recurrence of violence women have suffered, the fear of actions that may be taken against them and the fact that they refrain from consulting health specialists even when necessary. The third finding refers to the differential treatment Indigenous women received in hospital, while non-Indigenous patients received attention and care.

The testimonies we heard referred to degrading comments made in front of them and prejudices conveyed, as well as repeated proposals of a fallopian tube ligation. The fourth finding underlines the young age of the patients and the particular circumstances of their sterilization, since in several cases, they were offered no other contraceptive method, less risky and less invasive than ligature or hysterectomy. Finally, the juxtaposition of this report with the work of other academics and recent reports of inquiries on Indigenous issues reveals the presence and recurrence of systemic racism in Quebec. The 31 recommendations that come with the report include adequate training for health care staff, legislative changes and further research into the subject, as several people with experience to share have come forward following the publication of the report. In addition, it was impossible to meet many people during data collection due to the pandemic context.

Since the report was published, many initiatives have been launched. On the same, the Assembly of First Nations Quebec and Labrador unanimously adopted the *Declaration of Commitment to Ensure Free, Prior and Culturally Informed Consent in Health Services for First Nations Girls and Women in Quebec*. This declaration calls for compliance with the following principles: 1) access to culturally safe health services; 2) ethical medical appointments; 3) the right to free, prior and informed consent.[11] The following day, Minister Lafrenière of the Quebec government's *Secrétariat aux relations avec les Premières Nations et les Inuit* (First Nations and Inuit Relations Secretariat) announced a bill proposal on cultural safety, a project that had been left off the government agenda prior to the October 2022 elections.

The next day, the president of the *Collège des médecins du Québec* (Quebec College of Physicians) told the media that he wanted to meet with the research team to find short-term solutions. The *Groupe de réflexion sur les interruptions de grossesse et les stérilisations imposées aux femmes des Premières Nations et Inuit du Québec* (Focus Group on Pregnancy Interruption and Sterilization Imposed on First Nations and Inuit Women of Quebec) was created in February 2023. Within this group, three seats are held by the research directorate and the FNQLHSSC. The latter First Nations organization recently added a section on obstetric violence and consent to the fourth phase of its ongoing *First Nations Regional Health Survey (RHS)*, whose main objective is to provide "a detailed picture of the health and general well-being of First Nations living in communities" (FNQLHSSC, 2023). In addition to some twenty presentations of the research report findings to academics, governments and Indigenous and non-Indigenous civil society (*Commission des droits de la personne et des droits de la jeunesse* [Human Rights and Youth Rights Commission], Cree Nation Government, Indigenous Friendship Centres in Quebec), the research team has also been invited by Amnesty International to meet the UN Special Rapporteur on the Rights of Indigenous Peoples during his official visit to Canada in March 2023, and to submit him their report. He referred to our research report in his report on his visit to Canada submitted to the United Nations Human Rights Council.[12]

In May 2023, I was invited to share our research process with the Inquiry set up by the Greenland and Danish governments to investigate cases of forced contraception of Greenlandic women between 1960 and 1970. The research team has also joined forces with another research project on humanization of health care in Quebec, led by Professor Sylvie Lévesque (Université du Québec à Montréal). To date, 72 articles have been published in the media (Canada, France, England, Mexico) as well as 20 television, radio and web feature stories have been broadcast about our research report. An artistic performance was created and will be presented once again in September 2023 in Montreal. Other artistic projects are currently under development.

The second phase of the research project began in July 2023. This will make it possible for those we were unable to meet during Phase I, and those who have come forward since the report's publication, to tell the research team about their experience. We must now add obstetrical violence and forced sterilizations to the long list of traumas experienced by Indigenous families in Quebec. Let us conclude with this quotation from the first phase research report:

> In Canada, imposed sterilization fits into a continuum of colonial violence that continues to this day.[13]

Patricia Bouchard

Controlling women's fertility is a complex social, political, historical and legal reality whose repercussions are still being felt today. This control can manifest itself in different spheres of a woman's life, depending on where she lives, the group to which she belongs and her living conditions. A meaningful example is the right to abortion and how its exercise is threatened around the world: criminalizing women who want to terminate their pregnancies and the medical staff who perform this procedure, passing restrictive laws that curb its accessibility, forcing clinics that offer essential gynecology-obstetrics care to close their doors, etc.

This continuum of gendered violence also includes forced sterilization. Always from a control perspective, the idea is to deprive a woman of her ability to bear and give life by subjecting her to a surgical procedure that permanently compromises her fertility. It is hard to fathom the violence of this act and its impact on a woman's life. The aim is to damage their physical, psychological, emotional and spiritual integrity through a non-consensual operation that alters a biological function. In some cases, the sterilizing operation is performed without the patient's knowledge, usually during a caesarean section. In such circumstances, the bond of trust with care facilities and health professionals is completely broken. Even more frightening is the fact that this type of violence is documented in an impressive number of countries, and that this practice is not a thing of the past – quite the contrary.

In the 1960s, the Danish government introduced birth control policies in Greenland, now known as the "Spiral scandal" because of the IUDs' shape from those days. When they were very young, many Greenlandic women were forced to get IUDs (the largest model was used to prevent pregnancy), with long-term repercussions for their reproductive systems and preventing them from having children.[14] In 2023, the Greenlandic and Danish authorities officially launched a joint investigation to uncover the truth behind this practice. In Peru, "population control" policies introduced in the 1990s were used to legitimize the sterilization of thousands of Quechua women.[15] In 2015, the Quipu project gave those victims a voice by creating an interactive web documentary with audio recordings of their stories.[16] Finally, in Canada, Indigenous women from many provinces have experienced forced sterilization. In Alberta, under the *Sexual Sterilization Act* of 1928, a eugenics committee was responsible for evaluating sterilization requests from psychiatric hospitals and residential schools, among others:

> If upon such examination, the board is unanimously surgical of opinion that the patient might safely be discharged if the operation danger of procreation with its attendant risk of multiplication of the evil by transmission of the disability to progeny were eliminated, the board may direct in writing such surgical operation for sexual sterilization of the inmate as may be specified in the written direction and shall appoint some competent surgeon to perform the operation.[17]

The work of historian Jana Grekul has shown that Indigenous women were overrepresented in the number of patients sterilized under this law, which was revoked in 1972.[18] In the United States, the state of Vermont has decided to face its eugenics past by setting up a reconciliation commission to shed light on the laws and policies that legitimized the sterilization of Indigenous, French-Canadians and people with mental health problems, among others.[19] This important task will begin in 2023. Thus, the four cases mentioned above have two important similarities: these women belong to marginalized groups, and they live in countries with a colonial history. These factors tell us about the place they had yesterday and today on the political, social and economic scenes of their respective countries. From this perspective, forced sterilization is also part of a long history of colonial violence perpetrated against women.

Throughout my doctoral studies, I have read and analyzed numerous articles, theses, newspapers, testimonials and reports published all over the world, and I'm still haunted by a ton of questions. The literature review on the subject particularly shook me, because of the many harrowing testimonies coming from victims of these cruel and senseless policies. Conducting research is no small task, especially when it involves building trust, developing a culturally safe and relevant approach, and accompanying someone who is exploring such a sensitive part of her life with us. In this regard, I was plagued by doubts and fears about my ability to welcome such confidences and to live up to their courage.

In November 2022, the research report entitled "Free and informed consent and imposed sterilizations among First Nations and Inuit women in Quebec" was unveiled. It was widely echoed in the province and beyond, provoking outrage and indignation. This is the first time the phenomenon has been documented in Quebec, and these 35 testimonials make it no longer possible to deny this reality and to refuse to take action. The stories reported by the participants are shocking and cover a wide spectrum of violence. Making unacceptable comments about a new mother, deliberately ignoring a patient's pain, using pressure and threats to convince a woman to have an abortion, performing a hysterectomy or fallopian tube ligation without even discussing it with a patient: these are just a few of the examples reported to us. These facts are extremely shocking and beyond comprehension, especially as they occurred between 1980 and 2019. It is hard to understand how and why patients' rights could be blatantly disregarded in such a way, despite having legal protections related to the exercise of free and informed consent.

This report is the fruit of many months' work and it is thanks to a dedicated, sensitive and value-driven team that we've been able to achieve it. In my view, it is essential to highlight it, since we've taken each step together, with heart and conviction. Throughout this project, their thoughtfulness, thoroughness, attentiveness and support made all the difference: thank you to Nancy, Patricia, Caroline, Marjolaine, Jane, Debbie and especially Suzy. I'd like to thank each and every one of you; it has been a privilege to work and learn by your side.

I would also like to express my gratitude to each of the participants for agreeing to share this part of their lives with us. It is hard to put into words what it means to me to have had the privilege of meeting the women involved in this research. These moments seemed like interwoven multiple constellations coming together through dialogue, attentiveness, vulnerability and respect. These women still guide me and accompany my thoughts and every moment spent on this project. The trust that was placed in us is a real privilege, and I can never thank enough those who drew the strength to speak to us.

> To all the participants, without whom this process would have been in vain, to those who have shown unspeakable courage in telling their truth, to those who have honoured us with their trust: from the depths of our hearts, thank you. These simple

words cannot convey the gratitude and deep consideration we have for each and every one of you. Your sincerity, your voice and your profound humanity are the core elements of this process, and it's necessary to highlight them. You are the *raison d'être* behind every step of this process, and we hope that this research report will live up to the trust you have placed in us.[20]

A VICIOUS CAMPAIGN OF BIRTH CONTROL IN GREENLAND[1]

Ann-Sophie Greve Møller

Clutching her handkerchief, Hedvig Frederiksen calmly relates what happened to her.

"One by one the girls came out of the doctor's office, crying. I sat scared in the reception area, waiting my turn. I didn't know what was going to happen in there."

Talking about the incident that happened in 1974, Hedvig Frederiksen continues: "It was the matron of our dormitory who had informed us that we had to go see the doctor."[2]

To this day, 49 years later, Hedvig Frederiksen is unable to remember in detail what happened inside that doctor's office. It is blocked from her memory. But she knows she had an IUD (intra-uterine device) inserted. And she was far from the only one.

It caused a great outrage in Greenland, when the podcast "The IUD Campaign"[3] aired on the national Danish radio in May of 2022, exposing how thousands of Greenlandic women and girls had been fitted with IUDs in the 1960s and 70s as part of the Danish authorities' strategy to reduce the Greenlandic population growth.

According to Danish radio, more than 4,500 women had been fitted with an IUD between 1966 and 1970. At the time, the total number of women of childbearing age in Greenland was around 9,000.

Greenland had one of the highest birth rates in the world when the IUD campaign started. The birth rate peaked in 1966 when 1,781 babies were born.[4] At the time, Greenland was under Danish rule, and according to the Danish authorities, the high birth rate was an economic burden on Greenlandic society, as more schools, more housing, and better health facilities had to be built.

At the same time, the IUDs were viewed as a liberating tool in societies like the Danish one, where it was considered a benefit to women who wanted to avoid unwanted pregnancies. The same way of thinking may also have influenced the spread of the use of IUDs in Greenland, where they could be seen as a "help" to women and girls. However, for girls who were not given the option of deciding whether or not to have an IUD inserted, the experience became deeply traumatic.

Up through the 1950s and 60s, the Danish state had set in motion a modernization campaign in Greenland. These political strategies were referred to as "G50" and "G60," while colloquially it was labeled "Danification." These strategies resulted in forced relocations of settlement dwellers to towns, Greenlandic speaking children were required to speak Danish in the schools, while several older children and teenagers were sent to boarding schools in Denmark.

New housing was constructed, new schools built, and the healthcare system was optimized with Danish professionals at the helm. While the United Nations during this period focused on the decolonization of colonized countries, the opposite happened in Greenland. The focus of the Danish authorities was to get the population to become more "Danish."

To this day, stories of actions taken by the colonial government continue to emerge. One of the political tools used was the IUD, and it delivered on the Danish authorities' expectations. In the years that followed, the birth rate dropped drastically.

The IUDs that were used went by the name of "Lippes Loop" and were much larger than the ones we are familiar with today. In addition, they were only intended for women who had already given birth. Naja Lyberth was the first one to open up and publicly talk about having an IUD inserted at the age of 14 without having given prior consent. It happened in 1976 in Maniitsoq. The first time she talked about it was to the Greenlandic women's magazine "Arnanut." This subsequently prompted the journalists behind the IUD campaign; Anne Pilegaard Petersen and Celine Klint, to dig deeper into the case to uncover why Greenlandic girls were forcibly given IUDs. In "The IUD Campaign," Naja Lyberth relates how the girls in her year at school had been sent to the local hospital by the leading Danish doctor in the area. Neither Naja Lyberth nor her parents were ever asked if she wanted an IUD.

"It was like having knives cutting me up inside. It felt like an assault. The state took my virginity," Naja Lyberth says in the podcast.[5]

Since then, several women have come forward and told the same story. About being told to go to the doctor, being put on a gurney, and having an IUD inserted. In many of the stories, the scenario is the same: it was a school teacher who had told them to go to the doctor, while it was Danish doctors who inserted the IUDs. The health service was dominated by Danish labour, and the women were influenced by the general feeling in the society of a great belief in the authority of the Danish doctors.

At the same time, several women also revealed that they had had no sexual experience prior to the insertion of the IUD, and had no idea why they were required to have it. There were girls as young as 13 – yes, and some even younger than that.

During the autumn of 2023, while working as a journalist at KNR – Radio Greenland, I visited Arnaq Johansen at her home in Nuuk, to conduct an interview with her for our daily news program. To this day, this is still one of the interviews that has stuck most in my mind. The emotions were chiseled on her face as she plucked up the courage to let the words speak. Arnaq Johansen was only 12 years old when she had the IUD inserted in 1978 by a Danish doctor in Upernavik.

"I clearly remember how ashamed I felt. I had almost reached puberty at the time, and I had never exposed myself like that before. I just closed my eyes," she said.[6]

The traumatic ordeal of having an IUD forcibly inserted is the common thread in the stories of all these women. They unflinchingly refer to it as abuse by Danish doctors and Danish authorities. In the years that followed, they lived with massive pain and pelvic inflammatory disease as a consequence of the coils, which were far too large for a young girl's body.

Some of the women found their bodies rejected the IUD, after which they had been required to have a new IUD inserted. One of the affected women said that she had an IUD inserted five times in three years because her body kept rejecting them.

For other women, there were no medical follow-ups after the IUDs were inserted. A recurring story is that doctors refused to remove the IUD when approached by the women who requested to have it taken out. Other women say that the doctors allegedly were unable to find the IUD - that it had simply been set up so deep into the vagina that it had "disappeared." Some women even repressed the traumatic memory of the IUD or simply did not realize that they had been subjected to the insertion of one in the first place. Even now, gynecologists are finding old IUDs in women, when they examine them. A gynecologist revealed this fact to KNR in 2022.

"It happened during the 1990s and in the first decade of the 2000s, when women came seeking medical assistance, wondering why they were unable to get pregnant, resulting in the discovery of an IUD as the cause of their infertility. This situation did not involve a huge number of women, but still significantly enough to be noticed by all attending gynecologists working here," one gynecologist told KNR.[7]

For some of the women, the IUDs not only caused significant trauma and pain. They have subsequently been unable to bear children and accuse the forced insertion of IUDs as the cause of their infertility.

Although archival material and old newspapers demonstrate that the IUD campaign was not a public secret when it was rolled out, never-the-less this campaign has now become another trauma for the Greenlandic population to deal with. Articles in old newspapers and old files praise the campaign and its efficiency in drastically reducing Greenland's population growth. Yet, this is the first time several of the women affected have publicly voiced what happened to them. The IUD campaign is like an iceberg calving, the noise from it so loud it can be heard along the entire coast of Greenland. Each day more stories are surfacing. However, the big question remains: Have we only so far seen the tip of this iceberg?

An investigation has been launched

Over time, there has been a tendency in Denmark to talk about the colonization of Greenland as being "in the best interest of everyone." Greenlanders had to move to the cities so they could live in a more civilized manner, the children had to learn Danish so they could get a good education – and the "IUD strategy" was set up to "save" young girls and women from the burden of unwanted pregnancies.

Over time, as a journalist, I have delved into the backgrounds and reasons for several of the colonial measures that were once taken, and have often recounted personal stories by individuals on how the consequences of these colonial measures affected the lives of local people.

However, I wasn't prepared for the huge shock I experienced when the IUD case landed on my desk. And I'm far from the only one.

In the wake of The Danish Broadcasting Corporation's coverage of the IUD scandal, Greenlandic political leaders voiced their outrage. "Appalling," "cruel," "terrible"[8] and "vicious"[9] were some of the words legislators used about the case. One politician called it a clear violation of human rights, while his colleagues took it a step further, and referred to the IUD campaign as genocide.[10] In June 2022, the body of the Greenlandic parliament, Inatsisartut, agreed that an inquiry into the matter had to be launched. Additionally, the legislators also decided that the women affected by the IUD scandal were to be offered free mental health care.

By September 2023, 77 women had accepted the offer of mental healthcare.[11] However, this offer does not include Greenlandic women living in Denmark. A fact, which has drawn criticism of the Danish government from several of the women in question. In September 2022, the Greenlandic government, Naalakkersuisut, and the Danish government agreed to launch an investigation of the IUD campaign case. It will uncover the historical context of pregnancy prevention practices that were initiated in the 1960s, how Greenlandic women and girls experienced the process, and what the actual implementation in Greenland and for Greenlandic girls who were enrolled in post-secondary schools in Denmark entailed. The investigation will examine the period from 1960 to 1991 when the healthcare sector was handed over to the Greenlandic government. However, six months after an agreement had been reached by Danish and Greenlandic legislators to launch an investigation into the matter, it all came to a screeching halt. According to Naalakkersuisut, the Greenlandic legislators tried in vain to get the work started, with no response from Denmark. This lack of action resulted in a sharp criticism of the Danish government by the Premier of Greenland, Múte B. Egede. He did not believe that the Danish government viewed the matter with the seriousness it deserved.

"The trust that needs to be built between our countries dwindles when things like this are not prioritized," Premier Múte B. Egede commented to DR in May 2023.[12]

It started some things - at least Naalakkersuisut and the Danish government were able to announce shortly afterward that an impartial investigation, which is to be carried out by a research team including members from both Greenland and Denmark, could start. The investigation is expected to be completed in 2025 – until then, it is limited how many new revelations of the IUD case will see the light of day and be available for public scrutiny.

Perhaps you may have noticed that I mentioned earlier that the investigation must also get to the bottom of the policy used which insisted that Greenlandic girls, enrolled in post-secondary schools in Denmark, be given contraceptives in the form of an IUD.

After the airing of the podcast, more women came forward with their stories detailing how they too had been forced to get an IUD inserted while they were post-secondary students in Denmark in the 1970s. In the 1960s and 70s, it was common practice for several Greenlandic students to go to post-secondary schools in Denmark to improve their Danish, which was then seen as a way to further one's education. Shortly after the IUD case had gained momentum in Greenland, I got in touch with a woman who had had an IUD installed at a secondary school on the island of Bornholm in 1974.

She said that it was the principal of the secondary school who informed her that she was required to go see the doctor.

"I felt an intense pain in my abdomen when something cold was inserted into me. I didn't receive any explanation at all, and didn't understand what was happening," she said.[13]

Two years later, another woman, Judithe Kristensen, also had an IUD inserted when she was a student at the same secondary school on Bornholm. She had been a student at the post-secondary school for a week when the principal informed her that she had to have an IUD inserted. Judithe Kristensen was 16 years old at the time, was not sexually active, and had no idea why she was taken to the hospital to have an IUD inserted.

"It has been mentally challenging to think about how poorly we Greenlandic women were treated. It has made me sad and angry," Judithe Kristensen said about the incident that happened in 1976.[14]

On the other side of Denmark – specifically the village of Brørup in Jutland – 65-year-old Britta Mortensen was also subjected to an IUD assault. This happened while she was a student at Brøruphus Ungdomsskole, a school that saw the attendance of many students from Greenland. It happened in 1974. Britta Mortensen had also dreamed of improving her Danish and left the town of Ilulissat traveling to Denmark at the age of 15 ready for new adventures.

"One day the headmistress called me over and said I had to have an IUD inserted."

"I told her no. Then the headmistress said that it was not a decision I was free to make on my own. She said there was no option and that the decision was final. I had no say in the matter" Britta Mortensen told me in an interview I had with her.[15]

The IUDs damaged their bodies. Two of the women have subsequently been unable to bear children, and like several other women, they point to the IUDs as the culprit. The women's testimony about being forced to have an IUD inserted while they were students in Denmark opens up a whole new chapter in the IUD case.

Researcher Naja Dyrendom Graugaard, who researches the colonial relationship between Greenland and Denmark at Aarhus University, estimates that the forced use of IUDs can be categorized as genocide against the Greenlandic population.

"If you view the UN charter on the subject, it can be considered genocide when a country or people intentionally prevent pregnancy or births in a certain population group based on the group's nationality, ethnicity, or religious affiliation," she explains. "At the same time, the IUDs imposed on Greenlandic students in Denmark emphasize that they were fundamentally prejudiced or racist acts based on ethnicity," Naja Dyrendom Graugaard continues.[16] So far, no ethnic Danish women or girls have come forward with similar stories of a forced insertion of IUDs – most likely because the IUD campaign was not targeted at them.

Other researchers do consider this to be a violation of human rights but question whether it can be categorized as genocide. However, to some of the women who had the IUD inserted the consequences were devastating. This is why I am so full of admiration for these women, and grateful that they have opened up about their experiences and the pain they have endured and suffered for many years. Judithe Kristensen's words are still with me to this day, when she said during the interview:

"Even now, I scream in anger."

The women affected also showed a great deal of zeal and determination when they held a demonstration in Nuuk in connection with Danish Prime Minister Mette Frederiksen's visit to Greenland in June of 2023. Here they braved the wind and rain and stood for over an hour patiently waiting for the Prime Minister. Naja Lyberth was the first to speak when the Prime Minister appeared.

"Dear Prime Minister. We need recognition from the government for the wrongs we have been subjected to so that we can move forward. That you concede that the government's policy at the time was a torturous injustice against us and that the actions taken against us even violated the very laws the government had formulated," Naja Lyberth told the Prime Minister.[17]

It did not result in an apology from the Prime Minister, but she emphasized that "their plight touched her deeply" and that she would not forget them.

A demand for compensation from the Danish government

A good four months after the demonstrators came face to face with the Danish Prime Minister, they turned again to the Danish government. And this time it was with a compensation claim for violating their human rights. In October of 2023, 67 women, victims of the IUD campaign, demanded 300,000 Danish Kroner each – a total compensation of 20.1 million Danish Kroner. According to their lawyer, Mads Pramming from the Danish law firm, Ehmer Pramming Advokater, the Danish government violated several articles of the UN Human Rights Charter.

It is a breach of Article 3, which prohibits torture, Article 8, the right to have one's private and family life respected, and Article 14, which prohibits discrimination. Among other things, the lawyer stated to Radio Greenland that he found it difficult to see how a state could do more damage than had been done with the IUD campaign. According to a spokesperson for the group, Naja Lyberth, who was the first to speak out about the IUD, "it is important to act now, as several of the affected women are of advanced age."

"It is a demand for compensation for the suffering we had to go through. We have many physical and psychological aftereffects. For many of us, it was a torture-like experience," Naja Lyberth stated when I interviewed her for Radio Greenland in connection with the compensation claim.[18]

According to lawyer Mads Pramming, the compensation amount is determined based on similar cases in the Human Rights Court. At the same time, there is a high probability that the total compensation amount will grow even larger. When I spoke to the lawyer in November 2023, he claimed that the law firm is now in contact with around 140 women who are demanding compensation from the Danish government. The lawyers are collecting the women's stories.

The Danish government has not yet responded to this demand for compensation. The Danish Minister of the Interior and Health did not wish to be interviewed about the matter. Instead, she sent a written response to Radio Greenland alluding to the ongoing investigation "that it is important to get to the bottom of what occurred." However, several Danish politicians support the claim for compensation and call the IUD case "serious abuse."[19] At the same time, the women have also received support from the Greenland Government in Nuuk.

Naalakkersuisoq (Minister) of Health, Agathe Fontain, expressed to Radio Greenland how very sorry she is for the women affected and that the Greenland Government will help in any way they can.

However, during an interview with Radio Greenland, Agathe Fontain echoed her Danish colleague when she also pointed to the fact that the ongoing investigation needs to be completed "before there can be a thorough discussion and subsequent action taken by the Greenland Government on the matter."[20]

Time will tell whether the women take it a step further and challenge the Danish state in a court of law. In any case, Naja Lyberth said, when I spoke to her in November, "that there would soon be another reaction."

The IUDs continue to haunt

Another big issue has furthermore come to light which opens up a whole new chapter of the IUD campaign. It turns out that it was not only in the 1960s, 70s or 80s that women experienced IUDs being inserted without consent. Right up to today, there are now women who talk about receiving contraceptive treatment without first agreeing to it. In December 2022, the BBC published an article in which they had spoken to several women who had received involuntary contraceptive treatment without consent.[21] It put me on the trail of a woman, Emma Kuko, who was probably not one of the women interviewed by the BBC, but a woman my colleague knew about.

In 2010, Emma Kuko[22] had a surgical abortion at the hospital in Tasiilaq when she was 16 years old. Following the abortion, she had severe abdominal pain and irregular bleeding. On the internet, she read that there could be side effects if you had used an IUD as contraception. But Emma Kuko didn't use one. She knew that. She went to the doctor several times, and they viewed her medical journal, but she was told that there was nothing unusual in the journal. The pain continued over the next few years, but it wasn't until nine years after she had the abortion that she got the explanation. In 2019, a doctor found an IUD that Emma Kuko had no recollection of having been inserted. She believes that the IUD was inserted in connection with the abortion in 2010. Furthermore, there is no record of this IUD in her medical journal.[23]

After Emma Kuko's story went public several other women have come forward with similar accounts. About having a surgical abortion, subsequently experiencing great pain, and then the shock that hits when they find out they have been given an IUD. It appears the abortions were all carried out by Danish doctors.

Immediately after the BBC coverage in December 2022, the National Board of Health of Greenland[24] encouraged women to come forward with a complaint if they had been given contraception without consent. In October of 2023, the National Board of Health announced that they were aware of 14 cases of women having been given contraception without consent after the healthcare sector had been handed over to the Greenlandic government in 1991. Except for one complaint concerning a case in the 1990s, all the other cases happened after the turn of the millennium.[25] More cases may well be on the way. Recently, I spoke to several women who are victims of contraception without consent, but who have yet to launch a complaint with the National Board of Health. In October 2023, I also came into contact with a psychologist who told me that she was providing therapy to ten women, all victims of contraception without consent.[26]

The National Board of Health has emphasized that the latter cases are not part of a targeted strategy, as was seen with the IUD campaign.

At the same time, the office notes that these new cases have been found nationwide.

The questions are still many. How is it possible that women keep experiencing being given an IUD without consent? What kind of rationale – or lack thereof – is behind it? What will be done to rectify the negative experiences these women have had, and last but not least what can be done to restore women's trust in a healthcare system where they have experienced such a massive failure?

The Greenlandic healthcare system continues to be dominated by Danish labour, and it is no secret that language differences pose a significant challenge to the relationship between doctor and patient. The National Board of Health has pointed out that the language difficulties between doctor and patient may partially explain why some women have experienced being given an IUD without consent, but this is not the whole story, and additional explanations are needed.[27]

Thus, several stakeholders such as the Council of Human Rights, the Inuit Circumpolar Conference, and the UN special rapporteur for the Rights of Indigenous Peoples have called for the ongoing investigation to include current cases as well.[28] It is a demand that several Greenlandic and Danish legislators support.[29] The Greenland Government, Naalakkersuisut, has yet to state whether the ongoing investigation should include current cases after 1991.

I have been trying for months, with little success, to set up an interview with the Greenland Government's Department of Health. In response to my request for an interview, the Department issued a statement in which they claimed that the Government views this matter seriously and that they expect the ongoing investigation to be concluded by mid-December of 2023.

It is a vicious case - but there is also a bright spot. As a society, we now have the opportunity to face these abuses head-on and work on processing the colonial trauma of which the IUD campaign is a part. Both as a journalist and on a more personal level I have been greatly affected by the stories of these women.

As a woman, I can hardly bear to think what this situation has done to the women who have had an IUD forcibly inserted into their young bodies. That many were mere children at the time, some as young as 12 makes it even more unconscionable.

I gave the matter a lot of thought to how I should approach the interviews with the women who had experienced such intimate and invasive abuse. Furthermore, it was important to me to make room for the emotions swirling around everyone involved.

That the women would stand by their very personal stories when they became public knowledge was essential to me and I had a lengthy dialogue with them before we went public. The Greenlandic population is tiny. Everyone is more or less acquainted with everyone else. Coming forward to speak openly about such private matters on the national media scene takes great courage.

The IUD campaign is a new chapter in the ongoing saga of the Danish colonization of Greenland. As a journalist, I am fully determined to see this case through to the end.

The debate and discussion on Danish colonialism in Greenland covers a plethora of topics and some generate more emotional responses than others. However, we cannot avoid the fact that Greenlandic society continues to be dominated by the structures set in place by the Danish authorities, structures which for decades have set the framework for social development within Greenland.

There are still people alive today whose lives have been adversely influenced by colonization, and who have felt the impact of this colonization on their bodies – such as the victims of the IUD campaign. My heartfelt thanks - Qujanarujussuaq – goes to the women who so bravely have shared their private stories with the rest of us.

I JUST KNEW

Karen Lawford

In the course of writing this chapter, it became apparent that I was venturing into a sensitive area of my life. I wrote, rewrote, and deleted sections of my writing, a process that aligned with the way I write for Western academia. This approach, however, did not sit well with me. It seemed forced and inauthentic to the topic and to the person I am. After taking a week off of writing, I decided to write my chapter as five journal entries, labelled Days 1 to 5. I hope you can appreciate my thought process is complex, nuanced, and reflects my daily perspectives. None of them are incorrect, but rather, they change from day to day. I think this is the way I interpret life; it changes from day to day and is influenced by new information and reassessment.

Day 1

I just knew

When I was pregnant with my first child, I just knew I had to be careful. I had to protect my child and do everything just right so he wouldn't be taken away from me by government officials. I wasn't quite sure who these governments officials were or when they would intervene in my life, but I was keenly aware that I had to have the right relationship, the right housing, eat the right food, take my vitamins, do the correct amount and kind of exercise, keep all my appointments with care providers, get all the testing, and conform, conform, conform. Otherwise—and of this, I was certain—my precious baby would be apprehended at birth, even before we could meet each other.

I couldn't understand why it seemed other pregnant people were so happy and confident with their pregnancies and planning baby rooms, buying baby clothes, and having baby showers. How did those people know their baby was not going to be apprehended? How is it they had done everything the right way so they could enjoy their pregnancies and look forward to the future? What was so different between them and me?

I look back on those feelings and it seems strange to think of my pregnancy and the embedded insecurities that stirred in my guts until I was sick. Where did they come from? Where did I learn them? Who taught me to think like this? My son is now twenty, and I have had plenty of time to examine these questions. I am, thankfully, no longer worried he will be apprehended. I look back at my younger self and pray for her confidence and self-worth.

Since my son's birth, I have become a registered midwife, completed a master's and doctoral degree, and continue to dedicate my life to making sense of the maternity care that is offered to Indigenous Peoples. I best understand the details in Canada, but it seems maternity care experienced by Indigenous Peoples in the United States, Australia, and New Zealand are very comparable. Broadly, the similarities can be distilled down to the lived experiences and interactions with colonialism, Christianity, patriarchy, and the Euro-biomedical model. Taken as a whole, these intertwined attacks on Indigenous Peoples, regardless of the geopolitical boundaries, amount to genocide. It seems, then, that my feelings all those years ago were very well founded.

I just knew

Day 2

I dream for my children

I have returned from a five-day visit with Elder midwife, Carol Couchie, who lives on Nipissing First Nation. She and her husband, Kevin, are building an off-grid straw bale home. I spend time with them to help and lend my energy to their dreams. It is quite the task and will take many helpers to build their dream home. I am amazed by their vision and their dedication to their dream, to each other, their family, and their community. It is their ability to dream that gives me strength and sparks a question to my younger self: Are you dreaming enough?

I don't remember having many dreams as a child. Instead, they were nightmares. For the sake of keeping my childhood protected and safe from inquiry, I hold this time of my life close to my heart. Undoubtedly, you, the reader, get a sense that my childhood was less than ideal. As a family surviving poverty, Christianity, land theft, and other aspects of colonization that are not conducive to health and wellness, I don't remember the idea of dreaming as part of my life. But thinking back on this time, maybe my dream was to survive?

I have survived long enough to consider and reconsider my dreams. Long enough to dedicate my time to expanding dreams for myself, my children, my family, and the ancestral existences from all planes of time and space. I can see our People, across all generations, shifting towards a mindset of dreaming for more than survival. I dream for our People across all generations, timelines, and planes of existence. My dreams are now interconnected and entwined with all my experiences of life, the joyous, the difficult, and everything else that makes me who I am.

I am deeply honoured to witness the collective strength of our People, many of whom have survived the evils of colonialism, Christianity, and patriarchy. It is genocide that not all our People survived encounters with White settlers. Yes, genocide without any qualifiers or explanations.

I dream for my children

Day 3

I am a precious being

With all my heart, I believe that children are precious. Flowing from this belief is that each of us is a precious being. It is from this truth that I am learning that I, too, am a precious being. It will take time, patience, and self-care to shift into a space that is comfortable with being precious while simultaneously taking into account the entirety of my life experience. Certainly, there have been people and institutions that have greatly harmed me, but I too have acted in ways that were not good. I am sharing this truth for the sake of transparency and honesty. Not to you, the reader, but rather to myself. To be precious, I will need to see all parts of who I am and to make amends where I can.

I am confident that my younger self did not feel precious. Rather, I was a burden, unwanted, and a mistake of some sort. I now understand that living in a world significantly affected by colonialism, White supremacy, Christianity, and the Euro-Canadian bio-medical model results in the construction and maintenance of the right kind of human. These words are scary because they are meant to scare Indigenous Peoples into submission for the purpose of creating and maintaining systems of oppression and white supremacy. These are not just ideas that can be understood within academic spaces because we, Indigenous Peoples, understand they impart meaning and are accompanied by actions and material consequences.

It is the material consequences of colonialism, White supremacy, Christianity, and the Euro-Canadian bio-medical model, that some of our people are missing, murdered, and vanished from our homelands. It is through these interlocking systems of genocide that some of our people are targeted for forced and coerced sterilizations by healthcare professionals. It is the network of oppression that is underpinned by colonial legal systems that support the theft of our children and moves us away from family, community, and our homelands. The extent of the material impacts of our unequal and inequitable relationship with White settlers is just beginning to be understood.

I am a precious being

Day 4

I have choice

A dear friend posted a picture of her youngest son on Facebook. Her children are so important to my life and my family. I am proud to be their Aunty and kin. My friend is a kind and lovely partner and mother, and a friend to many. She has always wanted children, but pregnancy does not come easy to her. With the help of Western medicine and perhaps by chance, she has four children. We share many things but yearning for children is not one of them. Yes, I have two children who are the loves of my life and are the strongest teachers I know. But I seem to not have been born with a desire to have children. Irrespective of my choices in life and the path I am now on, I support—100%—people's decision to have, or not have, children.

Some of our People, however, have their children stripped from their lives even before conception. Our decision to have children is coercively, forcefully, and even violently taken away from us by health-care providers, government officials, and anyone else who has power and authority over our Peoples. Chemical sterilization through pharmaceuticals, such as Depo-Provera and Norplant, were injected into Indigenous women in the USA and Canada, even before either drug was approved for use in non-Indigenous populations. So, in addition to chemically sterilizing Indigenous Peoples without our knowledge and informed choice, government regulators and pharmaceutical companies used our Indigenous Peoples' bodies to test their newly developed drugs.

Forced and coerced physical sterilization of our People is happening in Canada and worldwide. In fact, it seems physicians and obstetricians are *still* performing forced and coercive sterilizations all across Canada! The Euro-Canadian bio-medical model has emboldened care providers to disregard human rights and choice. The reproductivity of Indigenous Peoples is still being purposefully targeted by those who adhere to white supremacy and nation building through the right kind of body. These acts are genocide conducted in medical industrial complexes by those who seem to be above professional ethics, national commitments, and international laws. Indigenous Peoples deserve choice and health care that is compassionate, attentive, and responsive to Indigenous relational ethics.

I have choice

Day 5

I can change

Lately, and perhaps especially because I am writing these journal entries, I have been considering how I have included Western, colonial ideals into my personal life. Now, I am taking time to use visioning and dreaming as a way to bring to life my imaginations of a self that is good and kind in an Anishinabe way. Part of this process, I realize, is that I must be gentle with myself as I come to recognize how Western, colonial ideas have become embedded into the person that I am. I am not sure what to call this process of purposeful and intentional change, but it is a path that feels right to me. I am self-ishly devoting part of my time and energy to becoming the person I want to be.

I know that I will be shifting in and out of spaces of comfort and distress, so I wonder how I will deal with these feelings. I mentioned in my biography that I work within a Western education industrial complex that is grounded in punitive assessment tools, such as grading. The processes of teaching and learning are also time limited and regulated at various levels of governance. How does this educational setup actually promote learning, reflection, and the potential for viewing the world in a new, complex, and nuanced way? I ask these questions because my education has been molded in this manner for almost thirty years! But these ways of learning can be unkind and harsh. To purposely walk toward new knowledge, I will need to explore new (or is it old?) ways of learning.

I want to be tender with the precious being that I am while I embark on a journey of change. I want to honour the prayers of my ancestors and those who have yet to come who brought me into this world as a sacred bundle. These ancestors left markers all over the world so that I could see I was part of their reality even before I came into existence. Their prayers brought me here. So, I honour their energy and dedication to me by continuing to become the person I want to be. It is my birthright to be an Indigenous person. I will honour this birthright.

I can change

Summary Thoughts

It is with immeasurable gratitude that I thank Morningstar for inviting me to contribute a chapter in her book. It is from her unqualified belief in me that I was able to create a chapter that reflects some of my innermost thoughts. Meegwetch, Morningstar.

171

Dedication

To my precious children, I love you so much. I love you so much.

THE AMAUTI AND THE NOOSE: REFLECTIONS ON POWER AND BIRTH

Ewan Affleck

My first-born arrived in a spring snowstorm. Gusts of wet wind blew flakes of snow through an open window. They gently settled on Susan, who seemed to welcome the cooling touch; "Leave the window open," she said, eyes closed between contractions. I sat by her side, timidly holding her hand, feeling small and inconsequential, awkwardly remote from her pain.

It was April 1993, three years before the doors of the last segregated Indian hospital in Canada were closed. I was fresh from medical school and had taken a post in Salluit, a remote Inuit village on the Hudson Strait. As Susan's belly grew, she was embraced by the local women, who made it clear that she – like all new mothers – needed an amauti, a traditional Inuit women's parka.

When the local women took Susan to be fitted for her amauti, I followed along. We approached a bright blue government-issue house that floated on piles driven into the permafrost. As we stamped the snow off our feet, the corrugated steel stair rang in the cold air; we stepped over frozen char and caribou piled on the front porch. Inside we met Elisapie, a traditional seamstress and Elder with weathered skin the color of copper. Settling into a couch beneath a small portrait of Jesus Christ, Elisapie padded softly from her kitchen in seal-skin kamiks with tea she had prepared on an electric hot plate. Swaths of fabric were brought out, and Susan joined the other women, who caressed the material like a newborn child. Drinking my tea, I watched from the side, trying to follow the stories of birthing; there was much laughter as the language alternated between Inuktitut and English. When the women finally rose to leave, I asked when the measurement would occur. "Oh, it is fine," they explained, "Elisapie just needed to look at Susan."

The amauti was delivered three days later, a beautiful white parka lined with plush duffle, embroidered with intricate sky-blue trim, and a hood bordered by delicate white fox fur. Fox fur, we were told, would do, although it was not as coveted as dog fur. The amauti was magnificent but didn't quite fit when Susan tried to slip it over her pregnant belly, so it was carefully folded and set in the closet, to quietly wait. Reverentially.

A month later we flew in a Twin Otter down the coast of Ungava Bay, stopping in every community to exchange passengers; Kangiqsujuaq, Quataq, Kangirsuk, Aupaluk, Tasiujaq; from above each hamlet a spit of brightly colored houses strewn like a distracted child's blocks on the white tundra. When we reached Kuujuaq, we changed planes, boarding an old jet bound for Montreal that lumbered down the runway – seeming impossibly heavy to leave the ground – carrying the amauti in its underbelly, secure in Susan's suitcase.

Manhood is a curious vantage from which to experience the birth of a child. There is an incidental quality to the role, that of a drone whose value is lost when their seed is spent. I had imagined an almost spiritual reckoning would accompany the arrival of my son; a deep sense of intimate deliverance, or some manner of transcendental firmament of the father-child bond. This did not occur. The baby born and brought home was unknown to me, a character introduced into my life by chance encounter, with a personality and habits that needed to be reckoned with. A new roommate, and one lacking even rudimentary life skills and demanding a lot of attention.

This was not so for Susan. She seemed to know him – intimately – bound by the union of their beings grown together. Coupled with the miraculous tools she possessed, ovaries, a uterus, breasts, she was a self-contained nurturing apparatus, ever-ready and in the moment, bonded in a deep union of familiarity. I watched her gift with a mixture of awe and longing, and privately felt a little outside the equation.

We had been very excited to have children. But after a year and a half without success, the monthly disappointment began to dampen the erstwhile gift of physical union, now becoming – unspoken, but understood – an act associated with predetermined failure. This had not been the plan for young love. Reluctantly, we visited a fertility clinic, feeling as though it represented an admission of guilt or shame.

Thinking back, now almost thirty years later, through the filter of a life lived with two beautiful children – grown and independent – the vigour of raw sadness we felt was but a brief moment in time, now grown faint. We bore the impatience of the privileged; where I grew up, success, prosperity, and joy of family were a birthright. We were entitled to be fulfilled and meant to have children; to imagine otherwise was an injustice.

Fortunately, this inconvenient hesitation was short-lived, and our birthright was served when one night the seed stuck. We were pregnant, spontaneously, without need of the speculums, centrifuges and semen cups we encountered at the fertility clinic. The positive pregnancy test confirmed that the righteous path was once more underfoot. Our little flirtation with infertility, our momentary disquiet – surely mistaken – was soon supplanted by the rightful odour of dirty diapers and cry for breast.

The amauti now fit Susan perfectly. We wrapped our baby boy in swaddling and slid him carefully into the warm space against his mother's back. Now a threesome, we walked in Jeanne-Mance Park in the spring warmth. Susan shone, her long blond hair catching the breeze. The white amauti, resplendent in the sunlight, drew curious looks from passers-by. Our son slept. "I can feel him breathing," Susan whispered contentedly.

A few weeks later, we returned home to Salluit, where Susan's amauti seemed more pedestrian, one among many. I returned to work at the Health Center, my step buoyed by fresh fatherhood enwrapping me in a newfound confidence.

Susan wanted our son to be baptized. I was not a church-going man but agreed to visit the local Anglican minister, a small Inuit man with a caring smile and big glasses, who made arrangements for a ceremony the following Sunday. We discovered that the Inuit communities that run along the coast between Hudson and Ungava Bay are either Catholic or Anglican, depending on whose version of God won the day during an antagonistic rush by competing Christian faiths to recruit souls in the 1930s. Salluit was Anglican, accented by a garnish of ardent evangelical missionaries who drifted through town from time to time.

On the assigned day, the church was full for Sunday service, the simple wood frame interior glowing in the morning light. The sermon was in Inuktitut, a language that proved just as difficult to master as it is beautiful to listen to, and was punctuated by periodic parishioners who stood or stepped forward and began to wail. This was speaking in tongues I guessed. No one acknowledged these people, other than to courteously step aside as they left or returned to their seats. I did not understand what it all meant, but it seemed quite magical, and I felt blessed to be sharing the moment. When called upon we carried our son to the front, dressed in an old yellowing baptismal gown used by three generations of Susan's family. After some words were spoken, the minister anointed our son's head with water. When it was over, we were given a document with a picture of an Igloo under the banner of the Diocese of the Arctic, certifying that our son had been adopted into Christianity.

Traditionally, the Inuit were nomadic people who followed the seasonal migration of food: fish, sea mammals, birds, berries, and sometimes caribou or muskox. The present-day Inuit settlements in the Canadian Arctic were established by the Government of Canada in response to American and Soviet threats to sovereignty prompted by the Cold War. Inuit, pawns in the machinations of global geopolitics, were forcibly moved into these settlements, whereupon the government and their agents slaughtered many of the dog teams to prevent people from leaving. Sled dogs were the principal means of transportation and hunting for the Inuit; their loss led to food scarcity, loss of kinship bonds, loss of identity, and starvation.

But at the time, I understood very little of this history. What superficial knowledge I had of the north and the Inuit was a by-product of my Eurocentric elementary and high school history curriculums, and popular media like the grainy silent film *Nanook of the North,* which portrayed the Inuit through the paternalistic lens of romantic primitivism. I grew up in the Canada of Pierre Trudeau, when multiculturalism and tolerance were hailed as core tenets of our national psyche, and the Canadian Charter of Rights and Freedoms was adopted to much fanfare. I understood *and believed* that all Canadians – irrespective of creed, culture, or race – were treated equally and fairly, and I was gratified to be working in our publicly funded health-care system, *known* to be the best in the world.

My son was born on April 1, 1993, seven days before the start of the Rwandan genocide. In the evenings after work, Susan and I would share dinner, play with the baby, and tune in to CBC Radio to catch up on the day's events. Sitting at our kitchen table, looking out over the sea ice that was broken into great hummocks by the cycle of the tides, we were vividly transported into a completely different world by a man named Romeo Dallaire, a Canadian general overseeing a small United Nations peace-keeping force in Rwanda. For a few weeks on the show *As It Happens,* General Dallaire described horrific scenes of men, women and children being lined up on jungle roads and systematically hacked to death with machetes. His impassioned pleas for assistance from the international community fell on deaf ears; no country forcibly intervened to stop the killing. When the dust settled, an estimated 800,000 people died in a little over 90 days.

The scale of barbarism was difficult to comprehend. I could not imagine this ever happening in Canada and reasoned through my Eurocentric lens that this event was a by-product of some sort of base tribalism that never had – and never would – be tolerated in our enlightened country. What I failed to understand at the time, sitting in a little Inuit community overlooking the Hudson Strait, was that it already had occurred in Canada, and was continuing, albeit in a less overt and immediate basis, borne out, over the years, through institutional intolerance and discrete acts of race-based cruelty. Although the methodology might be more nuanced, the impact was not dissimilar. Lives were being lost.

The first hint I had that all was not harmonious in our bucolic little nation was the number of local people I saw at the Salluit Health

Centre with suicidal intentions. One day, three different men presented to me wanting to kill themselves. The first gentleman, about 40 years of age, explained that he planned to shoot himself in the head with a rifle to spare his wife and five children the humiliation of his failure to provide for them. "There are no jobs," he explained. "I cannot buy food and cannot afford gas for the ski-doo to hunt. They are hungry."

A younger man revealed his plan to hang himself in the closet of his room – a preferred method – and had crafted a noose. I asked him to collect the noose from home and bring it to me, reasoning that if the weapon was removed, he would not be able to kill himself. Dutifully, he fetched it. I had never seen a noose before and was struck how intricately the thick rope had been knotted into a loop. I placed it in my desk drawer where it remained until my departure from Salluit a few years later. I was always aware of its presence; in idle moments, I would pull it out and feel its weight, the thoughtful craftsmanship told of a collective trauma. An epidemic of suicide had been slowly building since the forced relocation of the Inuit. In the decade after my departure suicide rates grew to be amongst the highest in the world, ten times the Canadian average.

Childbirth was another point of contention in the community. All pregnant women were forcibly shipped out at thirty-six weeks gestation to Povungnituk, to wait up to six weeks to give birth at the regional birthing centre. Women grumbled and resisted, not wanting to be separated from their families and young children. Some asked me to falsify their due date so they could deliver at home. I had to explain that evacuating women for childbirth was government policy and that there was a risk associated with childbirth in the community. "Whose risk?" I was asked. "Before, we used to have our babies in our camps, with our own midwives. Now we are forced to leave." I did not know how to answer the question. It was not lost on me that Susan and I had flown south at government expense to be close to our families for the birth of our son.

179

The medicalization of traditional birth harkened back to the era of the government Tuberculosis Ship that plied northern waters after the Second World War and forcibly – often without warning – removed Inuit thought to be suffering from TB, depositing them in sanatoriums in the south. Most were deprived of communication with their families, and many never returned home. What I did not understand at the time, was that forced relocation for birth, which continues across the north to this day, was not the darkest chapter in the government of Canada's Indigenous birthing policy.

The path of our life next led us to northwestern Ontario, where Susan and I welcomed our second child, a wilful baby girl, who was soon bundled in swaddling and stashed in the warmth and comfort of the amauti for family walks. My duties as a physician included covering two Ojibway reservations. Once again, I was clumsily naïve to their cultural traditions and history.

In 2001, we relocated once more, to Yellowknife, the capital of the Northwest Territories, a city of twenty-thousand built into Precambrian rock on the north shore of Great Slave Lake. Boasting traffic lights, fledgling office towers, and an abundant civil service, this was a far more cosmopolitan setting than we were accustomed to. I soon discovered that the clinical work seemed sanitized and dull compared to my practices in Salluit and northwestern Ontario; I was dealing principally with pasty white-collar ailments. Sensing my disappointment, Susan suggested I start an outreach clinic at the Centre for Northern Families, which functioned as a shelter for women from across the western Arctic disenfranchised by domestic violence, poverty, and addictions. I took Susan's advice.

Every Tuesday for the next seventeen years, I ran a drop-in clinic at the Women's Shelter, that catered both to residents and people living on the street. Being a white, educated male, I am certain I was viewed with doubt by the women when I first arrived, perhaps for the duration. But I kept returning, week after week, and gradually I believe, a modicum of trust grew. Over the seventeen years, I bore witness to all measures of dehumanization, pain, and suffering, the by-product of intergenerational trauma, lateral violence, and structural disdain for those less favoured. But I loved the service, the raw and unvarnished quintessence, the challenge of having to step outside one's comfort zone to grasp the thread of shared humanity, which I discovered was always there to be found. So often, I was honoured by the simple blessing of humour, wisdom, or grace, by those, whose suffering far outstripped anything I would ever know.

Needing a change, although not without regret, I stepped down from this service in 2017. Around the same time, the Saskatoon Regional Health Authority released a report documenting the cases of sixteen Indigenous women who reported being coercively sterilized between 2005 and 2010. Soon after, the United Nations Committee Against Torture (CAT) issued a condemnation of Canada, citing the extensive use of forced or coerced sterilization of Indigenous women and girls dating back to the 1970s, a practice they reported that continued until recent years. I learned that sterilization had been widespread, occurring across the country, and in many jurisdictions where I had worked, including Ontario and the Northwest Territories.

This gave me pause. After almost thirty years of providing health service in Indigenous communities across the country, I believed I had come to possess at least a basic understanding of the compendium of trauma that Indigenous people had suffered through colonization. How had I never heard about the forced and coerced sterilization of Indigenous women by the very health service I worked for? In a truly egalitarian society, there must be transparency and accountability. If one accepts that forced and coerced sterilization is a form of violence that deprives an individual of their freedom of choice, and that in a just society, violence is forbidden and freedom of choice is sacrosanct, then the practice of forced and coerced sterilization must be *named* and *accounted for*. It seemed to me it had never been named, or if it had, I had failed to notice.

In her seminal book on the sterilization of Indigenous women in Canada, author Karen Stote described the practice as a form of genocide. In 2018, Member of Parliament Rachel Blaney, speaking in the House of Commons, used the term genocide to describe the sterilization of Indigenous women in Canada. The same term was used to describe the consequences of the Residential School System in the report of the Truth and Reconciliation Commission. It turned out that the Canada of my youth, of social justice, equity, and the Charter of Rights and Freedoms, was a genocidal nation. One need not join Romeo Dallaire in Africa to find large-scale racially motivated killing; Canada has a domestic version.

My youthful belief in the sanctity of an egalitarian nation seemed to be reified by my personal experience. Although I was not naïve to a history couched in prejudicial beliefs, as a young man, I imagined that this described a remote history; that was then, not now. Hard work and diligence would be rewarded by success in Canada, irrespective of race, creed or culture. Was this wilful ignorance or unconscious bias? I guess it doesn't matter, because in the end the result is the same, the perpetuation of a mythology that benefits and supports those who occupy a position of power.

Our vision is framed by our birthright, by our learned perspective. My periscope arose from and was nested in a place of privilege, scanning the world myopically through a filter of implicit moral superiority and assumed beneficence, and emboldened by the liberty of righteous goodness that is a luxury of those born to a place of power.

In the 1970s, there was widespread sterilization of Inuit women in the Canadian Arctic. The order to sterilize women was meted out by southern white health officials, who did not speak the language and justified their decisions by ascribing to the woman "diagnoses" of mental deficiency, promiscuity or overcrowding of children. When Susan and I arrived in the Arctic, about fifteen years later, she was already pregnant. As her belly grew and the local women learned she was with child, they welcomed her unconditionally, as a sister united by the miracle of conception and birth. It did not seem to matter to them that her husband was a southern white health official who did not speak their language. In solidarity, they gifted Susan the amauti, a symbol of fertility, womanhood and future.

The counterpoint to the amauti is the noose, brought to the southern white health official by a young man who struggled to see a future, because his past had been damaged. The noose was not only emblematic of the young man's dysphoria, but of the constitutional trauma of a people, bled to the bone by structural racism. Both the noose and the amauti speak to a shared history. Both must be named and accounted for.

Ewan Affleck
Yellowknife, NT
February 1, 2021

STANDING AT THE DOORWAY:
FOR THOSE SPIRITS YET TO COME

Nathalie Pambrun and Cheryllee Bourgeois

Over the years, I have heard the stories of the violations, of forcibly, coercively, and involuntarily sterilized Indigenous women and gender diverse peoples. People quietly hold these deeply painful personal experiences, as well as those of their mothers, aunties, and grandmas. All yearning for and mourning those little spirits waiting to come through. I am deeply saddened that this is a reality here in Canada and want to acknowledge all those who have been affected.

Involuntary sterilization intersects with my role as a Métis midwife working within the health-care system, and this has left me with a deeply severed spirit. In spite of this, it is essential to call out this racist practice and end this violence so that forced or coerced sterilization will not be the experience of any other person and that it will not be the lived reality of the coming generations.

Deliberately taking life-giving abilities came with the colonization and medicalization of our sexual and reproductive health-care systems and the targeting of Indigenous bodies. Before this, our communities always relied on midwives, keepers of the most sacred ceremonies of life and death, medicine people with a deep understanding of biology and the reproductive life cycle. Our midwives were some of the most brilliant Indigenous scientists, providing care through reproductive physiologic events of menses, pregnancy, birth, abortion, menopause, and using life-saving skills when things deviated from the ordinary. Through relationships with midwives, women and gender-diverse people would learn about their bodies and what was happening throughout their life-cycle changes.

As life-givers, Indigenous people understood that we were powerful, and we knew how to harness that strength and the responsibilities we carried. In the past, our Healers, Elders, and Midwives were chosen and recognized by our communities for their skills sets and abilities as young children. They would start their learning young and be trained, as it would take over a decade of mentorship to learn and pass down the necessary knowledge they would need to fulfill their roles. Bound by the weaving of our strong kinship ties, we harvested plants seasonally and understood plants and food as medicine at the heart of our health and wellness practices. Many of these practices are still the foundation of our health and well-being.

Our bodies are not separate from our environment, including the moon cycles, the seasons or the animals, rocks, plants, stars, and winds. Our Indigenous health system continues to be revolutionary because it has always been grounded in the context and framework of our natural laws that define health and balance. The interconnectedness between all things is the basis on which our natural laws are built. The basis of our natural laws is relationship and consent. It does not include any type of forced and coerced practices.

As a young girl, I knew I would be a midwife and water protector. I am Métis from the Red River Settlement. I was born at the fork of the Red and the Assiniboine Rivers and I still live here. And this land and its waters hold the memory of my ancestors. I am filled with blood memory and oral histories that have linked me back to our Métis creation stories, the origin stories of my Nation continue to inform me of our emergence and the important relationships and responsibilities we have to these lands and waters. They have given me a clear vision and direction of what I must do. My role as a midwife is to raise our women up as the centre poles of our communities.

When I was eight, I attended my first home birth with midwives, and I remember my first thought: *I was not born this way.* I was not born in the hands of my aunties in a calm and loving space, where the birther was revered and cared for with such peace and harmony. I loved the feeling in the room. I could feel the openness of that sacred birth doorway, and I could feel the ancestors around us. And I remember thinking as I walked home that if I could be a part of birth in my life journey, I would live a blessed life. And in that same moment of clarity, I remember thinking that my kids would need to drink bottled water. These thoughts were separate truths in my mind at first. But I quickly came to realize how they were intrinsically linked. My understanding of being a water protector and a midwife were the same work. As Indigenous midwives, we are concerned about water, because our teachings tell us "Water is sacred, water is life." We know that all of human life is made of water. It's an essential part of our bodies, and, inside the womb, it helps life grow while also protecting it. For Millennia, Indigenous women have honoured this sacred relationship with water, and have in turn protected it through our traditions, ceremonies, and advocacy.

Katsi Cook, a Mohawk Elder and midwife, taught us "Women are the first environment," which reminds us that respect for women and the environment are one and the same. In this context, it's perhaps not surprising that we're confronting the multiple crises of missing and murdered Indigenous women and girls and forced and coerced sterilization while industries are simultaneously contaminating our environment and water. What we do to the land and water affects our first environment and vice versa.

Indigenous and non-Indigenous siblings, cousins, and families are fighting the pipelines, Energy East, Northern Gateway, the Tar Sands, the Site C Dam, and many other industrial development projects that harm people and place. These warriors are advocating for peace, prosperity, and protection of our lands and water for future generations. They are fulfilling the prophecy of resistance, seeking to stop the destruction and commodification of our cultures and environments on behalf of their mother – the earth.

Indigenous midwives are doing the same. Our education has taught us about the current Western landscape of sexual and reproductive health since colonization and pathologizing of Indigenous bodies. We work hard to bridge these understandings with the ancestral knowledge systems in our communities, centering Indigenous reproductive health teachings and practices without compromising modern medical advances. We believe Indigenous people have the right to decide when, where, and how we have children; to choose our own care providers; and to parent the children we have in a healthy environment. Our people have a right to access health care free of racism, racial-biases, and coercion. We are calling upon the regulatory bodies and professional associations to criminalize the behaviours and actions of practitioners involved in involuntary sterilization, looking at the Criminal Code to see where it can be opened to include appropriate investigation and follow-up.

There is a huge need to provide anti-racist and implicit bias training as a mandatory aspect of health-care education, including continuing professional development for those currently in practice. It is imperative to create clearly defined expectations for information sharing and decision making as well as transparent accountability measures. Survivors will be key in informing these processes and articulating the specific mechanisms of colonial and historical practices within the provider-patient relationship. Survivor-led analysis and critique of current policies and procedures around sterilization practices must be the foundation of both the critical examination of existing power structures and necessary changes to the health-care system. As midwives, we stand with survivors. Working in the community and within institutions, we commit to being a bridge to amplify the voices of survivors to advocate for real change.

Midwifery practice today does not operate within the typical Western biomedical model of a five-to fifteen-minute experience focusing on an isolated issue and compartmentalizing people's medical experiences. This medical model can be experienced as antagonistic toward people who desire truly informed choice, seek fulsome discussions of risks and benefits, or question their options in a pursuit to exercise autonomy in decision making. All midwives take the time to be with people, creating the conditions for dignity and trust to grow. The Canadian Midwifery Model of Care includes the principles of:

- Partnership: recognizing a non-authoritarian and supportive partnership with clients is integral to the provision of care that is responsive to the unique cultural values, beliefs, needs, and life experiences of each client.
- Informed Choice: sharing knowledge and experience, providing information about community standards and offering evidence-based recommendations while respecting the right of each person to be the primary decision-maker about their care.
- Continuity of Care: prioritizing sufficient time during routine visits for meaningful discussion and ongoing health assessment to create the opportunity for building a relationship of familiarity and trust, resulting in excellent health outcomes.

In addition to this, midwives are advocates in navigating the health-care system in more complex situations, always with an aim to upholding client autonomy over her body. Midwives in rural and remote communities often work in an expanded scope that includes sexual and reproductive care beyond the childbearing year. Indigenous midwives participate in coming-of-age teachings and ceremonies, where speaking about forced and coerced sterilization will be central to the protection of Indigenous youth.

There is a role here for Indigenous midwives in this dialogue around safe care for future generations. It's going to take time to see anti-racist interventions transforming practitioners, systems, and institutions. It's also going to take time to build the necessary trust between the medical systems and our communities. It is time the medical community realized that all the deficit-based statistics reported about Indigenous health outcomes are deficits in the current system, not deficits of Indigenous Peoples.

As a Metis midwife, I refuse to be part of the atonement in the current discourse on forced and coerced sterilization that wants everybody to "play nice" and use soft words to describe what is defined as one of the acts of genocide. When implicit bias goes unexamined, it allows white supremacy and anti-Indigenous practice a place at the table, which are powerful deterrents in the honest self-examination and awareness of health-care providers. I am outraged that Indigenous women and gender-diverse people have overwhelmingly embodied colonial violence. And perhaps worse is that this racism and violence is amplified when accessing health care.

Now is the time to ensure that we clear the path for those who have experienced involuntary sterilization to come forward. We need to create safe spaces for those who are questioning or concerned about interactions they had within systems intended to provide care and security. Survivors need to know they will be listened to, believed, and valued when they come forward. These voices need to be recognized and valued, as they will be the seed of change for the next generations. It is time to support Indigenous survivors of reproductive violence and put an end to these practices. Survivors' circles will highlight the journey required for individualized resources related to emotional grieving, physical healing, and addressing mental and spiritual trauma. Like the sound of the drum steadily beating stronger, the voices of the survivors will wake us up, stir us up, and help us to understand the way forward.

We call for survivor-centered solutions. We call on health-care institutions to commit to implementing real systemic change. We call on health-care providers and professional associations to engage in deep and challenging self-reflection, and to consider how good intent can sometimes cause harm. We call on regulatory bodies to demonstrate accountability by developing transparent processes for prevention and discipline related to unacceptable individual provider practices.

Let us take meaningful action to repair the deficit-based relationship between health care and Indigenous Peoples. Let us take this opportunity to honour our Indigenous Nations, past, present and future.

TRIGGER WARNING: H(A)UNTED

Keri Cheechoo

(Re) Position

Wachiye. My name is Keri Cheechoo. I am a Cree woman. An *Iskwew*. My community is Long Lake #58 First Nation. I am a daughter, mother, kookum, sister, auntie, cousin, and niece. I am all of these. I am also an Indigenous scholar. Being an Iskwew and daughter to parents who experienced the atrocities of the Indian Residential Schooling system and intergenerational abuse, my occupation of an academic space could be considered catalytic for other Indigenous women.

(Re) Search

My dissertation documents a doctoral study that employs my Cree Knowledge, arts-based methodology, and poetic pedagogy in the form of poetic inquiry. This research engaged a Cree *Nisgaa* methodological framework that is framed by protocol, *Mamatowisin*, or engaging inner mindfulness, and reciprocity. The research question asks: *What do Indigenous women's stories reveal about public and customary practices, and policies and practices of forced sterilization?* This question was explored with twelve Indigenous women from different First Nation communities and Treaty areas across Ontario and

191

Quebec, where sterilization was carried out in the absence of legislation. The women participated in semi-structured interviews and in a sharing circle. Questions ranged from requesting participants to position themselves, to inviting them to share personal and ancestral stories. The shared stories included subjects such as reproductive racism, reproductive violence, and racisms experienced from health-care professionals and institutions. With regards to my positionality and reflexivity, I am therefore an Iskwew researching within the shadows and shades of violence. *Before we continue, let me share this with you: this is a dangerous space.*

(Re) View

To be candid, I was stopped in my tracks so many times while I was writing my dissertation. The violence I was absorbing, embodying – from articles and garbage-rhetoric voices about Indigenous women and their bodies – was so painful and scarring that I would just abruptly get up from my desk, crawl into bed, and sleep. This is a trauma response.

Some of the information I gathered for my thesis was incredibly problematic and violent. In fact, I had to transform a paragraph of health-care provider perceptions of Indigenous women (page 27 of the External Review conducted by Boyer & Bartlett (2017)), into a poem using a Documentational Poetry method. The method involves pulling words and phrases from a document to provide a different lens through which to (re)view information. In my case, I had to (re)read the perceptions through the vehicle of a poem to ease some of the harms I was feeling from it.

The Documentational Poem is below.

Spectrum/Continuum of Ignorance, Bias, Racism & Discrimination

Health providers indicated
they see coercion-conversation

One health provider indicated
"This person had so many children
she's not taking care of them;
shouldn't we tell her stop?"

One health provider complained to the charge nurses
[about] bias [toward "Aboriginal" women]

Another health provider Related
"It's a constant struggle…" nurses ask

"Aren't you apprehending that baby?"

Health provider comments reflect
systemic discrimination
toward Aboriginal populations.

One provider stated
"What has been happening with apprehensions
is similar to residential schools"

A health provider indicated
"It's a fight
to convince people that this stuff
[tubal ligation]
is wrong

... yet we have to conduct our ways where we try not to
make white people feel uncomfortable"

Interviews reveal
covert and overt
racism in the hospital environment.

This health provider stated
"...the nurses in our hospital
are all races
I don't think
racism is involved"

One resident on labour/delivery Said,
"I fucking hate you people more than any other race on this
entire earth"

Another provider attempting to understand Aboriginal
women indicated
"...and so when you talk to them [about tubal ligation]
I'm sure they're not attentive ..."

An Indigenous woman survivor
of coerced sterilization
was quoted as saying
"The doctor took away my gift."

I stepped away from all writing for well over a month after I crafted
this Documentational Poem. Those words seemed to *spill* so effort-
lessly from health providers' mouths, these staunch notions about
how Indigenous women and their autonomous, sacred bodies and
even how our future ancestors should be treated, regulated. Stereo-
typical, colonial default demands that we are infantilized, sanitized,
and then apprehended if we even make it earth-side. Just casualties
of colonialism. I am fatigued, being h(a)unted disrupts my peace,

my spirit. Colonialism makes Indigenous Peoples pay for their existence with their lives. Commerce through pain-trading. *Pain equity.*

(Re) Surge

B.O.L.O.

Colonial acronym
Authorities
Should
Be. On. The. Lookout.

Be On The Lookout
For my friends
Missing

Be On The Lookout
For my friend's
Murderer

Be On The Lookout
For my childhood
Innocence

Be On The Lookout
For consequence
Intergenerational trauma

Be On The Lookout
For my missing memories
And my perpetrators

Be On The Lookout
For my kids
Oppressors

Be On The Lookout
For self-harm
Signals

Be On The Lookout
For my dad's siblings
Indian Residential School

But that lens
That lens
Is distorted

And oh man, it's white

When that lens
Swings my way
I become a kaleidoscope
Of every stereotype

Better Be On The Lookout

I'm manifesting
Ancestors
Brawling colonization
Together

(Cheechoo, 2019)

THE ARSENAL OF GENOCIDE AND THE POLITICS OF HEALTH

Gary Geddes

It's an early fall morning, my house on Thetis Island not yet warm. Across the narrow cut that separates Thetis from Penelakut Island, low-lying rays of a rising sun are gilding the ragged tips of the dense wall of Douglas fir. It's a beautiful sight and I am acutely aware of my privilege to be living here. But behind those trees, the Penelakut people continue to struggle with the intergenerational trauma caused by the infamous Kuper Island Residential School and Nanaimo Indian Hospital, which, though now demolished, have left a criminal legacy of neglect, abuse and murder that lingers on. It's a sobering thought.

Several years ago, I was writing a chapter about eugenics for *Medicine Unbundled: A Journey Through the Minefields of Indigenous Health Care*, appalled but not surprised to learn that Canada's Indigenous population of 2.3% accounted for 25% of the sterilizations administered under that program. Thanks to racist attitudes and a set of perverse laws supported even by enlightened public figures such as Tommy Douglas and Nelly McClung. As I struggled with these appalling statistics and contradictions, an email arrived from Yvonne Boyer, a Métis nurse who went on to become a lawyer and holder of a Canadian Research Chair in Indigenous Health and Wellness at

Brandon University, and is now a member of the Senate. Her note included a brief alert: "I'm attaching an article from an interview out today that I did at the *Star Phoenix*, I can't believe forced sterilization is still happening" The in-depth article in bold, upper-case type by Betty Ann Adam, dated November 15, 2017, was titled:

"SASKATCHEWAN WOMEN PRESSURED TO HAVE TUBAL LIGATIONS."

The story, as it unfolded, mainly concerned the plight of Brenda Pelletier, who had been badgered by nurses, doctors and social workers to have her tubes tied. Intergenerational trauma had created havoc in her early life, making it necessary for her children to be raised by her grandmother. Eventually, she recovered from substance abuse and was happy to be pregnant again with the opportunity to create for herself and the baby something resembling a normal family life. However, as so often happens, the systems in place operate on the assumption that authorities know what's best in all situations, so the pressure to comply continued until Brenda gave in and signed the permission document. However, in the delivery room she announced that she had changed her mind and did not want to be sterilized. This was not enough for the medical staff. They insisted that Brenda, having signed the agreement, had given up her right to refuse the operation. Besides, they added, it can always be reversed. When Brenda woke up to the smell of her own burnt, cauterized flesh, she knew there would be no reversal.

Like displacement, residential schools and Indian hospitals, forced sterilization is just another deadly weapon in the arsenal of genocide. It was clearly an unwritten policy of the Canadian government to encourage and pay doctors for such "services". I can't overemphasize the importance of these iniquities finally being acknowledged. The national narrative must now change. We've had to abandon the Myth of Innocence, stop hanging on the coattails of Lester B. Pearson and his Nobel Peace Prize, and admit that we've perpetrated a slow-motion genocide. As former playwright and SFU political science professor Herschel Hardin wisely observed in 1958: "Creating a simulacrum of innocence is only a way colonials have of avoiding their condition." If you think this is a hard truth to swallow as a Canadian, imagine for a minute being a target or victim of this genocide, where your land, language, children, dignity—even your right to participate in the Sun Dance or celebrate the Potlatch—have been taken away. I share the view of psychologist Carl Jung that maturity for the individual, or the nation, can only be achieved by coming to terms with the dark side of our nature and history.

But it's not over. The racism goes on. While I was working on *Medicine Unbundled*, I was often asked why I was writing about Indian hospitals, when they had disappeared decades earlier. Isn't this old hat, stale news? If that's the case, I replied, how was it possible, as recently as 2009, for Brian Sinclair to wheel himself into the emergency department of a Winnipeg hospital for help, only to be found dead in his wheelchair after waiting unattended for thirty-four hours, with a kidney infection that could have responded to penicillin? Brian was ignored to death. It's a horrific example of what I call psycho-social triage, where a doctor, nurse or receptionist makes the decision, based on skin colour and a host of old racist stereotypes, that this person is not worth trying to help or save.

As I sat down to write this piece, Chris Moonias, Chief of the Neskantaga First Nation in Northern Ontario, was being interviewed on CBC Radio about the boil water advisory that has been in place on his reserve for twenty-five years. A quarter of a century without proper drinking water – how does that reflect on the seriousness of the government's promises to decolonize and reconcile with First Nations, Inuit, and Métis peoples? Chief Moonias, not surprisingly, is skeptical about the government's promises: "It will take another generation to trust the water after the BWA has been lifted … if it's ever going to be lifted."

"This continued water crisis goes beyond boiling contaminated water," he said in an earlier statement, speaking of the psychological damage being done to his people. "The bigger issue is that peoples' basic fundamental human rights are being contravened and continually ignored."

Colonialism is driven by greed, and racism greases the wheels. Belittling and demonizing the other—denying his or her humanity, as the Indian Act does—is an essential step in the process of stealing land. And the racism of colonizers dies hard. Despite the Truth and Reconciliation Commission revelations, the Saskatoon hospital that sterilized Brenda Pelletier being sued, and the large class action lawsuit mounted against the Canadian government for the travesty of the Indian hospitals, much work remains to be done. News has just emerged from the Joliette Hospital in Quebec that Joyce Echaquon, an Atikamekw woman from Manawan, about 180 km north of Montreal, had, just prior to her death, posted a frantic cell-phone video from her hospital bed that recorded the words of medical practitioners making racist comments about her, saying she was stupid and would be better off dead.

During the fifty-odd talks I've been asked to do in Canada and abroad about *Medicine Unbundled* and the still sorry state of Indigenous health care, I've witnessed some powerful moments when doctors, health-care workers and young nurses in training have been deeply moved by the stories of what we have done, and are still doing, to Indigenous Peoples in Canada. I recall two students in the Nursing program at Queen's University in Kingston, a man and a woman, approaching me in tears after my talk, asking what they could do personally to bring about change. I thanked them for their concern, which is very much in line with the words of Paulette Regan, who reminds us in *Unsettling the Settler Within*, that we have to stop talking about the so-called Indian problem and start focusing on the settler problem. You might start by studying the recommendations of the TRC, I said, and keep in mind the wise words of Australian Aboriginal Elder and activist Lilla Watson: "If you've come here to help me, you are wasting your time. But if you have come because your liberation is bound up with mine, then let us work together."

It's high tide. Shadows of the Thetis tree-line cast by the setting sun are now reflected on the water's surface. Eagles have returned from their annual feeding trip to the salmon spawning grounds at Goldstream in Saanich Inlet. One of them catches an upward draft of air and glides easily and comfortably between the islands and their troubled histories. It's a skill I'd like to emulate.

BREAKING THE BRITISH MYTH: FROM A COLONIAL CURRICULUM TO THE HISTORY OF INDIGENOUS STERILIZATION

Genevieve Johnson-Smith

"They took our past with a sword and our land with a pen. Now they're trying to take our future with a scalpel."

— Women of All Red Nations

Growing up in England, Indigenous history was not on the cards for my history lessons at school. Our history lessons were overwhelmingly Anglo-centric and sought only to educate us on the positive ways in which Britain had affected the world. When we learned about events in other countries, they were used as a mechanism to glorify Great Britain. There were what seemed like constant lessons and exams about the Second World War throughout my education, only to drill it into us that we won. It was Britain that defeated Hitler. Winston Churchill was a hero. When I was around 13 years old, I do remember several lessons about the Atlantic slave trade, only so they could emphasize that Britain outlawed slavery before the USA did. They conveniently left out that Great Britain enthusiastically perpetuated the slave trade, that Britain became enormously wealthy from the profits of it. There was a lot of emphasis on the fact that the Industrial Revolution started in Britain, but no mention of the fact that this was funded by slavery. We learned in great detail the life of King Henry VIII, his six wives, and the Tudors and Stuarts, with no mention of his descendants' colonization of North America. Indeed, if your only knowledge of history came from the lessons I experienced, you would assume white people had always been in North America. You would have no clue who Indigenous people, Native American people, or First Nations people were. You might make the connection between these groups of people and the words "Red Indian" but only as something almost mythical from the past, or from a Disney cartoon. It would be entirely possible, and probable, as an English person to grow up never knowing that Indigenous people still exist at all. To an English child, they may only seem a people who existed long ago, like the Ancient Greeks, for example.

For me personally, I only initially learned that Indigenous people existed through Caucasian-authored fiction. The aforementioned Disney movie, and an old book of my grandparents called *The Song of Hiawatha* were my only clues. At the end of the book, of course, Ojibwe warrior Hiawatha accepts Christianity as the truth.

Visits to Canada are what opened my young eyes to the fact that Indigenous people were not simply cartoons or book characters, but people who still existed in the world. My older brother was born in Canada and lived between the UK and Canada, meaning that as a child and a teenager, I made several visits to Edmonton, Alberta. One summer I was there, a family friend told me that her First Nations boyfriend was being bullied in school because he lived on the reservation. I heard adults complain about "Indians" getting cheaper bus tickets, or reduced tuition for university education. When I was 18, I moved to Vancouver for a year. There, though I witnessed less overt racism, it was still present. There was one instance on a bus, where I had noticed a First Nations man with a long thick braid sitting near the front of the bus. People getting on the bus actively avoided sitting by him until there was nowhere else to sit. In downtown

Vancouver, the overwhelming majority of homeless people there appeared to be Indigenous.

A curiosity was stoked in me that ensured I learned for myself the true basics of the history of European-Indigenous relations and the colonization of North America. A basic Google search did for me what my education system would not. I learned that Indigenous Peoples exist all the way across North America still. I learned what a reservation really was, and why they exist. I learned about "Indian wars." I learned the true history around Christopher Columbus and the "discovery" of the Americas. As I began my history degree at university, I was finally in a position to gain as much knowledge as I could about the topic. The more I learned, the more I burned with the injustice of what I came to understand as a long campaign of genocide carried out against the Indigenous people of North America by Europeans. I began reading about the American Indian Movement and protests in the 1970s. I discovered the music of Buffy Sainte-Marie and hung on every word she sang. I watched Sacheen Littlefeather accept Marlon Brando's Oscar on his behalf, only to be booed and have her speech cut short. Yet beyond trying to learn and engage with existing and historical activism as much as I could, as a young woman in England, I frustratingly could not find a way in which to positively contribute. I was a first-year undergraduate when the Dakota Access Pipeline protests took place in early 2016. Due to the power of social media and YouTube I was able to follow very closely everything which was happening. Again, I wanted to make a positive contribution, but I was limited in what I could do. I bought an "I stand with Standing Rock" T-shirt, the proceeds of which went to the protesters. My students' union organized a protest at one of our local banks, which had ties with the pipeline – seven of us turned up to picket. With very few other people who were interested or cared about the past, present, or future of Indigenous people, there was little to be done, activism-wise, from the UK. It was then I resolved that my opportunity was to do my bit as a scholar – if I could use the resources my privilege had placed at my fingertips, perhaps I could make a contribution that way.

Later, when I was researching during my Masters degree, I came across an article that mentioned the forced sterilization of Indigenous women in the USA in the 1970s. I was sickened by what I read as I began to research what was undoubtedly modern eugenics. As a woman, I was horrified at the idea of my body being violated in that way, at my agency being literally torn from me. As a white, English woman, I was safe in the knowledge that nobody would ever do that to me simply because of who I was. As a historian, I wondered why nobody seemed to be talking or writing about this. There were a handful of articles, some biased documents from the US government, and two books on the topic. Other than that, it seemed to me that this was something that was just slipping away from the memory of academic history, to become a footnote somebody might notice one day, be temporarily outraged about, and move on.

Upon further research, I discovered the work of Women of All Red Nations. A quote from their "Theft of Life" article in one of their newsletters is featured at the beginning of this piece. This article led me to Dr. Connie Redbird Pinkerman-Uri, the woman who really drove the pushback against the forced and coerced sterilizations in the 1970s. Her discoveries about forced hysterectomies and tubal ligations were absolutely vital, and her research into what was happening is arguably the most important research in this area from that period and even since. Yet, her original research is nowhere to be found. Search and search as I might for days and nights on end, I could not find anything written by her – only secondary works that referenced her research, as almost every work on this topic does. After weeks of research, I managed to find a video clip of her talking about her research on the television program *Women's Hour*. As far as I can tell, this clip has never been used as a source in any academic paper on Indigenous sterilization. This is the persistent problem with this area of historical research – resources are severely lacking. So few historians have researched or written about this topic that there is very little out there for people to learn from. This was one of my key drivers toward investing myself so heavily in the topic.

It may seem strange that a white, English woman could feel such a strong affinity with the struggles of Indigenous American women, but it is in fact the stark difference that compelled me. In all cultures, to varying degrees, women are expected to produce children. It is sometimes a duty, sometimes an honour, sometimes a privilege, a miracle, expected, sacred. Throughout my life, there has always been an expectation that all women should want children, and many people can't comprehend that pregnancy and motherhood are not something all women want. Even in my own culture, the idea of a woman not becoming a mother is abnormal – yet here comes the stark difference. In my country, as a woman, there is no option to permanently prevent pregnancy. Unless you are seriously ill, the British health service will not remove or permanently alter your reproductive system if you are a woman. A man can be sterilized as he pleases, but a woman cannot, except in the most extreme of situations. In most circumstances, a British woman who is completely indifferent, opposed to, or put at risk by pregnancy and motherhood will retain her ability to reproduce until it naturally leaves her. There are already over 51 million white people in the UK alone, yet I cannot decide to relinquish my ability to reproduce, just in case I want a baby. In North America, Indigenous women have had, and still do have, the exact opposite experience. To many Indigenous Peoples across North America, a woman's identity as a life-giver is sacred. As part of a population that has been so brutally dwindled, the responsibility of the life-giver seems ever more important, to ensure the endurance of minority peoples who have no gene pool in another country or continent.

To be sterilized is often to feel half a woman. Yet the health services responsible to Indigenous people in North America feel they have the right to take the ability to give life away from them. The governments of both the USA and Canada allow physicians to take away the autonomy of Indigenous women, to take control of their bodies and the future of their communities simply because they are Indigenous. It is forcible, coercive, and a calculated, hidden continuation of eugenics.

It is a bitter injustice.

I believe that I have a responsibility to at least try to ensure that this is not a topic that fades away and becomes a forgotten history. I believe that historians have a unique opportunity as story-tellers, to inform the present in order to ensure that the future does not reflect the past. I also understand and feel very deeply that the colour of my skin allows me enormous privilege and opportunity. I believe that my position allows me to be a mechanism through which the female Indigenous voice can be amplified. These are the things that drove me to write my Master's dissertation, *"Trying to take our future with a scalpel": Sterilization and American Indian Women's Reproductive Rights until 1979.* It consisted of a chapter on the eugenics movement, another on the sterilizations themselves, and a third on the intersection of gender and race in colonial practices. The aim of my work was to establish the sterilizations of Indigenous women as part of a centuries-long genocide, and to place them firmly within the history of eugenics in North America. I consider this piece of work to be my greatest, proudest achievement. Yet what I really wanted to achieve was to get this history out into the academic world, where despite the efforts of many before me, it still remains swept under the rug. I have applied twice for funding to do a PhD on this topic, and twice have been rejected. Whether due to the controversy of the topic itself, or the lack of scholars of Indigenous history in the UK, the institutions that control the money to fund doctoral study will not fund me to further my work.

Perhaps if I wanted to research the Second World War or King Henry VIII, they'd be more willing to pay for it.

I honor my voice

Memories buried
Deep within my psyche
Chase me
A hologram
Of
Vignettes
Grieving
Tears of terror
Silent spaces
can only
Trace the outline
Of Momentous
Milestones
Living in the periphery
Of my life
Heartfelt happiness
Evaded
Robbing
Joy
Chained
In a chamber
Of isolation
occasionally
Hidden behind a smile
Laughter became
Cathartic lapses
Of brief freedom
Sometimes for years
Until I forgot
To forget

Images beyond words
Now demanding
A voice
Or
My life
Mute death
Or
Speaking out
Recanting events
I never had
Courage
To utter
Aloud
Until now
Live
Or
Die
Whisper
Or
Cry
Or
Scream freedom so loud It pierces and shatters
Glass
Ivory towers
For a change
I dare to do more than
Survive
Now that I can breathe
I AM ALIVE!

INDIAN HOSPITALS: THE EVOLUTION OF INTENTIONAL COLONIALITY AND THE BIOLOGY OF ANTI-INDIGENOUS RACISM

Cassandra Felske-Durksen

A radical revision of socially defined pathology

Operated between the early 1930s and well into the 1980s, Indian hospitals in Canada are clear examples of eugenics in practice: segregated health care anchored in Euro-white-settler, race-based ideologies and beliefs that First Peoples were fundamentally unfit for treatment and care amongst the broader non-Indigenous population.

Indian hospitals were benignly marketed as tuberculosis (TB) sanitoriums to the general Canadian public. First Peoples, and their perceived pathologies, were "treated" away from their communities-of-origin and away from mainstream society's gaze.

Often located on-reserve, but also operated in larger, centralized urban centers, Indian hospitals subjected First Peoples to Euro-Canadian medicine while the care delivered did not reflect the best practice and evidence that was being offered to Euro-white-settler society.

Undoubtedly, TB was an epidemic among First Peoples. What the TB epidemic allowed for, however – and what Indian hospitals delivered – was justification for Canadian authorities to legislate, through the *Indian Act*, the forcible removal of Indigenous peoples from their families and communities for non-consensual "care and treatment."

Indian hospitals are infrastructural representations of large colonial assumptions about the rights of (mostly) Euro-white settler Canadian health experts to deny patient autonomy within a larger colonial agenda of land dispossession and genocide.

Indian hospitals represent a fundamentally flawed colonial health assumption: non-Indigenous peoples know what's best for Indigenous peoples and communities. By way of rhetoric about a disease, the TB epidemic became the logic for colonial oppression and violence.

Once in place, the logic expanded: Indian hospitals were sites of nutritional, medical, and surgical experimentation. Unindicated physical and chemical restraint of both pediatric and adult patients was routine. Apprehension at birth was a well-developed procedure. Graves went unmarked - nearby residential school students were commissioned (forced) to dig them.

Indigeneity was pathologized, institutionally segregated, "managed" and either "cured" or eliminated.

I have trained and worked in communities across two provinces. In both those provinces, I have worked with people and families deeply impacted by nearby Indian hospitals, namely the Nanaimo Indian Hospital and the Edmonton Charles Camsell Indian Hospital.

The Charles Camsell Indian Hospital was home site (ground zero) of the *Alberta Sexual Sterilization Act*. Disproportionately to their percent of the population, Indigenous peoples with gestational biology were deemed "mentally deficient" and met the diagnostic criteria for non-consensual sterilization. Charles Camsell Indian Hospital is now closed and the *Sexual Sterilization Act* has been revoked and put on trial.

Nevertheless, an increasing body of evidence, captured in research by former nurse, lawyer, and now Senator Dr. Yvonne Boyer, makes clear that forced and coerced sterilization of Indigenous women is actively practiced today in Canadian health care settings.

This unquestionably has roots in Alberta's eugenics program and is perpetuated by provider unconscious bias and through unspoken curriculum. This kind of anti-Indigenous racism and violence in the health care system is stealthy, inconspicuous, implicit and sophisticated – with purpose and progression.

Indian hospitals and eugenics have not been eliminated; their phenotypes have evolved.

While the physical infrastructure of most Indian hospitals has been dismantled, their legacies are ever-present. Arguably, the legacies reach into the present day. Certainly, as has been documented in recent months across the country, anti-Indigenous racism in the health care system is very much alive and thriving.

Canada is described by some as a "post-colonial" state. For those of us upon whom colonial violence is focused however, we are at best still surviving in a neo-colonial state. Neo (or "new") colonialism includes:

- settler economics (capitalism)
- globalization (prioritization of worldwide social relations over local community relations)
- conditional aid (exerting power and privilege)
- cultural imperialism (maintenance of unequal relationship through an imposition of settler-colonial social norms and status quo, including in health care)

Colonization, which often refers to direct imperialism and acquisition founded on force and military action, has evolved.

The role of health care in relation to colonialism has also evolved: so too have the roles of health care providers and sites of health care.

Many health care facilities across Canada today are located on both unceded lands, where no numbered treaty applies, and contested lands, where treaty obligations are frankly breached. The very presence of these clinics and hospitals represents:

- Dispossession and displacement (including forcible confinement on reserve and coerced migration to no fixed address in large urban centers) which leads to unsafe and unstable housing.
- Chemical restraint (historically delivered by Indian Agents but now often administered by health care providers) have led and continue to lead to multi-generational polysubstance use disorder.
- Criminalization of Indigenous Peoples (including within the confines of health care facilities) can contribute to unorganized and organized illicit, and sometimes violent, effects.

Indigeneity continues to be geographically segregated, pathologized, "managed," and either "cured," certified or incarcerated.

These contemporary realities represent subtle yet deeply unsettling ways that ideologies and practices of Indian hospitals have shifted over time, allowing the concepts of health and health care to continue as antithetical to Indigenous personhood and wellness.

Unfortunately, we physicians who hold so much privilege and power in the health care system, along with our predecessors, have been unwitting participants in the colonial agenda. Without insight or intent, we have been trained to be tolerant of epistemic (bodies of knowledge and ways of sharing them) racism and developed dependence on a neo-colonial health care system.

We have been taught that Indigeneity is a pathology.

Indigeneity is not the pathology. Coloniality is the pathology.

We have not learned how to stand against a state body that thrives on pathologizing others. Our hospitals embody and express the pathology of coloniality.

How will Indigenous peoples ever find good health outcomes when we continue to be pathologized?

As physicians, it is impossible for us to extricate ourselves from a colonial history. We are embedded within it, suffused in the ongoing legacies that our profession has been an agent of.

But like Indian hospitals, we physicians too can evolve. We can evolve in good and kind and culturally humble ways.

Before we can learn to hold space for Indigenous self-determination in health and wellness, we must first learn how to hold space for ourselves in our own recovery from the pathology of the coloniality of power and bolster protective factors against it.

With gratitude, for their contributions, to Tibetha Kemble (Stonechild) and Sarah de Leeuw.

This work previously appeared in Alberta's Doctor Digest (March-April 2021): https://add.albertadoctors.org/issues/special-issue-indigenous-health/indian -hospitals/

GET YOUR SKIN IN THE GAME: COMMODIFICATION OF INDIGENOUS BODIES

The explicits on legislated human trafficking for the state's purpose of extractive body economics

Dear colleague,

Please hold space for me while I try to explain something to you.

Please let me hold your face with my kind eyes – my warm, respectful, physically distant embrace.

So that I know you too are now listening with more than just your ears. An act of reflective attention you have clearly not afforded yourself in some time.

Let me hold your face with my deceivingly kind warm embracing eyes, while I explain to you the explicit nature and underpinning of your logic.

You ask me to 'stay in my lane.'

You intend this to mean: stick to my prescribed role and responsibilities. You intend this to facilitate the interdisciplinary procedures: the communications, encounters and documentations.

You mean this as if it were a good thing.

As if it were well informed by years of clinical rhetoric and experience; knowledge and skills; policies and best practices. You intend this in the best possible way.

You refer to your years of experience and dedication: how much skin you have in the game.

Your interest in 'helping'
                        'protecting'
                        'the safety of'
                        'the Aboriginals..

Your unconscious bias is showing.

You speak of your time at the Indian Hospital fondly, how you came here following its closing in '93. You infer that 'the good work' you do now is credited to your time as
an officer
            – sorry, I mean social worker,
            in the Federal Prison
            – sorry, I mean Federal Hospital.

My conscious bias is showing.

You think your suggestions are apolitical, pragmatic and well informed.

Your lack of self-reflection and cultural humility has abolished our opportunity for ethical space. Your epistemic and ontological racism is so pervasive it permeates from your very pores. I can smell it on your skin — I don't even have to open my eyes to know who you are. Your superficial white savior complex reeks of Holy Sweat.

And so instead of saying it within a non-existent ethical space, I write this.

In my colored words, on your white pages. From the voice of my spirit, in your English language.

You say: stay in your lane.

I say:

> You mean stay out of the way.

> > You mean stay in the lane that you've made for me.

> > You mean stay in the lane that is paved on stolen lands.

> > > You mean stay in the lane that is plowed, packed and paved over the bodies of my stolen sisters and children.

> > You think you have skin in the game?

National commissions, inquiries, human rights tribunals notwithstanding:

You say YOU have skin in the game.

You treat Indigenous prenatal patients as disposable incubators. To be sterilized and decommissioned back to their chemical, physical and physiological restraints; to their certifying psychiatrists, incarcerating judges and gaslighting exes. The various faces of coloniality of power; the faces of the master and his narrative.

You treat Indigenous infants as commodities to be monetized, premiums paid for an investment in genocide – selling of body, mind, heart and spirit for the profits of the state. Trafficked to foster care, only for a limited lifespan, to continue the cycle of demand. Given the ongoing supply.

> You say YOU have skin in the game.

From the comfort of your ivory tower: the bleachers: a device screen.

What skin of your own have you thrown into the eugenics game?

Here, take my skin. Stretch it over your displays of capitalistic freedoms obtained by corruption and mutilation of the organic and original. Take my skin, stretch it for your economic games: over your appropriated Token Tipi, your Edmonton Eskimos football, your War Drum of white feminist neoliberalism. See my skin, not for its color or texture, but for its spirit and culture.

You say you have skin in the game: Get down from your ivory bleachers and get your ass in here.

I have so much skin in the game, every single part of me that shares embryologic origins with skin is rebelling:

I can hear my melanocytes moving when your blinding ignorance hits my face.

I can feel every neuron vibrating with unmitigated rage when your words hit my ears.

I can taste the residual volume forced on my lungs from the hit of your gaslighting white fragility.

I have skin in the eugenics game.

You want me to stay in my lane?

Your lanes are not real.

This land is not yours.

Our peoples are not your commodities to

sell, trade or consume.

I have skin in the game: my oocytes have been free bleeding all over your plowed, packed and paved track. All these lanes are mine now and belong to us. My blood memory both fractures your tracks and fertilizes our interred sovereignty.

Our stolen lands, women and children are alive, well and prolific – despite you saying you have skin in the game, the game that you can't name. Eugenics.

What you have made is finite, destructive and meaningless. And actually belongs to us to recover.

Look me in the face, while hold you with my deceptively kind eyes and warm respectful physically distant embrace:

Your game

is genocide.

You (un)wittingly continue to be both master and mouth-piece of naturalisation of the evolution of body economics, the trafficking and contractual expiry of Indigenous bodies, when you say to me, in this place, the phrases 'stay in your lane' and 'I've got skin in the game.

Welcome to our playing field.

Trackless.

Laneless.

Non-linear.

No boundaries.

Where we are more than just our bodies - but mind, heart and spirit as well.

This is how we endure, drive and ride our revolution.

Our revolution of love; radical compassion

– hence my warm kind eyes, as I say:

You are not welcome here – get in your fucking lane and pray to your god that I don't come for you.

In the way that you have come for me.

Because where you offer blight, I thrive.

Cassandra Felske-Durkse

MATRIARCHAL MEDICINE OF GRANNY ANNIE

To understand, you must know of her, and those who came before me, those among us, and those unborn.

Memories of my maternal Granny Annie are visceral and intuitive. I have photos of her, yet my impression of being in her presence is stationary, safely nuzzled near her, these memories warm my heart. Her dark brown eyes showed a depth of love and loss. Granny was tall, at least 5'9. She was a humble, striking Dene woman with high cheekbones, deep-set eyes, and a soft kind smile, her hair held back with bobby pins. In her day, she always wore a skirt and was neatly kept. On occasion she adorned herself with a floral scarf loosely tied around her shoulders when not wrapped over her head.

Granny Annie on the left. 'Laviolette' sisters; Annie Piche, Agnes Piche, Celine Flett, Maryanne Bruno.

Granny Annie had fifteen children. My late Mom, Rita Florence Mercredi (Piche), was one of four of granny's surviving children. Granny Annie's story and what happened to my late aunts and uncles may never be known in full account, the medical records once archived in the Charles Camsell Indian hospital were destroyed.

If I could have talked with my late granny in our Dene language, I would have silently listened to her-story. Though I'm not sure she would have talked about her life, some of her experiences may have been too painful, nonetheless, there was so much more to granny Annie than the events she overcame.

Busy hands, calm hands, wrinkled and strong, cooking over a crackling fire outside or a wood stove. Scents reminiscent of her. Smoked tanned moose or caribou hides, juniper, birch, spruce gum medicine sap, her cooking fish, duck soup, caribou or moose meat fried, or smoked and dried. The sound of tin and paper peeling open a can of Klik, eggs frying, hot bannock cooked on the woodstove lingered in the bush tent as a gentle breeze carried the aroma of smoked dried fish hanging in the smoke hut.

Granny's shuffling moccasins on earth, over spruce branches in our bush tent boreal forest floor, peppermint muskeg tea with surround sounds of birds, mosquitoes, flies, all things crawling and buzzing nearby, my auditory reminisces of granny's voice as she visited aunties, grandpa, and all our relations.

When my grannies visited one another, they often played cards, one granny had a sedative monotone voice, another granny had a high-pitched voice when angered yet she spoke softly. Granny Annie spoke in a neutral tone, kind and funny. Together, they would visit over tea, treats, playing cards which soon became a string of harmonics of Dene or French chords reciting antidotes of life. They were fluent in French, Dene, Cree and English, their conversations were often a fusion of Dene and French, ebbing and flowing in no random order, one granny would speak in French, another granny would reply in Dene, or French, depending on who was talking.

During these visits, in between silent stares of unspoken heart-ache, a faint faraway look intuitively nudged a gentle gaze of empathy amongst each other. There was a kind understanding having lived her-stories together. There is something to be said when the unspo-ken is louder than emotions or words. Brief seconds in a blink of an eye overshadows distant recollections, feelings of grief, and if the soul had more tears from the gaunt of life it wouldn't be at a card game where trauma was permitted to trump.

The Queen of Spades, Queen of Diamonds, Queen of Clubs with two aces is a full house, metaphorically speaking, the Gran-nies shared a 'full house.' Bidding spare change, sharing stories and laughter as a passage of time. Card games weren't the place to retrace the traumatic trails they endured. The grannies wore Catholic rosa-ries and an emblem of Saint Mary strung together with glass, plastic or wood beads, replacing the seeds of rosary peas once used. Rosaries they held in the palm of their hands in Church, or in their own privacy reciting prayers. Prayers for their children, those who passed on and those unborn. And for those who lived to grieve the children who did not survive. Amongst each other, safely harbored beneath floral scarves, they held in their hearts precious memories.

When granny's grandchildren were born, she held us lovingly in the cusp of her soft wrinkled palm, her smiling eyes of adoration, endearing glances of sentimental nostalgia holding a newborn and then wrapping her gran-babies snuggly in a blanket before safely placing us in a baby swing.

Our grannies were kept busy scurrying around grandchildren when we were in their company.

For me, her-story was of coping with and overcoming being a prisoner of the Patriarchal Hierarchy Government of Canada through siege and war, the Indian Act, and hundreds of thousands unaccounted children murdered and missing in Residential Schools and Indian Hospitals, where medical experiments and forced steril-izations of women, girls, young men and boys were also common in her lifespan. Separate laws of the land for 'Indians' were established by the Dominion of Canada in an effort to assimilate the remaining populace that could not be terminated with disease and wars.

The assault remains on the most vulnerable, women and children in the masses. If I could say anything to Granny I would tell her, "Granny, it's still happening. We're still being sterilized in the twenty-first century. It happened to me too…"

I imagine her gentle gaze as I tell her this, "But they won't break our spirit Granny…"

She probably wouldn't say much other than smile at me, she knows what she witnessed, what she survived.

If I could, I would hold her hand and say nothing more. Silence is loud. Yet the faint echoes of granny speaking Dene, stern, soft, silly, sounded of love and adoration from her Dene soul. I am not fluent in Dene however, I know when I'm told to go to sleep, I love you, money, nothing, yes, no and greetings.

She was forced to live her life, as hundreds of thousands of First Nations people, in accordance with the Indian Act.

As children, how were we to understand what our grannies endured? We were a group of squabbling kids running amok, screaming, giggling, fighting, fueled with the vigor of youth, often acting out what children should not witness nor be subjected to, tarnishing our innocence, yet we spun a spool of thread in stitches of laughter, sewing childhood memories. I imagine in granny's eyes we carried variations of resemblances and mannerisms; eyes, lips, walk, temperament, hair colour, something as subtle as the stride in her/his walk. We were DNA imprints, reminiscent of our late aunties and uncles. Granny Annie's grandchildren personified someone in the family in some small way. Did Granny notice who among us reminded her of a child she lost in the Charles Camsell Indian hospital?

We were their grandchildren to watch within eavesdrop distance, crying, boisterous little chip-munks chasing each other in constant squirrelly chaos as children do.

They were conscious of how brief childhood is when you're not permitted to raise your own children, when it was against the law to do so. Those stolen moments with your babies are replayed in slow motion, in black and white footage, until the film reel is finished, only to be archived in a dark room in their psyche along with how her child sounded when he or she laughed. My boy. My girl. Each child stored in their hearts to be revived and revisited through a grandchild's intricate little ticks and traits, reminders of one of their children, stolen.

These are the muses of a child's memory, brief as childhood is borrowed, nonetheless a limited edition of experiences that etched my character as I emanate my Granny's influence on my innocence and wonderment as one of her grandchildren. Granny's matriarchal sustenance nurtures my spirit, birthed of my mother's lineage, her womb, our umbilical cord severed, not our spirit or our maternal instincts, both remain intact, despite the efforts to assimilate and break our bond.

I know who I am and where I come from.

Our lineage predates Canada, founded on July 1, 1867. Treaty 8 signed in 1899 in Fort Chipewyan, and the Province of Alberta established in 1905. My great-grandfather, Chief Alexandre Laviolette, is the signatory for Treaty 8 in our traditional territory. He was my late granny Annie's father. We are the K'ai Tailé Dené, *people of the land of the willow.*

Known as, Athabasca Chipewyan First Nation, among Provincial, Federal Governments.

All first peoples' lineages are undated on Turtle Island, we have been here since time immemorial.

Eleven of Granny Annie's children did not survive the Charles Camsell Indian Hospital, of the four that survived, only my late mom Rita, and my late aunt Celine were able to have children.

Granny Annie's generation was one of profound historical trauma and loss, even so, she was a humble woman living her life with her husband, my late Grandpa Jonas Piche, a traditional trapper and hunter.

In her own right, Granny resisted the apprehensions and institutionalization of her children in the Residential School, even though it was the law. When she wasn't advocating for the right to see her children in the Holy Angels Mission, she was in Edmonton to be close to her children that were in the Charles Camsell Indian hospital. Granny was also ill for a period of time and she too was a patient.

I remember clearly my late mom telling me she hadn't spent a lot of time with her mom, Granny Annie, because mom was in the Holy Angels Mission until she was sixteen and when she left, she met my dad. They got married and moved to Uranium City Saskatchewan where dad sought work at Gunner mine.

Dad was a proud, strong man who worked hard all his life, "chasing work" as he put it. He was a Union man.

He soberly told me in conversation one day, "I never wanted to be thought of as a lazy Indian. It wasn't how my dad raised me." Pausing, "You can feel it when people look at you with racism, like you're nothing."

My parents eventually separated and then mom moved all of us to Edmonton a few years after they moved to Uranium City. I choose to remain on the periphery of my parent's lives, as I too moved on with my life at a very young age, and as life does, decades came and went like waves on a beach, washing away past imprints along the shoreline.

We didn't sit around the table talking about their time in the Holy Angels Mission. Mom and dad rarely mentioned it. Why would they?

As my parents aged, they gradually needed geriatric care in long term seniors' residences in Edmonton, it didn't take long for me to understand both of my parents were triggered living in rooms similar to the dormitory rooms of the Holy Angels Mission in Fort Chipewyan Alberta, the four walls closing in on them as flashbacks of being institutionalized resurfaced. The rooms were small, Dad's room had a bathroom which he didn't have to share, some of the rooms had a shared bathroom between two rooms.

There was a table with two chairs situated by his window, he had a television and enjoyed watching wrestling and older movies. The walls were concrete, adorned with family photos of sentimental value. A braid of sweetgrass carefully placed on the wall. His closet was spacious enough to store his personal belongings and clothes. His meals were provided in the main cafeteria, which he had to be able to get to on his own. He liked where he was living because it was a Métis residence, Nihgi Metis Seniors' Lodge, there were elderly who also spoke Cree and Michif. The staff and other seniors liked dad, he was jovial, a bit of a trickster and quick to speak his mind when annoyed. Yet, despite the comfort of three meals a day, a clean bed, and kind, compassionate staff, dad's onset of dementia triggered him, resurrecting dormant flashbacks and nightmares.

After several months of living in the senior's residence, he had heart surgery. Dad was constantly in and out of the revolving doors of hospital emergency and doctor appointments. And with this dementia he slowly began disclosing his Residential School days, there were specific incidents he repeated. I hoped the retelling of his trauma lessened the burden of what he internalized as I witnessed a scared boy in a grown man's body, to no fault of his own.

"They fed us rotten fish for supper! If you didn't eat it, they fed it to you for breakfast... while the priests and nuns are like Kings and Queens... we had to swallow a spoon of cod liver oil every morning, they used the same spoon for all of us. Lots of kids were sick."

His eyes held a disturbed look. "I could write a book about what happened in there, it was no good. No good..."

He felt safe enough to talk to me, and if that gave him a reprieve, that was all that mattered.

Although my dad was taking a myriad of prescription drugs due to his physical health issues, I became aware that he was being heavily medicated, prescriptions readily prescribed by his doctor. As it turned out, my mom was kept in an induced comatose state by the staff at the senior residence she lived in, as was my dad (although unlike my mom, the staff were not medicating my dad intentionally) I am aware the staff sedated my mom with the intent to restrain her from attempting to leave her bed, though she couldn't walk anymore, she was strong and stubborn. Nonetheless, the staff's method of restraining my mom was sedation. It is no wonder she wanted to leave the seniors residence she was in, she was being triggered, sedated and abused through neglect.

Approximately 60 percent of the prescribed drugs given to both of my parents were unnecessary, as well as experimental, prescribed by doctors at the request of pharmaceutical corporations. I made sure both of my parent's medications were limited to only what was absolutely necessary, and through the assistance of the pharmacist and I, my parents regained their basic motor skills and became more aware of themselves and their environment. They were no longer docile.

It has been my observation, and the observation of family and community members that the misdiagnosis of First Nations, Métis, and Inuit peoples' psychological evaluations is rampant, especially in northern communities, where there are no hospitals and patients have to be flown south for medical reasons. Although a physician is not a mental health practitioner, I'm aware of physicians abusing their authority as practitioners by prescribing pharmaceutical prescription drugs, opioids, and antipsychotics, whether warranted or not.

Medical malpractice and systemic racism
are as interwoven as a spider's web.

A spider weaves its web, creating a fine silk dragline,
should a dragline break, the spider spins its silk and the web
is easily rewoven, like systemic racism, it is all linked.

After 'what happened' to me in Saskatoon City hospital, I was brought back to Uranium City SK with the social worker who picked me up in Saskatoon. I slowly came out of my comatose state by compartmentalizing 'what happened' while slipping into an abyss of no longer wanting to live. In January I attempted to take my life the first time, three months after I was released from Saskatoon City hospital.

A childhood friend found me on his bathroom floor after I emptied their medicine cabinet of any and all pills I found, I had swallowed the pills and passed out. My friend brought me to the hospital where my stomach was pumped and when I came to, I remember being disappointed I was still alive, everything else was noise; nurses, lights, puking, falling asleep. I couldn't talk about 'what happened" at Saskatoon City Hospital. I couldn't talk much about anything for that matter. There wasn't a psychologist, therapist, psychiatrist, or mental health practitioner at the hospital and even if there was a qualified mental health practitioner in the hospital, I was only in the hospital overnight.

A physician briefly spoke to the nurses who pumped my stomach, then wrote on my medical file his ***misdiagnosis*** of me which became a life sentence of medical mistreatment, constant patronizing and dismissive medical assessments thereon. I was released under the care of my dad who was once again in my life, thankfully. His words were unkind, angry, and harsh. I understand now, his fear of almost losing me caused chaos and pain.

Most of my life I wondered why doctors looked at me with indifference once they reviewed my medical records.

The following is what remains, to date, on my medical file.

(For confidential purposes, some details are removed.)

Birth Date: XXXX
Sex: F
Hospital Location: Saskatchewan

Hospital: XXXX Uranium City Municipal Hospital

Level of Care: Acute Care

Admission Type: Urgent

Admission Date: January 30, XXXX

Discharge Date: January 31, XXXX

Length of Stay (days): 1

D i a g n o s i s X: XXXX

MANIC-DEPRESSIVE

PSYCH/DEPRESS

D i a g n o s i s X: XXXX

PERSON DISORD SOCIOPATH/ASOCIAL

Cause of Injury: NOT APPLICABLE

Primary Procedure: NOT APPLICABLE

Separation Type: Medical Discharge

The above assessment was based on an overnight emergency crisis, whereby there wasn't adequate time to assess my mental health, and there wasn't a mental health practitioner available to evaluate me properly, what more as an underage youth. Nor was my dad made aware of this *misdiagnosis*. The *misdiagnosis the physician placed on my medical record* remains on my electronic medical record to date (medical records are presumably deleted after ten years). Yet 'what happened' to me at Saskatoon City hospital three months prior has no paper trail.

The interwoven links of medical systemic racism and *misdiagnosis* are intricate and illusive, especially when it comes to mental health. It will take the ongoing collective efforts of grassroot activists, aunties, grandmothers, mothers, and fathers, alongside allies, to create change within a medical system determined to justify racial bias that perpetuates medical mistreatment, malpractice and sterilizations. Forced or coerced.

Yes, there are days my well runs dry and I'm too exhausted to keep moving forward with the weight of systemic generational trauma.

I've experienced burnout more than once, yet I've learned through time, trial and error, to make selfcare priority.

Then I looked around only to find myself in a minefield of lateral violence among social media trolls, online junkies fueling online toxicity because social media likes or dislikes are more or less than others. So, I also decided to unplug from online apathy and dug deep into the recesses of my inner reservoir and realized, no matter how I express my lived experience as a survivor of sterilization, there will always be someone willing to deflate or debunk me.

So, I decided to be my own refuge. Own my voice.

If not for the warrior women, allies, and support peers, life would be overwhelming. I am grateful to those who have the courage to walk alongside me/us.

I've also walked alongside others in a supportive, caring capacity.

I too am a matriarch, like my grannies.

I come from a long, long line of strong women.

My grannies taught me how to bead and make moccasins. I learned to sew traditional clothing and make jewelry as a form of creative meditation, quiet moments to myself. I bead and sew moccasins as well as make regalia for my two grandchildren, Walker and Nahanni. He is a grass-dancer and she is a jingle dress dancer at Pow Wows.

If I had the choice there would have been many, many more grandchildren I would have sewn for. I wanted more children and I live with this reality; generations of my lineage were denied life.

Seven generations would have been hundreds of my great, great... grandchildren's children...

Isn't that the point?

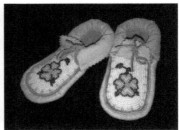

"IN CLOSING"

Proud Father and Devoted Husband, Alika Lafontaine

When my daughter was a toddler, she had nightmares so frequently we moved her single bed next to ours. Sometimes the nightmares would cause her to mumble and a soothing hand on her arm, or head, would calm her enough to settle her down into a deep sleep. Other times, she'd crawl into our bed, tear filled eyes red with fatigue, asking me to hug her tightly and not let go. I'd talk to her as she fell asleep, asking her what had made her so afraid. The details she'd remember were often sparse, though the strong, negative feelings she felt seemed to linger. As her father I would never question whether her nightmares were real. Her visceral reactions and the feelings she felt were enough for me to acknowledge and comfort her. This is how I chose to respond to her as she was experiencing her trauma.

This is not how the medical system responds to the harm it causes. Although medical ethics are built around the four pillars of; doing good, doing no harm, justice, and informed choice. When those pillars are violated, the burden of proof is placed on the shoulders of the survivors. Health systems demand details. They demand dates, names, words from conversations, and for patients to see into the minds and hearts of the persons providing them care, years after those events occurred. Health systems have normalized the interrogation of survivors of healthcare harm before even considering acknowledgment and comfort. For those who've gone through this process of reporting and investigation, the words "I'm sorry" ring empty in the context of further traumatization.

Compounding this is the masterful way that health systems make this trauma invisible. We are not taught how colonial approaches to Indigenous Peoples and popularized medical eugenic theory in the early 20th century, which led to policy and legislation that sanctioned a culture of violating Indigenous women's rights. Instead, it sets decades of history within a footnote, content in a belief that repealing legislation, updating policies, and closing segregated Indian hospitals somehow corrected the harms done within their walls. It is implied that the past should be left behind as we wade into the current exchanges around paternalism, unconscious bias, partial consent, and coercion. As we compartmentalize the past, we will fail to connect today's hostile medical cultures to a continuation of historical abuse. The abuse never stopped, it just moved places, and was relabeled with different words. Indigenous women have lived for a century within health systems that normalize the questioning of whether they should retain the power of life and creation. Ongoing harm is hiding in plain sight.

Throughout this book you've read thoughts and experiences clear and concise. They have been powerful, direct, and moving. Each chapter has woven together the stories of those who've survived forced sterilization, and those who stand as witnesses. In the real world outside this book however, these stories are not so apparent. Shame, guilt, and fear prevent many Indigenous women from sharing their stories. For those who choose to share openly, the memories may be incomplete though the physical scars and the strong feelings remain.

Conversely, the justifications flow easily on the side of the health system.

"This should never happen in medicine, but [insert excuse]."

"The physician didn't mean harm; they were trying to help."

"Why didn't she speak up?"

"Can we be sure they remembered this right?"

"I know that person, they could have never done this."

"That's impossible. That would never happen here."

"If only they had more detail, I could believe them. Why can't they remember?"

An Elder once taught me that survivors are always ready to share their trauma, but it's us who are not ready to hear their experiences. They went on to explain that understanding the trauma of others forces us to acknowledge its reality and reflect on how we can prevent that trauma from happening again. Lasting prevention requires each of us to change our priorities away from what we personally need, to what trauma survivors need. The traumatized have an intuitive sense for when others are ready to understand, acknowledge and act.

In that teaching is a challenge to prepare ourselves, and the health systems we work in, to accept its failures and history. It is our work to educate ourselves and each other on trauma-informed care, hidden histories, and the horrors of forced sterilization. It is our work to question the justifications of harm and dig deeper into the responsibility and obligations of the health system to treat Indigenous women with the care and respect that is their inherent right. It is our work to create safe spaces for survivors where we are quick to comfort and slow to interrogate.

In the retelling of their stories, survivors want to bring meaning to the trauma they experienced. They are asking us to shift the burden of change onto our shoulders as well.

A SURVIVOR'S STORY OF STERILIZATION AND THE NEED TO BE HEARD.

NOTE: These are only *suggestions* if you know a survivor of sterilization and she, or he, choses to disclose their trauma of forced or coerced sterilization.

Practice active listening, especially if it's the first time a survivor is able and willing to talk about their trauma.

Offer non-judge-mental support. Allow the survivor to decipher what their psyche and body is remembering.

The survivor may have to retell their story over and over, allow them to talk about it as often as they are comfortable with talking about it. PTSD and traumatic memory are not black and white; memories, images, feelings etc., fall into place by retelling over time. Or not.

It is different for each person.

(Healthy boundaries are encouraged for a survivor if the survivor is not being supported in a nurturing, safe manner.)

If you are a family member, partner, friend, whomever you are to the survivor, be honest with yourself, and the survivor if their trauma is too overwhelming (imagine how difficult it is for her or him).

DO NOT judge or interrogate. The survivor has likely blamed herself, or was led to believe it was somehow her fault. If you don't know what to say, ask if there is anything she needs, or what you can do to be more supportive.

DO NOT imply she is seeking attention, or being dramatic, or selfish for needing to talk about her trauma.

Understand that after disclosure, she may feel incredibly uncomfortable and question whether she should have talked about it. She may experience psychosis of any variation. She is NOT TO BE BLAMED. If she talks about self-harm, suggest seeking professional help to process what she is experiencing. Again, if you are having a difficult time coping with her trauma, be honest and gentle with yourself and her, and then recommend she create, or seek a support base.

DO NOT imply she is lying, unstable, or anything that dismisses her as a human being coping with a very traumatic memory.

I am not a mental health practitioner.

I base these suggestions on what I experienced and what was helpful when I needed to process 'what happened.'

Personally, I sought therapy and continue to see my therapist. Sterilization is not something anyone 'gets over,' however I now understand, I am NOT TO BLAME. It was not my fault and I am NOT crazy (as I was led to believe).

In all honesty, if you are unable to be there for a survivor, that is okay. However, express this in a kind, loving manner.

The priority is that the survivor feels safe. As well as yourself.

Morningstar Mercredi.

INTRODUCING
THE FIRE KEEPERS

Daphie Pooyak is Nakota-Cree from Sweetgrass First Nation, Treaty 6 territory. A social media influencer, storyteller, and a traditional knowledge keeper, traditional dancer, and foremost; a mother and grandmother. Daphie travels extensively throughout Indian Country on Turtle Island, she is well respected and known for her teachings, which she generously shares. She is a medicine knowledge keeper, a ceremony woman who devotes her time to those in need of healing and spiritual guidance.

Joseph Naytowhow is a gifted Plains/Woodland Cree (nehiyaw) singer/songwriter, storyteller, and voice, stage and film actor from the Sturgeon Lake First Nation Band in Saskatchewan. As a child, Joseph was influenced by his grandfather's traditional and ceremonial chants as well as the sounds of the fiddle and guitar. Today he is renowned for his unique style of Cree/English storytelling, combined with original contemporary music and traditional First Nations drum and rattle songs.

Dr. Unjali Malhotra, Medical Officer, Women's Health First Nations Health Authority, Daughter of Drs Tilak and Lalita Malhotra, mother, auntie, is from Prince Albert, Saskatchewan. She completed her residency in Winnipeg, Manitoba, where she created and completed a women's health residency program after family residency. She is the Founder and former Program Director of the UBC Women's Health Residency Program (for training family doctors in advanced women's health skills for delivery in rural and remote communities). She is outgoing Medical Director of Options for Sexual Health BC and the outgoing Chair of the Society of Obstetricians and Gynaecologists of Canada's Canadian Foundation for Women's Health. She previously served on the Board of the Federation for Medical Women. She is an author and speaker for Continuing Medical Education both provincially and nationally, and in her various roles, Dr. Malhotra has co-created provincial programs focused on advocacy, community support, and education as much as clinical services.

Adrianne Vangool is an author, licensed physical therapist and certified yoga therapist. She is passionate about making the benefits of physiotherapy and yoga accessible to all. This passion has driven her to start Vangool Wellness, a holistic clinic with a focus on addressing and eliminating barriers that prevent people from taking part in yoga and receiving health services. Adrianne's podcast, "Awaken To Your Body's Wisdom," where she speaks with thought leaders and change-makers who are making a difference in their community and fields of study. Adrianne has published two books: *Yoga for the Stages of Pregnancy and Early Days Postpartum* and *The Journey of Self-Care to We-Care*. Adrianne has a passion for spreading the joy and holistic benefits of yoga through her clinical practice, continuing education courses, speaking engagements, podcast, yoga teaching, and writing. Stay up to date on Adrianne's offerings @vangoolwellness. Adrianne lives in Saskatoon, SK, with her husband, Matt, and their children, Walker and Nahanni.

Dr. Yvonne Boyer is a Michif, who is a member of the Métis Nation of Ontario with her ancestral roots in the Métis Nation-Saskatchewan, Manitoba and the Red River. She acknowledges her Chippewa, Nehiyawak and Treaty 1 territory roots as well as her Irish ancestry. She was the Associate Director for the Centre for Health Law, Policy and Ethics and part time professor of law at the University of Ottawa. She was appointed to the Senate of Canada in 2018.

Dr. Karen Stote has Irish, Scottish and English roots. She grew up on the unceded territories of the Wəlastəkwiyik (Maliseet) and L'nu (Mi'kmaq) Peoples. Karen is Assistant Professor in the Women and Gender Studies program at Wilfrid Laurier University, where she teaches on Indigenous-settler history, feminism and the politics of decolonization and issues of

reproductive and environmental justice. Her research focuses on the coerced sterilization of Indigenous women in Canada. She is the author of An Act of Genocide: Colonialism and the Sterilization of Aboriginal Women (Fernwood Publishing, 2015).

Dr. Lucía Isabel Stavig received her PhD in Cultural and Medical Anthropology from University of North Carolina at Chapel Hill (2022), a Master's in Anthropology from the University of Lethbridge, Canada (2017), a Master's in Justice and Social Inquiry from Arizona State University (2013), and a Bachelor of Arts from New College of Florida (2010). She is Peruvian-American and has had the honor to learn with *Las Abejas* and the zapatistas in Chiapas, Mexico; the Rama people in Nicaragua; the Ñhäñhú (Otomí) in Hidalgo, Mexico; the Kainai (Blackfoot) in southern Alberta, and the Runa (Quechua) of the Cusco area. Lucía's research explores how Indigenous peoples' struggles for health are also political defenses of their lands and more-than-human relations. Her work in reproductive and Indigenous justice follows the efforts of First peoples from Canada to southern Peru to heal from colonial reproductive violences (including forced sterilization, forced contraception, obstetric violence, and genocide) to create Indigenous futures for generations to come.

Alisa Lombard is a multi-lingual lawyer practicing specific claims, human rights and civil litigation on behalf of Indigenous Peoples. She represents Indigenous women in collective actions against those responsible for their forced sterilization and other forms of obstetric violations. A citizen of the Mi'kmag Nation, Alisa raises her two young girls (Zoe and Amaya) with her husband (Allan), a citizen of the Nehiyewak Nation and extended family residing on unceded, and unsurrendered Algonquin territory, and Treaty 6 and 10 Territories. Alisa has appeared before all levels of court, including the Supreme Court of Canada, and international treaty bodies, and the Committee against torture and other forms of cruel and inhuman treatment. She was instrumental in the operationalization of the Specific Claims Tribunal and in court proceedings leading to a judicial confirmation of its powers. Her legal expertise in matters involving power inequalities and various structures designed to address them. Her academic research focuses on the reproductive injustices suffered by Indigenous women worldwide, and the constitutional accountability of medical professionals and their regulators in law. https://lombardlaw.ca/

Dr. Suzy Basile comes from the Atikamekw community of Wemotaci, Quebec, Canada. She is professor at the School of Indigenous Studies of UQAT, at the Val-d'Or campus. In 2017, she set up a Research Laboratory in Indigenous Women Issues – Mikwatisiw and since January 1st, 2020 is hold a Canada Research Chair in Indigenous Women's Issues. She is member of the steering committee of Aboriginal Peoples Research and Knowledge Network (DIALOG), and member of the UQAT's Research Ethics Board (REB). Between 2017 and 2019, she was co-director of the research sector at the Public Inquiry Commission on relations between Indigenous peoples and certain public services: listening, reconciliation and progress, known as the Viens Commission. Since 2022, she has co-chaired the Task Force to ensure the leadership of Indigenous Peoples in research of the *Fonds de recherche du Québec (FRQ)*. Dr. Basile was involved in the development process of the Assembly of First Nations of Quebec and Labrador's Research Protocol (2005, 2014). She has published and co-leaded diverse issues on the subject of the ethics of research with Indigenous peoples, including the Toolkit of Research Principles in Aboriginal Context: Ethics, Respect, Fairness, Reciprocity, Collaboration and Culture published in 2014 (1st edition), 2018 (2nd edition) and 2021, (3rd edition).

Patricia Bouchard is a graduate of the criminology program at the University of Ottawa and completed a field placement at the Ottawa Drug Treatment Court. In 2017, she completed a master's degree in criminology (intervention option) at the University of Montreal, with an internship at the Philippe-Pinel Institute and the writing of a research report entitled Schizophrenia, violence and stigma: the experience of families. Subsequently, she held a position as project manager and community worker at CALACS l'*Étoile du Nord* in Val-d'Or. In September 2017, she joined the research team of the Public Inquiry Commission of Inquiry on relations between Indigenous Peoples and certain public services in Quebec. As part of this mandate, she conducts an in-depth analysis of investigation reports from the Coroner's Office and focuses on the subjects of suicide and violence in Indigenous communities. She was responsible for a literature review concerning the forced sterilization of Indigenous women, in collaboration with Professor Suzy Basile of the School of Indigenous Studies at the University of Quebec in Abitibi-Témiscamingue (UQAT). In September 2019, she joined the UQAT Continuing Education team as a research agent then project manager and trainer. In September 2020, she began doctoral studies on the subject of imposed sterilizations of indigenous women in Quebec. With Professor Basile, she is the co-author of a research report entitled

Free and informed consent and the imposed sterilizations of First Nations and Inuit women in Quebec (Basile & Bouchard, 2022). This is the first report on the subject in the province; it documents the multiple attacks on the reproductive rights of Indigenous women and highlights a continuum of violence in a context of gynaeco-obstetric care.

Ann-Sophie Greve Møller received her education in Journalism and Cultural Encounters from Roskilde University. She works as a journalist at KNR, the Greenlandic Broadcasting Corporation (Kalaallit Nunaata Radioa), and as a freelance journalist, with numerous articles in several Danish newspapers. She grew up in Denmark and has lived for several years in Nuuk, the capital of Greenland. She's now based in Copenhagen in Denmark. Throughout her career as a journalist, Ann-Sophie has particularly focused on Greenland and the relationship between Greenland and Denmark. She's especially been following cases related to the colonial history of the area, such as the IUD-scandal. She has both Danish and Greenlandic roots.

Dr. Karen Lawford, (Namegosibiing, Lac Seul First Nation, Treaty 3) Ph.D., R.M., A.M. is Associate Professor in the Midwifery Program at McMaster University. She is the first registered midwife and Indigenous midwife in Canada to obtain a doctoral degree and hold a university appointment. She advocates for maternity care that allows community members to give birth in their communities and on the land, and has explored the resiliency and resistance of women evacuated from their communities for birth. She is a founding member of the National Aboriginal Council of Midwives. Her growing recognition nationally and internationally as an expert in her field recently led her to be named Co-Chair of the 2019 conference for the International Health Workforce Collaborative.She continues to work with Indigenous midwives in Canada, the USA, and New Zealand, with plans for forming relationships in Australia. She was the 2020 Indspire Laureate in Health for her research and policy work on mandatory evacuation for birth.

Dr. Ewan Affleck, CM., BSc., MDCM., CCFP. is a graduate of the McGill School of Medicine, and Dalhousie University where he studied history. Ewan Affleck has worked and lived in northern Canada since 1992. He is currently serving as the Senior Medical Advisor - Health Informatics, College of Physicians & Surgeons of Alberta, and is the past Chief Medical Information Officer of the Northwest Territories. A nationally recognized digital health information systems expert, he pioneered the implementation of an enterprise electronic medical record system in the Northwest Territories that is unprecedented in Canada in its level of integration. He has served on boards in both the public and private sector, is a faculty member of the University of Calgary, maintains a half-time clinical practice, and was the Executive Producer and co-writer of The Unforgotten, a film about inequities in health service to Indigenous people living in Canada that was released in June 2021. In 2013, he was appointed to the Order of Canada for his contribution to northern health care. Ewan is married and has two children.

Nathalie Pambrun   Cheryllee Bourgeois

Nathalie Pambrun is a Franco-Manitoban Métis midwife who has practiced for 17 years in urban, rural and remote communities across Canada and the world. Committed to midwifery care that is accessible, equitable, and culturally safe, Nathalie works primarily in Winnipeg with Indigenous teens and newcomers to Canada. Nathalie is a mother of three children. As the Past-President of the Canadian Association of Midwives (2018-2020), Nathalie is CAM's first Indigenous midwife to serve as President of the organization and served on the board for 9 years. She is a founding member of the National Aboriginal Council of Midwives (NACM).. Nathalie has been instrumental in building a unique partnership between these two midwifery associations that respects self-determination, reciprocity and humility. This relationship has informed CAM's global framework and success in association strengthening. Currently Nathalie is NACM's Advocacy and Policy Advisor focusing on federal files related to eliminating anti-Indigenous racism in the

Canadian health care system through Indigenous-led education initiatives to grow the Indigenous midwifery primary health workforce. Nathalie is a board member of Grand Challenges Canada with a cross appointment to the Indigenous Innovation Council empowering First Nation, Inuit and Métis innovators and communities to identify and solve their own challenges, transform lives and drive inclusive growth and health through innovation.

Cheryllee Bourgeois is a Mother of three, Aunty to many and a Métis Midwife at Seventh Generation Midwives Toronto. She graduated from Ryerson Midwifery Education program in 2007 and worked as a registered midwife for eleven years before giving up registration to work under the authority of the Indigenous community under Ontario exemption clause for Aboriginal Midwives. While she grew up on the west coast, her Cree and Assiniboine ancestry are rooted in the Red River District of southern Manitoba and the Missouri River Basin in North Dakota. Cheryllee has taught in the Ryerson Midwifery Education Program since 2008. She sits on the Core-leadership of the National Aboriginal Council of Midwives and has been involved in multiple projects supporting Indigenous communities to bring birth closer to home. Her work includes international Indigenous partnerships to support the education, skill development and practice of traditional Indigenous midwifery in Peru and Mexico. Cheryllee worked as co-lead in the establishment of the midwife-led and Indigenous governed Toronto Birth Centre, where she continues to serve as President of the Board. Most recently, through her work with NACM, Cheryllee led the collaborative process to develop Indigenous Midwifery Core Competencies, which is a tool that Indigenous midwives, communities and health programs will use to bring midwifery back to the people. She has been involved in several research projects all with the aim of building community capacity and grounding process and governance in Indigenous community knowledge and ownership. Cheryllee has dedicated her work as a midwife to supporting Indigenous midwifery students, working to both change systems to provide better integrity and Indigenous lived reality – believing wholeheartedly that the practice of self-determination supports the health and well-being of our Nations. She is thankful to live and work on the traditional territory of the Anishnawbe, Haudenasonee, Huron-Wendat, and Mississaugas of the New Credit peoples.

Wachiye. My name is Dr. Keri Cheechoo. I am a Cree woman from the community of Long Lake #58 First Nation. I am a mom, kookum (grandmother), and professor who resists daily the systemic and institutional racism that is deeply embedded within society and higher education. I am Assistant Professor in Indigenous Studies and the first  Grundy Scholar at Wilfrid Laurier University. About my research: As a published poet, I use poetic inquiry (an arts-based methodology) in a good way that connects my spiritual aptitude for writing with educational research. By linking poetic inquiry with my Cree Nisgaa Methodological Framework, I am seeking to share the missing histories and the intergenerational and contemporary impacts of colonial violence on Indigenous women's bodies, as a part of the educational and reconciliation process toward Indigenizing school curricula.

Gary Geddes has written and edited more than fifty books of poetry, fiction, drama, non-fiction, criticism, translation and anthologies and won a dozen national and international literary awards, including the Commonwealth Poetry Prize (Americas Region), the Lt.-Governor's Award for Literary Excellence and the Gabriela Mistral Prize from the Government of Chile. His most recent books are *Medicine Unbundled: A Journey Through the Minefields of Indigenous Health Care* and *The Resumption of Play.* He taught at Concordia University in Montreal and now lives on Thetis Island with his wife, the author Ann Eriksson.

Genevieve Johnson-Smith is completing her PhD at Newcastle University, working on a project around fugitive abolitionism, emancipatory activism and anti-slavery radicalism in the UK, particularly Wales. She has carried out extensive research on forced and coerced sterilisations of Indigenous women and remains dedicated to this very important work of raising awareness on this ongoing genocide. Genevieve is from a working-class village in the North-East of England and has English and distant Irish and Scottish ancestry. She spent some time living and working in Surrey, British Columbia, on the unceded traditional territories of the Semiahmoo, Katzie, Kwikwetlem, Kwantlen, Musqueam, Qayqayt, Tsleil Waututh and Tsawwassen First Nations and has family connections in Edmonton, Alberta, on the unceded traditional territory of Treaty 6 First Nations.

Morningstar Mercredi is Wolf Clan and a member of the Athabasca Chipewyan First Nation in Treaty 8 Territory. She is an accomplished author, poet, artist, researcher, social activist, producer, actress, and filmmaker with a background in multimedia communications. Her work suffuses and moves across multiple genres of writing and mediums of storytelling. In addition to publishing several articles, she is the author of three books: 'First edition; Sacred Bundles Unborn,' 'Morningstar: A Warrior's Spirit', and 'Fort Chipewyan Homecoming' which explore the multifarious impacts that colonialism and persistent anti-Indigenous racism play in shaping definitions of personhood and how this, in turn, informs how one relates to and experiences a sense of self in the world, as well as home and community as an Indigenous person in Canada. Recently, Morningstar's voice work was featured in The Unforgotten, a five-part film exploring the health and wellness experiences of diverse First Nations, Inuit, and Métis peoples across five stages of life. The film uncovers systemic anti-Indigenous racism in the health care system, colonialism's impacts, and the ongoing, and often intergenerational, trauma experienced by First Nations, Inuit, and Métis peoples. The film premiered in Canada in the summer of 2021 and remains a critical vehicle for raising awareness and catalyzing conversations about the anti-Indigenous racism in the healthcare system and the persistent cultural and social ideologies underpinning medical colonialism. Her 40 years of activism and activation work are expansive; a five-minute introduction could only begin to touch on the breadth of her work and its far-reaching impact. Morningstar's activism focused on raising awareness of Missing and Murdered Indigenous Women and girls, and members of the LGBTQ2S communities. Today, she is a vocal advocate for the criminalization of the coerced and forced sterilization of First Nations, Inuit, and Métis women and girls in Canada. Morningstar describes her 'advocacy' work as an ongoing creative process, which she approaches as an 'artist.' Her gift as an oratory storyteller naturally evolved into various genres of writing and film, which she continuously challenges herself to explore. She regards herself as perfectly imperfect; a constant work in progress, with no ambition to be anyone other than herself. Passionate about her creative process and advocacy, she remains grounded in her 'self.' Morningstar regards her most treasured contribution in 'her-story' is her role as *Setsune* (Granny) as well as 'Aunty' and matriarch. Her activism as a storyteller is grounded in her awareness of her roles/responsibilities which she embraces with utmost respect for her grandchildren and community, she reverently acknowledges 'our' ancestors who have gone before 'us,' those among 'us' and those unborn. www.morningstarmercredi.com

Dr. Cassandra Felske-Durksen. I was taught by Leah Walker of
Seabird Island First Nation that when I speak (write) on topics such
as these: Indigenous Peoples and their health, it is important to
locate oneself socially and ethno-geographically. I am Otipemisiwak
and Citizen of the Métis Nation within Alberta and our Otipemisiwak Métis Government. This is what my plains Nêhiyawak relatives
refer to my Peoples as. I am told it literally translates to: "The free
People; The People who own themselves." I hail from the Northern Prairies of Turtle Island, which is a common territory to many
Original Peoples. I trained in the Unceded Coast Salish Territories,
specifically in Indigenous health. My practice is based out of the
Indigenous Wellness Clinic, located at the Royal Alexandra Hospital
in Amiskwacîwâskahikan, and is focused on Indigenous reproductive and sexual health. I feel like my responsibility as an Indigenous
person and physician is to act as observer and witness. And my role
is to make space and hold it for others – for their stories, their resilience and their (body) sovereignty. I stand on the shoulders of giants.
I am humbled by the knowledge, skills and ways of my colleagues
and communities. I learn every day. I am humbled by my mistakes
and missteps, every day.

Dr. Alika Lafontaine (MD, FRCPC) is an award-winning physician, social innovator, and the first Indigenous doctor listed in Medical Post's 50 Most Powerful Doctors. He was born and raised in Southern Saskatchewan with a mixed Indigenous ancestry of Métis, Anishinaabe, Cree, and Pacific Islander. Alika has served in senior medical leadership positions for almost two decades with the Alberta Medical Association, Canadian Medical Association, Royal College of Physicians and Surgeons of Canada, HealthCareCAN, Canadian Medical Association Journal, Indigenous Physicians Association of Canada, and Alberta Health Services. He is a respected authority on health systems, change management, social innovation, anti-racism, and reflective practice. From 2013 to 2017 Alika co-led the Indigenous Health Alliance project, one of the most ambitious health transformation initiatives in Canadian history. Led politically by Indigenous leadership representing more than 150 First Nations across three provinces, the alliance successfully advocated for $68 million of federal funding for Indigenous health transformation in Saskatchewan, Manitoba and Ontario. He was recognized for his work in the alliance by the Public Policy Forum, where Prime Minister Justin Trudeau presented the award. In 2020, Alika co-founded Safespace Networks with his brother Kamea, an Indigenous dentist and software developer. Safespace Networks is a learning platform for safe and anonymous reporting of healthcare harm and waste. Patients and providers use the platform to share their lived and observed experiences and insights of healthcare systems without risk of retaliation; enabling decision-makers, advocates, and funders to make more impactful decisions. He continues to practise anesthesia in Northern Alberta, where he has lived with his family for the last ten years.

Emma Voyageur is a 22-year-old Denesųłiné artist from Fort. Chipewyan, Alberta. She is a proud member of the Athabasca Chipewyan First Nation in Treaty 8 territory. Emma is attending her 1st year at Athabasca University working towards a Bachelor of Commerce in Indigenous business. Emma is a visual artist and often brings her identity and culture into her artwork. She has created clothing such as jerseys for Keyano College and orange t-shirts with SMS Equipment in 2022. Creating indigenous artwork like portraits and landscapes help her express her thoughts, values, and beliefs with an indigenous perspective.

ENDNOTES

Fairy Wings and Gossamer: The Forced Sterilization of Indigenous Women in Canada

1   Indigenous Peoples carry intergenerational trauma of the residential school system. The policies that governed the schools were rooted in racism, colonial superiority and wardship beliefs. Unfortunately, today, a substantial power imbalance continues to exist between non-Indigenous health care providers and Indigenous peoples, which underpins their negative experiences in the health care system – yet this problem is not well understood, or even perceived, by many health professionals.

2   Law Reform Commission of Canada, *Sterilization: Implication for Mentally Retarded and Mentally Ill Persons* (Working Paper 24) (Ottawa: Minister of Supply and Services Canada, 1979) at 25 [Law Reform].

3   See https://www.merriam-webster.com/dictionary/eugenics.

4   *Sexual Sterilization Act* (S.A.) (1928) c.37; *Sexual Sterilization Act* (R.S.A) (1955) c.311 [repealed 1972].

5   *Sexual Sterilization Act*, R.S.B.C. 1960, c. 353 repealed by S.B.C. 1973, c. 79.

6   Of patients approved for sterilization [in Alberta] 35.3% were male and 64.7% were female. Thus, not only did the Eugenics Board approve the sterilization of more females, but a disproportionately high number of them were sterilized. See Law Reform supra note 2 at 42.

7   See for instance, guardian and ward theory in Yvonne Boyer, *Moving Aboriginal Health Forward: Discarding Canada's Legal Barriers* (Saskatoon: Purich, 2014).

8   Red Lake First Nation became a reservation in 1863, see online: https://www.redlakenation.org/wp-content/uploads/2019/12/old_crossing_treaty.pdf.

9   This was a term of respect used in my family.

10   See Mercredi, Morningstar & Firekeepers, eds. *Sacred Bundles Unborn*, 2021 (Friesen Press, Altona MB); Yvonne Boyer and Judith Bartlett, *External Review: Tubal Ligation in the Saskatoon Health Region: The Lived Experience of Aboriginal Women*, 22 July 2017: https://senatorboyer.ca/wp-content/uploads/2021/09/Tubal-Ligation-in-the-Saskatoon-Health-Region-the-Lived-Experience-of-Aboriginal-Women-Boyer-and-Bartlett-July-11-2017.pdf.

11   See for example: *CBC News*, Print & Radio March/November 2018; *Toronto Star* November 2018/January 2019; *Globe & Mail* November 2019; Washington Post, December 2018, https://www.washingtonpost.com/opinions/2018/12/04/end-forced-sterilizations-indigenous-women-canada/; *The Guardian*, November 2018, https://www.theguardian.com/world/2018/nov/18/canada-indigenous-women-coerced-sterlilization-class-action-lawsuit; *Live Action* (Spain), February 2020, https://www.liveaction.org/news/measure-spain-forced-sterilization-disabilities/; *The Japan Times* (Japan), December 2018, https://www.japantimes.co.jp/opinion/2018/12/15/editorials/admit-error-eugenics-law/.

12   *Scars we Carry*, https://sencanada.ca/content/sen/committee/441/RIDR/reports/2022-07-14_ForcedSterilization_E.pdf at 10.

13   Review the Recommendations in the *Scars we Carry*. It is a very good starting point.

Reflections on the Coerced Sterilization of Indigenous Women: Toward Seeing the Humanity of Indigenous Peoples

[1] The following thoughts are not mine alone. They have been shaped by relationships, conversations, and learning with and from others over many years.

[2] Jana Grekul, Harvey Krahn and Dave Odynak, "Sterilizing the 'Feeble-minded': Eugenics in Alberta, Canada, 1929-1972," *Journal of Historical Sociology* 17, 4 (2004), 358-384.

[3] Gail van Heeswijk, "'An Act Respecting Sexual Sterilization:' Reasons for Enacting and Repealing the Act" (MA diss., University of British Columbia, 1994).

[4] *D.E. (Guardian ad litem) v. British Columbia* 2003 BCSC 1013.

[5] Karen Stote, *An Act of Genocide: Colonialism and the Sterilization of Aboriginal Women* (Halifax: Fernwood Publishing, 2015).

[6] *Leader Post*, (1964, September), "Poorest in the World Promised Action – Indian Situation Deplorable"; *Globe and Mail*, (1966, May), "Indians Breed Like Rabbits, Thatcher says." Provincial Archives of Saskatchewan, R-327, File 1.226, "Indians"; David Quiring, *CCF Colonialism in Northern Saskatchewan* (Vancouver: UBC Press, 2004), 67.

[7] Bali Ram and A. Romaniuc. *Fertility Projections of Registered Indians, 1982 to 1996* (Ottawa: Indian Affairs and Northern Development, 1985), 1.

[8] Karen Stote, *The Genocide Continues: The Sterilization of Indigenous Women in Modern Times* (Halifax: Fernwood Publishing, Tentative Title – Forthcoming).

9   Yvonne Boyer and Judith Bartlett, *External Review: Tubal Ligation in the Saskatoon Health Region: The Lived Experience of Aboriginal Women* (July 2017).

10   Indigenous suicide rates are three times higher than non-Indigenous people, with some communities having no suicides and others having youth suicide rates 800 times higher than the non-Indigenous population; the life expectancy of Indigenous peoples is up to 15 years shorter; the Inuit experience tuberculosis at a rate 290 times higher than non-Indigenous peoples. These are just some examples. M. Patterson, S. Flinn and K. Barker, "Addressing Tuberculosis Among Inuit in Canada," *Canada Communicable Disease Report* 44, 3/4 (2018), 82-85; Michael Chandler and Christopher Lalonde, "Cultural Continuity as a Hedge Against Suicide in Canada's First Nations," *Transcultural Psychiatry* 35, 2 (1998), 191-219; Mohan Kuman and Michael Tjepkema, *National Household Survey: Aboriginal Peoples Suicide Among First Nations People, Métis and Inuit* (2011-2016) (Statistics Canada, Catalogue no. 99-011-X, 2019), 3-23; Michael Tjepkema, Tracey Bushnik and Evelyn Bougie, "Life Expectancy of First Nations, Métis and Inuit Household Populations in Canada," *Health Reports* 30, 12 (2019), 3-10.

11   Poverty rates are 3.8 times higher for First Nations children than non-racialized, non-Indigenous children; non-status First Nations children face poverty at a rate that is 2.5 times higher; for Inuit and Métis children, poverty rates are twice as high. Drinking water advisories are highly concentrated in First Nations communities. There are currently approximately 27 long term drinking water advisories on reserves. Indigenous peoples in Canada are disproportionately located in close proximity to actual and potential sources of toxic exposure like refineries, pipelines, landfills, incinerators, and other waste disposal sites. Natasha Beedie, David MacDonald and Daniel Wilson, *Towards Justice: Tackling Indigenous Child Poverty in Canada* (Assembly of First Nations, July 2019); Government of Canada, "Ending Long-Term

Drinking Water Advisories," *Indigenous Services Canada* (January 2024); United Nations Human Rights Office of the High Commissioner, "End-of-Visit Statement by the United Nations Special Rapporteur on Human Rights and Hazardous Substances and Wastes, Baskut Tunkat on His Visit to Canada, 24 May to 6 June 2019," *News and Events* (6 June 2019).

12   National Inquiry into Missing and Murdered Indigenous Women and Girls, *Reclaiming Power and Place: Final Report* (Ottawa, June 2019).

13   Andrea Bear Nicholas, *Linguistic Decline and the Educational Gap: A Single Solution is Possible in the Education of Indigenous Peoples* (Office of the United Nations High Commissioner for Human Rights, 2009).

14   Indigenous women account for 4 percent of the total population of Canadian women and girls but approximately 38 percent of those in custody. The rate of incarceration of Indigenous women has increased by 60 percent from 2007-2017. Elspeth Kaiser Derrick, *Implicating the System: Judicial Discourses in the Sentencing of Indigenous Women* (Winnipeg: University of Manitoba Press, 2019), 5.

15   Alison Bashford, *Global Population: History, Geopolitics, and Life on Earth* (New York: Columbia University Press, 2014), 320.

16   Kim Anderson, *Life Stages and Native Women' Memory Teachings, and Story Medicine* (Winnipeg: University of Manitoba Press, 2011), 40-2; 'Vital Signs: Reading Colonialism in Contemporary Adolescent Family Planning' in Bonita Lawrence and Kim Anderson, eds., *Strong Women Stories: Native Vision and Community Survival* (Toronto: Sumach Press, 2003), 175-81.

17   First Nations Center, *Birthing Through First Nations Midwifery Care* (Ottawa: National Aboriginal Health Organization, 2009).

18   Karen Lawford and Audrey Giles, "An Analysis of the Evacuation Policy for Pregnant First Nations Women in Canada," *AlterNative: An International Journal of Indigenous Peoples* 8, 3 (2012), 329-42.

19 Truth and Reconciliation Commission, *Honouring the Truth, Reconciling for the Future: Summary of the Final Report of the Truth and Reconciliation Commission of Canada* (Truth and Reconciliation Commission, 2015), 3.

20 National Inquiry into Missing and Murdered Indigenous Women and Girls, *Reclaiming Power and Place: Final Report* (Ottawa, June 2019), 53, 266-7, 309, 405; Karen Stote, *An Act of Genocide: Colonialism and the Sterilization of Aboriginal Women* (Halifax: Fernwood Publishing, 2015), 127-52.

21 *Convention on the Prevention and Punishment of the Crime of Genocide,* Adopted by Resolution 260 (III) A of the United Nations General Assembly on 9 December 1948, art. 2.

22 Matthew Lippman "The Convention on the Prevention and Punishment of the Crime of Genocide: Fifty Years Later," *Arizona Journal of International and Comparative Law* 15, 2 (1998), 457.

23 It also left out b) causing serious bodily or mental harm to members of the group and e) forcibly transferring children from one group to another. *An Act Respecting the Criminal Law [Criminal Code],* R.S.C. 1985, c. 46, s. 318-320 (formerly s. 267A).

24 *Crimes Against Humanity and War Crimes Act*, R.S.C. 2000, c. 24.

25 George Vincent, *The Rockefeller Foundation – A Review of Its War Work, Public Health Activities, and Medical Education Projects in 1917* (New York: Rockefeller Foundation, 1918), 31-2.

26 Robert Arnove, editor. *Philanthropy and Cultural Imperialism* (Bloomington: Indiana University Press 1982).

27 Eve Tuck and K. Wayne Yang, *Towards What Justice: Describing Diverse Dreams of Justice in Education* (New York: Routledge Press, 2018), 10-11.

28   Christi Belcourt, "The Revolution Has Begun," in *Toward What Justice: Describing Diverse Dreams of Justice in Education*. Eve Tuck and K. Wayne Yang, eds. (New York: Taylor & Francis, 2018), 113-22.

"Why Do This Work?: A History of Solidarity through Roots and Rhizomes"

1   I was granted permission to share this story coming from ceremony.

2   Pseudonym.

3   Pseudonym.

JIJAQEMIJ (Spirit or Shadow Women)

1   *Disclaimer: not legal advice, and not medical advice. Created for educational and discussion purposes. Thank you to Professor V. Gruben, expert in health law and policy, for her thoughtful review; thank you to the brilliant women of the International Justice Resource Center in San Francisco, USA – Lisa Reinsberg and Citlali Ochoa for all that they do to protect the reproductive fights of Indigenous women; and, thank you to Aubrey D. Charette for her tireless commitment, skillful contributions and unwavering support of survivors and the work required to achieve a measure of justice on their behalves. Thank you to the senior and managing partners at Semaganis Worme Lombard, Helen G Semaganis and Donald E. Worme, who tirelessly and generously contribute to the advancement of these matters towards a measure of justice for survivors and systemic change for future generations of Indigenous girls. Of course, greatest thanks to the courageous women who have shared their stories with us and trust us to champion justice on their behalves – MRLP, SAT, DDS, SDP, PDI, EAE and Morningstar Mercredi – and the over 100 other warrior women patiently awaiting justice in the form of prevention, punishment, and reparations.

2   *The Provincial Health Authority Act,* SS 2017, c P-30.3.

3   Dr. Yvonne Boyer & Dr. Judith Bartlett, *External Review: Tubal Ligation in the Saskatoon Health Regions: The Lived Experience of Aboriginal Women,* July 22, 2017, at page. 27.

4   Dr. Yvonne Boyer & Dr. Judith Bartlett, *External Review: Tubal Ligation in the Saskatoon Health Regions: The Lived Experience of Aboriginal Women,* July 22, 2017, at page. 27.

5   Dr. Yvonne Boyer & Dr. Judith Bartlett, *External Review: Tubal Ligation in the Saskatoon Health Regions: The Lived Experience of Aboriginal Women,* July 22, 2017, at page 31

6   Dr. Yvonne Boyer & Dr. Judith Bartlett, *External Review: Tubal Ligation in the Saskatoon Health Regions: The Lived Experience of Aboriginal Women,* July 22, 2017, at page. 31.

7   Dr. Yvonne Boyer & Dr. Judith Bartlett, *External Review: Tubal Ligation in the Saskatoon Health Regions: The Lived Experience of Aboriginal Women,* July 22, 2017, at page. 31.

8   Note: a large amount of the information contained in this section, and all sections prior to the section entitled "Sterilization Without Proper and Informed Consent on the International Stage" is drawn from an unpublished paper written by myself and entitled, *"Human Dignity and Constitutional Cautions: Curtailing the Non-Consensual Sterilization of Indigenous Women,"* submitted on January 5, 2021 in an LLM course addressing special topics in human rights and focussed on privacy law at the University of Ottawa.

9   Part I of the Constitution Act, 1982. Canadian Charter of Rights and Freedoms, s 7, Part 1 of the Constitution Act, 1982, being Schedule B to the Canada Act 1982 (UK), 1982, c 11.

10   *Cataford v. Moreau* (1978), 114 DLR (3d) 585 (Que. SC).

11   *Cataford v. Moreau* (1978), 114 DLR (3d) 585 (Que. SC).

[12] *Blencoe v. British Columbia (Human Rights Commission)*, [2000] 2 S.C.R. 307, at para 55.

[13] *Carter*, supra note 14, at para 65.

[14] *E. (Mrs.) v. Eve* [1986] 2 SCR 388. [Eve].

[15] Defined by Merriam-Webster, "the state in its capacity as the legal guardian of persons not sui juris and without natural guardians, as the heir to persons without natural heirs, and as the protector of all citizens unable to protect themselves": https://www.merriam-webster.com/legal/parens%20patriae, accessed December 16, 2020.

[16] *Eve*, supra note 18, at para. 20.

[17] Note: the elements of consent are drawn from the framework in *Robertson & Picard*, supra note 27, at pages 74-121, and 141-150.

[18] *Reibl v Hughes* (1980), 114 DLR (4th) 1 at 9 (SCC) [*Reibl v Hughes*], and many other cases. cited in *Robertson & Picard*, supra note 27, at page 74, footnote 124.

[19] *Norberg v Wynrib*, [1992] 2 SCR 226 at 246.

[20] *Norberg v Wynrib* (1992), 92 DLR (4th) 449 (SCC), at 457.

[21] *Latter v Braddell* (1881), 50 LJQB 448 (CA), at footnote 126, referenced in *Robertson & Picard*, supra note 27, at page 75.

[22] Re. T (1992) 4 All ER 649 (CA).

[23] *Norberg v Wynrib* (1992), 92 DLR (4th) 449 (SCC) at 457.

[24] *Robertson & Picard*, supra note 27, at page 76.

[25] Stokes, *Consent in Captive Circumstances*, (1981), 2 Health Law in Canada 83, referenced *Robertson & Picard*, supra note 27, at p 77.

[26] *Kelly v. Hazlett* [1976] 1 CCLT 1 (Ont. H.C.).

[27] *Reibl v Hughes*, supra note 32.

28 *Kita v Braig* (1992) 71 BCLR (2nd) 135 (CA), leave to the SCC refused (1993).

29 *Starson v Swayze*, 2003 SCC 32.

30 *Robertson & Picard,* supra note 27, at page 85. [internal citations omitted].

31 *Smith v. Tweedale*, [1995] BCJ No. 229. [*Smith v Tweedale*].

32 *Smith v. Tweedale*, Ibid, at para 6, citing the Trial decision.

33 *Starson v Swayze*, 2003 SCC 32 at para 80.

34 *Starson v Swayze*, 2003 SCC 32 at para 80.

35 *Reibl v Hughes*, supra note 32, at 10.

36 *Kanis v Sinclair* (1989) BCJ No. 588 (SC).

37 *Murray v McMurchy,* 1949 2 DLR 442.

38 *Cuthbertson v Rasouli*, 2013 SCC 53 at para 18.

39 *Cuthbertson v Rasouli*, 2013 SCC 53 at para 18.

40 *Reibl v Hughes*, [1980] 2 SCR 880 at 891-92; *Norberg v Wynrib*, [1992] 2 SCR 226 at 246.

41 *Reibl v Hughes,* supra note 32, at 8-9.

42 *Taylor v. Hogan*, (1994) 370 APR 37 (Nfld. CA); *Augustine v Lopes*, [1994] OJ No 2646 (Gen. Div.).

43 *Smith v. Tweedale*, supra note 44, at para 9.

44 *Murray v McMurchy,* [1949] B.C.J. No. 74.

45 Marshall v Curry, [1933] N.S.J. No. 6.

46 *White v. Turner,* [1982] O.J. No. 2498, 120 D.L.R (3d) 269.

47 International advocacy is guided by the sage and expert assistance of the brilliant women at the International Justice Resource Center in

San Francisco, California, USA. Lisa Reinsberg and Citlali Ochoa were instrumental in developing the information contained in this section in submissions provided to international human rights Treaty bodies.

48 *See, e.g.,* International Justice Resource Center, *Forced Sterilization: Developments in International Human Rights Law (2016-2018)* (Mar. 2019), https://ijrcenter.org/wp-content/uploads/2019/04/FS-IHRL-Developments-Summary-w-links.pdf.

49 *See* I/A Court H.R., I.V. v. *Bolivia.* Preliminary Objections, Merits, Reparations and Costs. Judgment of 30 November 2016. Series C No. 329, *available at* http://www.corteidh.or.cr/docs/casos/articulos/seriec_329_esp.pdf (Spanish only). For an English summary, see International Justice Resource Center, *IACtHR Holds Bolivia Responsible for Forced Sterilization in Landmark Case,* IJRC News Room (Jan. 3, 2017), https://ijrcenter.org/2017/01/03/iacthr-holds-bolivia-responsible-for-forced-sterilization-in-landmark-judgment/.

50 For additional detail and documentation related to this advocacy, please see International Justice Resource Center, Forced Sterilization of Indigenous Women in Canada, https://ijrcenter.org/forced-sterilization-of-indigenous-women-in-canada/.

51 Press Release, United Nations Office of the High Commissioner for Human Rights, Canada: UN Expert Urges New Measures to Target Gender-based Violence, Especially against Indigenous Women (Apr. 27, 2018), https://www.ohchr.org/EN/NewsEvents/Pages/DisplayNews.aspx?NewsID=22999&LangID=E.

52 *Id.*

53 *Id.*

54 *Id.*

55 UN Human Rights Council, *Report of the Working Group on the Universal Periodic Review – Canada (Addendum),* UN Doc. A/

HRC/39/11Add.1, 18 September 2018, para. 17, *available a*t http://lib.ohchr.org/HRBodies/UPR/Documents/Session30/CA/A_HRC_39_11_Add%201_AUV_Canada_E.docx.

[56] OHCHR, Preliminary observations - Country visit to Canada, 5 to 16 November 2018, (16 November 2018), *available at* https://www.ohchr.org/EN/NewsEvents/Pages/DisplayNews.aspx?NewsID=23896&LangID=E.

[57] *Id.*

[58] *Submission Regarding Examination of Canada's State Report, 65th Session,* October 15, 2018, *available at* https://tbinternet.ohchr.org/_layouts/treatybodyexternal/Download.aspx?symbolno=INT%2fCAT%2fCSS%2fCAN%2f32800&Lang=en.

[59] *See* UN Web TV, Consideration of Canada - 1695th Meeting 65th Session of Committee Against Torture, 21 Nov. 2018, http://webtv.un.org/meetings-events/human-rights-treaty-bodies/committee-against-torture/watch/consideration-of-canada-1695th-meeting-65 th-session-of-committee-against-torture/5970060614001; UN Web TV, Consideration of Canada (Cont'd) – 1698th Meeting 65th Session of Committee Against Torture, 22 Nov. 2018, http://webtv.un.org/meetings-events/human-rights-treaty-bodies/committee-against-torture/watch/consideration-of-canada-contd-1698th-meet ing-65th-session-of-committee-against-torture/5970826548001; Committee against Torture, *Concluding Observations on the seventh periodic report of Canada,* UN Doc.CAT/C/CAN/7, 7 December 2018, para.50, *available at* https://tbinternet.ohchr.org/_layouts/treatybodyexternal/Download.aspx?symbolno=CAT%2fC%2fCAN%2fCO%2f7&Lang=en.

[60] Committee against Torture, *Concluding Observations on the seventh periodic report of Canada,* UN Doc.CAT/C/CAN/7, para.50.

[61] *Id*. at para. 51.

[62] *Id*. at para. 54.

[63] Press Release, Inter-American Commission on Human Rights, IACHR Expresses its Deep Concern over the Claims of Forced Sterilizations against Indigenous Women in Canada (Jan. 18, 2019), *available at* http://www.oas.org/en/iachr/media_center/PReleases/2019/010.asp.

[64] *Id.*

[65] Canada, National Inquiry in Missing and Murdered Indigenous Women and Girls, *Supplementary Report, Reclaiming Power and Place,* at page 16 (Ottawa: Privy Council Office, 2019).

[66] Canada, National Inquiry in Missing and Murdered Indigenous Women and Girls, *Supplementary Report, Reclaiming Power and Place,* at page 17 (Ottawa: Privy Council Office, 2019). [internal citations omitted].

The Story of a Research Study on Free and Informed Consent and Forced Sterilization of First Nations and Inuit Women in Quebec

[1] Basile, S., Lévesque, C., Brodeur-Girard, S., Gabriel, W., Gabriel, E., Michel, V. and Siouï, M. (February 18, 2019). "Silence de Québec sur la stérilisation forcée des femmes autochtones." *Plateforme web Espaces autochtones de Radio-Canada.* https://ici.radio-canada.ca/espaces-autochtones/1153624/silence-quebec-sterilisation-forcee-femmes-autochtones-lettre-ouverte?

[2] *Act to authorize the communication of personal information to the families of Indigenous children who went missing or died after being admitted to an institution,* adopted by the Government of Quebec in September 2021.

[3] Public Inquiry Commission on relations between Indigenous Peoples and certain public services in Québec: listening, reconciliation and progress. (2019). *Public Inquiry Commission on relations between*

Indigenous Peoples and certain public service in Québec: listening, reconciliation and progress Final Report, https://www.cerp.gouv.qc.ca/fileadmin/Fichiers_clients/Rapport/Final_report.pdf; National Inquiry into Missing and Murdered Indigenous Women and Girls. (2019). *Reclaiming Power and Place: Final Report. Vol. 1b.* National Inquiry into Missing and Murdered Indigenous Women and Girls. https://www.mmiwg-ffada.ca/wp-content/uploads/2019/06/Final_Report_Vol_1 b.pdf.

4   Shaheen-Hussain, S., Lombard A. and Basile, S. (2023). "Confronting medical colonialism and obstetric violence in Canada." *The Lancet, 401,* 1763–1765. https://doi.org/https://doi.org/10.1016/S0140-6736(23)01007-3.5.

5   In English, those institutions are called "Indian residential schools." Volume 4 of the Truth and Reconciliation Commission of Canada Report (2015) documents the thousands of children who went missing or died in residential schools and unmarked burial grounds.

6   Here is the class action web page: https://www.dionneschulze.ca/class-action/imposed-sterilizations-at-the-cisss-de-lanaudiere/?lang=en.

7   Stevenson, V. (2023, August 22). Quebec judge authorizes class action by Atikamekw women alleging forced sterilizations. *CBC Montreal.* https://www.cbc.ca/news/canada/montreal/class-action-authorized-forced-sterilizations-1.6943855.

8   Standing Senate Committee on Human Rights (2022). *The Scars that We Carry: Forced and Coerced Sterilization of Persons in Canada—Part II.* Senate of Canada, 26. https://sencanada.ca/content/sen/committee/441/RIDR/reports/2022-07-14_ForcedSterilization_E.pdf.

9   International Criminal Court. (2002). *Rome Statute.* https://www.icc-cpi.int/sites/default/files/RS-Eng.pdf.

10   Basile, S. and Bouchard, P. (2022). *Free and informed consent and imposed sterilization among First Nations and Inuit women in Quebec. Final Report.* First Nations of Quebec and Labrador Health and Social Services Commission, 8.

11   Assembly of First Nations Quebec and Labrador. (2022). *Declaration of Commitment to Ensure Free, Prior and Culturally Informed Consent in Health Services for First Nations Girls and Women in Quebec* Assembly of First Nations Quebec and Labrador, 1. https://sterilisationsimposees.cssspnql.com/?lang=en.

12   Cali Tzay, J. F. (2023). *Visit to Canada - Report of the Special Rapporteur on the rights of Indigenous Peoples* (Human Rights Council, Issue HRC/54/31/Add.2). United Nations. https://turtletalk.files.wordpress.com/2023/08/report-of-the-special-rapporteur-on-the-rights-of-indigenous-peoples-jose-francisco-cali-tzay.pdf.

13   Basile and Bouchard (2022). *Free and informed consent and imposed sterilization among First Nations and Inuit women,* 10.

14   Murray, A. (September 30, 2022). Inuit Greenlanders demand answers over Danish birth control scandal. BBC News, https://www.bbc.com/news/world-europe-63049387.

15   Vasquez Del Aguila, E. (2006). Invisible women: forced sterilization, reproductive rights, and structural inequalities in Peru of Fujimori and Toledo. Estudos e Pesquisas em Psicologia, 6(1), 109-124. http://pepsic.bvsalud.org/pdf/epp/v6n1/v6n1a10.pdf.

16   Court, M. and Lerner, L. (2015). The Quipu Project. MIT Docubase. https://docubase.mit.edu/project/quipu-project/.

17   Assembly of the province of Alberta. The Sexual Sterilization Act, SA 1928, c 37, Article 5. https://www.canlii.org/en/ab/laws/astat/sa-1928-c-37/latest/sa-1928-c-37.html.

18 Grekul, J. (2002). The Social Construction of the Feebleminded threat: Implementation of the Sexual Sterilization Act in Alberta, 1929–1972. (Doctoral thesis.) University of Alberta.

19 The Associated Press. (April 28⋅ 2023.) Vermont forms reconciliation panel after eugenics apology. NBC News. https://www.mynbc5.com/article/vermont-forms-reconciliation-panel-after-eugenics-apology/43738841#.

20 Basile, S. and Bouchard, P. (2022). *Free and informed consent and imposed sterilization among First Nations and Inuit women in Quebec. Final Report.* First Nations of Quebec and Labrador Health and Social Services Commission, 7.

A Vicious Campaign of Birth Control in Greenland

1 A heartfelt thanks to the women from the IUD-scandal who shared their stories with the world. In order to develop our society, it's important to get to know our past. But I know it took personal courage to open up for this chapter of your lives. Thank you, Celine Klint and Anne Pilegaard Petersen, the journalists behind the IUD-scandal, for uncovering this part of Greenlands history. And a thank you to Grace Heindorf Nielsen for helping me translate this chapter. It means a lot to me.

2 Møller, Ann-Sophie. 2023. KNR: After many years of pain and shame, Hedvig Frederiksen is now demanding compensation from Denmark. Retrieved: 28-11-2023.

3 DR.dk. The IUD campaign. Retrieved: 28-11-2023.

4 Vinther Nielsen, Helena. DR: The IUD campaign. Retrieved: 28-11-2023.

5 Lyberth, Naja. 2022. The IUD campaign. dr.dk.

6   Møller, Ann-Sophie. 2023. KNR: Arnaq Johansen received an IUD when she was 12 years old. Now she wants compensation from the Danish government. Retrieved: 28-11-2023.

7   Tobiassen, Nukaaka. Pedersen, Signe. 2022. KNR: Gynecologists still find old IUDs in women who got them during the IUD campaign. Retrieved: 28-11-2023.

8   Møller, Ann-Sophie. 2022. KNR: Politicians commenting on the IUD campaign: Shocking, cruel, and terrifying. Retrieved: 28-11-2023.

9   Veirum, Thomas. 2022. Sermitsiaq.AG: Strong reactions to the IUD cases: Creepy and shameful. Retrieved: 28-11-2023.

10 Hyldal, Christine. 2022. KNR: Women in crisis after the IUD scandal - now help is on the way. Retrieved: 28-11-2023.

11 Kristensen, Kassaaluk. 2023. Sermitsiaq.AG: The IUD cases: 77 women have received therapy. Retrieved: 28-11-2023.

12 Dall, Anders. Lindegaard, Lasse. 2023. DR: The government of Greenland criticizes Denmark for hesitation regarding the IUD. Retrieved: 28-11-2023.

13 Møller, Ann-Sophie. 2023. KNR: Judithe, Arnannguaq, and Britta were forced to get IUDs at Danish post-secondary schools. Retrieved: 28-11-2023.

14 Møller, Ann-Sophie. 2023. KNR: Judithe, Arnannguaq, and Britta were forced to get IUDs at Danish post-secondary schools. Retrieved: 28-11-2023.

15 Møller, Ann-Sophie. 2023. KNR: Judithe, Arnannguaq, and Britta were forced to get IUDs at Danish post-secondary schools. Retrieved: 28-11-2023.

16 Møller, Ann-Sophie. 2023. KNR: Researcher on the spiral scandal: We should consider it genocide. Retrieved: 28-11-2023.

17 Møller, Ann-Sophie. 2023. KNR: Mette Frederiksen face to face with protesters: I will not forget you. 28-11-2023.

18 Møller, Ann-Sophie. 2023. KNR: Women, victims of the IUD scandal, demand more than 20 million Danish Kroner in compensation from Denmark. Retrieved: 28-11-2023.

19 Sørensen, Helle. 2023. KNR: The IUD case: SF (The Green Left) and the Social Democratic Party support the women's demand for compensation. Retrieved: 28-11-2023.

20 Møller, Ann-Sophie. Kristiansen, Ivik. 2023. KNR: Naalakkersuisut supports the 20 million Kroner compensation demand in the IUD case. Retrieved: 28-11-2023.

21 Jung, Elaine. 2022. BBC: 'Doctors fitted a contraceptive coil without my consent'. Retrieved: 28-11-2023.

22 Møller, Ann-Sophie. 2023. KNR: 28-year-old Emma Kuko had an IUD for nine years without knowing it: It makes me very angry. 28-11-2023.

23 Cramon, Lærke. Møller, Ann-Sophie. 2023. Dagbladet Information: New IUD cases in Greenland: "The nurses started whispering while I was lying on the examination table." Retrieved: 28-11-2023.

24 The National Board of Health in Greenland is a government institution that, among other things, advises the Government on health issues, provides information to the public on health matters, and conducts supervision of health personnel and institutions.

25 Møller, Ann-Sophie. 2023. KNR: 116 women have submitted reports of getting an IUD without consent. Retrieved: 28-11-2023.

26 Møller, Ann-Sophie. 2023. KNR: The IUDs are still haunting the victims: Arnaq Knudsen-Frederiksen no longer trusts the doctors. Retrieved: 28-11-2023.

27   Cramon, Lærke. Møller, Ann-Sophie. 2023. Dagbladet Information: Danish and Greenlandic politicians demand a deeper, more comprehensive investigation of the IUD campaign. Retrieved: 28-11-2023.

28   Møller, Ann-Sophie. 2023. KNR: The IUD investigation should continue to include the present: Human rights have been violated. Retrieved: 28-11-2023.

29   Cramon, Lærke. Møller, Ann-Sophie. 2023. Dagbladet Information: Danish and Greenlandic politicians demand a deeper, more comprehensive investigation of the IUD campaign. Retrieved: 28-11-2023.